RENAISSANCE STUDIES

RENAISSANCE STUDIES

by

Wallace K. Ferguson

Professor of History
University of Western Ontario

✦
HARPER TORCHBOOKS
Harper & Row, Publishers
New York, Evanston, and London

To Peggy

RENAISSANCE STUDIES

This book was originally published by the University of Western Ontario in their Studies in the Humanities series. It is here reprinted by arrangement.

First HARPER TORCHBOOK edition published 1970 by Harper & Row, Publishers, Inc., 49 East 33rd Street, New York, N.Y. 10016

Library of Congress Catalog Card Number: 75-111241

Table of Contents

PROLOGUE

HISTORIOGRAPHICAL ESSAYS

STUDIES IN RENAISSANCE HUMANISM

ESSAYS IN INTERPRETATION AND SYNTHESIS

Preface

For the past thirty odd years I have been preoccupied with problems of historiography, interpretation and synthesis in relation to the period we know as the Renaissance and to the humanist movement which was one of its most characteristic cultural manifestations. The major results of these years of study have been published in book form. The articles here collected and republished through the generosity of the University of Western Ontario are in a sense by-products, although each was conceived as an independent study designed to illuminate some aspect of my chosen field. With one exception they were originally written as papers to be read before various learned gatherings, and their introductory paragraphs bear the marks of *ad hoc* presentation. The single exception—the article, "Humanist Views of the Renaissance"—was later partially incorporated in my study of *The Renaissance in Historical Thought,* but since it was frequently cited in the decade between its publication and that of the later book it seemed worth while to include it here. Parts of the article "The Revival of Antiquity or the First Century of Humanism" have also been incorporated in my recently published book, *Europe in Transition, 1300 - 1520,* but without the documentation that justifies its reproduction here in its original form.

The articles as presented here are arranged with slight regard to the chronological order of their publication, but rather with a view to grouping those which have most in common together under three general headings. Although they can be thus divided into more or less distinct groups, they all deal with closely related problems, and as a result there is a certain amount of repetition, which could not be avoided without depriving articles which are complete in themselves of essential parts of their argument. The temptation to rewrite and revise in the light of second thoughts or more fully developed concepts has proven difficult to resist, but I have felt that to do so would be a procedure of questionable honesty. The articles are therefore presented here just as they were written, save for the correction of an occasional minor error.

I am happy to take this opportunity to thank the editors and publishers of the publications in which these articles originally appeared for permission to reprint them in this volume. As always, too, I owe a debt of gratitude to my wife, who not only read the proofs, but also read with a critical eye the manuscript of most of the essays here reprinted, as well as the proofs of the original editions.

W. K. F.

Prologue

SOME PROBLEMS OF HISTORIOGRAPHY*

As one of my predecessors in this distinguished office remarked on a similar occasion, presidential addresses generally fall into one of two categories. Most commonly they are discussions of some subject in the speaker's special field of interest. More rarely they are essays on the general subject of history and historical writing. Professor Creighton characterized the former as the safe way. The latter is obviously more hazardous. On this occasion I have decided to live dangerously and to deliver myself of a few random *obiter dicta* concerning some of the problems of historiography. I have been tempted to adopt this rash course by the tradition that the presidential address is not open to discussion. It is the one occasion on which a scholar may address his peers without fear of immediate and overt question or contradiction. Nevertheless, I embark upon this undertaking with a good deal of trepidation. I fear that much of what I will have to say will be merely laboring the obvious. With the permission of my contemporaries, then, I would like to direct my remarks principally to the younger members of the profession, who may not yet have had time to think as consciously about the problems of their craft as they will later do.

What do I mean by the problems of historiography? This is a question that my wife frequently asks and does not stay for an answer. There are, in fact, a great many, and I can touch on only a few to-day, principally those problems of a practical sort which the working historian will have to face sooner or later and to solve to the best of his ability.

I intend to say very little about the problems of research. No one will question its fundamental importance, but after a hundred and fifty years of increasing emphasis upon research I think we can take it for granted. The first point I want to make is that without communication research is sterile. Now it is true that there is no more fascinating game in the world than historical research; but it is not an end in itself. The historian cannot fulfil his function in society or justify the princely salary paid to him unless he communicates his knowledge. If he fails to do this, his research is, to use Bolingbroke's

*Presidential Address, read before the Canadian Historical Association, University of Montreal, Montreal, Quebec, June 8, 1961. Reprinted from Canadian Historical Association *Report of the Annual meeting*, 1961.

phrase, "at best but a specious and ingenious form of idleness." I use the term communication, despite its deplorable aura of jargon, because I do not wish to imply that the historian can fulfil his function only by publication. The academic historian is fortunate in having a captive audience which he can reach directly, and this is undoubtedly his most important audience—one that he can influence in its formative years. But there is a still larger audience composed, we fondly hope, in part of those former students in whom we have awakened an interest in history, which can be reached only through the printed word. Historical research can, in fact, fulfil its social function to the fullest extent only when it is translated into literature.

The concept of history as literature is one that seems unfortunately to have faded somewhat in the last century or so. Until the arrival upon the scene of the professional academic historian the writers of history were primarily men of letters. Their books were directed toward the general reading public and they found their place, with the pages, it is true, sometimes uncut, on the shelves of gentlemen's libraries. Gibbon could write happily in his *Autobiography* "My book was on every table, and almost on every toilet". I am sure that few historians to-day could claim as much, nor can many compete with Gibbon's style. One reason for the decline in the literary quality of much historical writing may be that historians began to write for other historians, and scholars have a notoriously high boring point. Another reason may be that in many places history has been evicted from its time-honored place among the *studia humanitatis* and has been classified as a social science. As such it has acquired an esoteric terminology comprehensible only to the initiated members of the guild. In the strictly medieval sense of the word it has become a mystery. It might be well at this point to recall the humanist ideal of learning as expressed by Leonardo Bruni in his essay *De studiis et litteris*.

> To enable us to make effectual use of what we know [Bruni wrote in the opening years of the Quattrocento] we must add to our knowledge the power of expression. These two sides of learning, indeed, should not be separated: they afford mutual aid and distinction. Proficiency in literary form, not accompanied by broad acquaintance with facts and truths, is a barren attainment; whilst information, however vast, which lacks all grace of expression, would seem to be cut under a bushel or partly thrown away. Indeed, one may fairly ask what advantage it is to possess profound and varied learning if one cannot convey it in language worthy of the subject.

May I repeat that if history is to fulfil its social function fully it must recover its status as literature. How then is this to be accomplished? I can suggest no easy formula. Writers, like teachers, are born, not made. Young scholars can, however, be encouraged to develop such native literary talent as they possess, and can be taught that prose rhythm is as necessary to historical writing as poetic rhythm is to poetry. They can be disabused of the idea that literary form is somehow suspect, that a readable history is probably unscholarly. It might even, God save the mark, be popular! Now, few people acquire a fine literary style without wide reading and much practice. I once heard a distinguished professor of history say that he would advise any aspiring student of history to concentrate during his undergraduate days on literature and languages: the requisite training in history could safely be left to graduate school. This is perhaps an over-statement, but it suggests an emphasis which is, I think, increasingly necessary in these days when audio-visual aids are becoming accepted as substitutes for the written word. We are, I fear, in danger of breeding a race of illiterate and inarticulate historians. Our graduate schools commonly require a knowledge of two foreign languages as pre-requisites for the Ph.D. degree, and very properly so. There are times, however, when I feel that I would be willing to settle for a knowledge of English.

It is not enough, however, to say that written history should possess a literary quality. There are all sorts of literary styles and not all of them are appropriate to history. Let us consider for a moment the qualities most necessary to historical writing, and, while doing so, let us maintain a firm grip on the obvious.

The subject matter of history calls primarily for two forms of prose: narrative and exposition. We may consider narrative first, for history began as story. Historical narrative requires of the writer something of the novelist's gifts: imagination, the ability to evoke an atmosphere and to recreate the actions of men vividly and concretely. This does not mean that the historian is free to mingle fact and fiction. He is bound by his professional honor and the exigencies of his craft to recount events, so far as possible, exactly as they occurred. But the story he tells is the story of living men, and he will approach no closer to the truth by draining his story of all semblance of life. Unfortunately our sources seldom tell us all that we would like to know. Imagination must fill in the *lacunae* before the story comes to life in the historian's own mind, which it must do before he can infuse life into his narrative. I have always thought the story of Henry IV standing bare-foot in the snow before the castle of Canossa one of the most dramatic in medieval history, but it took the question of a girl student to make me vividly aware that this was something happening to real people. She asked, not too naively, what the Countess Mathilda said to the emperor when they met at dinner that night. She could scarcely use the weather as an opening gambit of conversation, and she would have to decide whether, as a solicitous hostess, she should enquire concerning her guest's health and possible chilblains or whether it would be more tactful to ignore the whole incident. Not an important point, perhaps, and one on which the monastic chronicler is regrettably silent, but for me at least the unanswerable question lent a new immediacy to a more than twice-told tale. Finally, imagination is necessary if the historian is to become emotionally involved with his characters, as I think he should be. This, I know, is contrary to the prevalent notion that the scientific historian should maintain an attitude of strict objectivity, and, of course, he should never allow his involvement to lead him into distorting the story. But, if he does not become in some degree involved, he cannot care what happens to his characters, and, if he does not care, it is certain that nobody else will.

Narrative, however, is but one form of historical writing and in recent years it has become a decreasingly important one, since we have added to political and military history the newer disciplines of economic, social, constitutional, cultural, intellectual and religious history and many others. Here the primary form of expression is expository. Imagination is necessary here, too, but for exposition the most necessary quality is that it should be clear. It has often occurred to me irreverently that the virtues an historian most needs are faith, hope and clarity. Without the first two he will never get anything written, and without the last he will not get anything read. Now, clarity is not something easy to attain. In my experience it can be approximated only as the result of much writing and rewriting. Carl Becker used to say that if the author didn't sweat, the reader had to. Such a division of labor may make mass production possible, but it is ruinous to craftsmanship. We are all too familiar with the massive works which reviewers characterize as mines of information, not alwaysy noting that the reader will have to do his own mining. Verbal clarity, of course, is impossible without clarity of thought. When I get tangled in an inextricable web of involved syntax, I find it useful to stop and ask myself what *am* I trying to say? Sometimes it works. Neither clarity of thought nor of expression, however, will avail unless your work as a whole, whether it is a lecture series or a book, is clearly organized. Without a solidly constructed scheme of organization, the main outlines of which are clearly discernible, the best you can hope for is, as Faguet said of Voltaire's thought, "un chaos d'idées claires".

This brings me to the second, and closely related, category of historiographical problems: that of organization. Now, organization is not only essential, as I have suggested, to clarity of presentation and hence to effective communication; it is fundamental to the very nature of historical science. History is a science in so far, and I think only in so far, as it is an organized body of knowledge. Abstractly considered, history may be said to include everything that has happened to mankind, every thought, every action of every individual man since "in this world's unpleasing youth our Godlike race began". But, in this sense, history simply cannot be known, much less communicated. Of all the thoughts and actions of men only a fragmentary record survives. The basic problem of historical epistemology, however, is not that we have too little data, but that we have too much to grasp unless the available facts are selected and organized in some comprehensible pattern. Only when this has been done can history be qualified as a science,—something that can be known. This becomes apparent as soon as we move away from the strictest form of detailed narrative and begin to think about history. We cannot consider every individual fact or event as an isolated unit. We are forced to generalize to a greater or lesser degree if any statement we make is to have meaning beyond the mere reporting of the individual fact or event. Generalization, then, is the first step in the organization of our historical knowledge, and an indispensable tool for the communication of that knowledge to others. Only when we have taken this step can we draw inferences from our data which will help us to explain the factors which have conditioned the course of historical development.

There are, of course, certain hazards which accompany the process of generalization. We will probably find that the accuracy of our statement varies in inverse ratio to its significance and general usefulness. This is something that young scholars find disturbing, but it is a risk that I think we must take. We may discover, for example, that in a given English manor in the year 1200 seventy-five per cent of the tenants were serfs. In this case we have the evidence of the manor roll and can be fairly sure of the accuracy of our statement, but the inferences we can draw from it are limited. After further research we may conclude that in that year the majority of the tenants on English manors were serfs. This is a more significant statement, but due to inadequate data it cannot be as precise. Nevertheless, in our thinking about English society in 1200 this generalization serves its purpose by organizing our knowledge and enabling us to communicate it. The significance of such a generalization, however, depends not only upon its lateral or geographical extension, but also upon its vertical or chronological scope. For what area of time is it valid? There was a previous time when it was not yet true and a later time when it had ceased to be true. Thus, if our generalization is to be useful it must be limited by both place and time, to, let us say, England in the High Middle Ages. In short, if we are to discuss medieval serfdom, we must have some periodic concept that will indicate briefly the time for which our generalization is valid.

But, if we grant the need for a term denoting a period of time for discussion of the kind of fact I have just mentioned, do we have the same need when dealing with a unique event like, for example, the Battle of Waterloo? I think we do, once we try to assess its historical significance. Ideally, of course, what happened to every single individual in that battle was an historical event. When I was young, someone told me that on the field of Waterloo there is a tombstone on which is to be found the following inscription:

> Here lie the bones of Alexander McPherson
> Who was a most extraordinary person.
> He stood two yards high in his stocking feet
> And kept his accoutrements clean and neat.
> He was slew
> At Waterloo.

I have not verified this, and with the years my faith in it has faded. If, however, the event thus recorded did indeed take place, it was a personal tragedy, but it can hardly be regarded as historically significant. Even the battle itself, dramatic though it was and vitally important to those who fought and died in it, has for us little historical significance if shorn of its context of cause and effect. And when we begin to think about, or to describe, the varied factors which culminated in that day of battle and its far reaching results for France, for England or for all Western Europe, we cannot deal with these day by day or even year by year. We need some periodic devices like, perhaps, the Napoleonic Era and the Age of Metternich.

I may have seemed to labor this point unduly, but the problem presented by periodization as an instrument for the organization and communication of historical knowledge seems to me sufficiently important to merit some further consideration. It is a problem beset by many difficulties, for the point at which our generalizations become doubtful is nearly always the point of time. In most areas of historical activity conditions change gradually, and it is one of our most difficult problems to decide for what period of time any given generalization is sufficiently valid to serve the purpose of our science. Nevertheless, we cannot do without periodic devices of some sort. Analogies drawn from the natural sciences are generally misleading when applied to history, but it seems to me that chronological periods serve the historian in much the same fashion as genus and species serve the biologist. They enable him to organize his knowledge and hence to think about it, to interpret it and to communicate it.

There are historians who have objected to any form of periodization on the ground that it imposes arbitrary divisions upon the unbroken stream of history, and, in fact, no form of periodization should ever be taken as marking a break in the continuity of historical development. Yet the stream of history *does* at times reach a turning point at which it seems to veer off in a new direction, and here and there it *is* broken by rapids which accelerate its tempo, and it will help our understanding to mark these places. Or, to use another analogy dear to historians, history is a seamless web woven on the loom of time; but I submit that it must be cut into manageable lengths if it is to be handled conveniently and conveyed to the consumer.

A second and somewhat more serious objection to periodization is that the terms commonly applied to historical periods are so frequently loaded, and that they indicate a fundamental bias. Such terms as the Dark Ages, the Age of the Reformation, the Enlightenment, the Romantic Era, the Age of Nationalism, not to mention the Renaissance, suggest a point of view which limits their applicability and may, indeed, distort the interpretation of the age. They are, however, hallowed by custom and rich in accumulated connotations. They have, themselves, a history, and there seems little reason to substitute for them less familiar guide-posts. We may delude ourselves by the hope that we can find less prejudiced and more chronologically exact periods in the reigns of outstanding monarchs or in such purely chronological terms as decades or centuries. If, however, these terms correspond in fact to a phase of historical development sufficiently distinctive to make them useful as periodic devices, they will acquire overtones and connotations which rob them of their apparently innocuous character. Such terms, for example, as the Elizabethan Age, the Age of Louis Quatorze or the Victorian Age, the Thirteenth Century, the Eighteenth Century or the Quattrocento have become concepts as loaded as the more apparently biased terms I have already mentioned. Certain decades have also acquired this conceptual character. For those of us who lived through those hectic years, the term "the Twenties" carries as distinct a connotation as though we called it the Aspirin Age. Even certain years have acquired the character of concepts or symbols. For Americans, if not for Canadians, 1776 is as potent a symbol as 1066 and all that, something that awakens in almost every mind the memory of a great moment in history. When I first went to New York the memory of the late Mayor Hylan was still green, and people still recalled the occasion on which he delivered a Fourth of July address. Hizzonor was doing very nicely, all things considered, with close attention to his manuscript, until he reached his peroration: "What this country needs is more of the spirit of — One Seven Seven Six."

Now, I am not arguing that there is anything deplorable about the fact that these various periodic terms have acquired through use an aura of qualifying connotation. On the contrary, it is only when they have acquired this aura that they become useful as a kind of shorthand symbol, compressing into a word or a phrase what it would take us pages to explain. I can only suggest that when we use these terms we think about them instead of merely taking them for granted, that we use them carefully and with due consideration for their applicability to the historical facts, and that, when necessary, we warn the reader to be on his guard against accepting them at their face value. This is particularly necessary in works of synthesis, where we are dealing with the whole civilization of an age. For a periodic term that may be irreproachable in the history of art or religion or economics may warp the picture of the whole. Moreover, the broader our canvas the more danger there is that our periods will overlap or become fuzzy at the edges. This is unfortunate, but it is unavoidable.

The foregoing observations suggest another historiographical problem, that of interpretation and synthesis. Like other problems it is not an easy one to solve, and I think it has been somewhat neglected by professional historians in the past two or three generations. Let me repeat that I do not depreciate original research or its immediate products in the form of editions of sources, monographs or articles in learned journals. These are the essential materials with which the historian works, but they are not the end of his craft. In any case, the audience for works of detailed research, or monographs dealing with a restricted field, is almost inevitably limited to the membership of the historical profession. If historians are to fulfil their social function, they must put together the materials made available by research into some larger synthesis, and interpret the facts so as to give them meaning for the interested but untrained reader, as well as for that perhaps only potentially interested audience composed of our helpless students. Not that we should think of synthesis and interpretation as a kind of popularization fit only for consumption by the uninitiated. Even professional historians may find an interpretive synthesis of inestimable value, and that not only because as specialists they cannot be equally conversant with all fields. Such a work may contain no single fact that is unknown to them, but they may see the facts in a new light as the result of some scholar's thoughtful consideration of the known data. We are too accustomed to thinking that a learned article or monograph to be respectable must present original research. It might be more valuable if it presented original thought. It is a hopeful sign that the editor of the *American Historical Review* has recently issued appeals for more interpretive articles, and I understand that other editors would welcome articles of that kind, but find them in short supply.

I fear that our system of graduate study must bear some of the blame for this state of affairs. Certainly it does little to encourage either interpretation or synthesis. Perhaps this is unavoidable, since it is essential that the apprentice scholar should be given basic training in the technique of research, and there is time for little else. It may be assumed that independent thought will come later, when the maturing scholar no longer feels an examining committee breathing down the back of his neck. Unfortunately, the doctoral dissertation frequently sets a pattern which the scholar will follow for the rest of his life, devoting such energies as he can spare from his academic duties to learning more and more about less and less. For many graduate students, too, in this age when students marry young and acquire the title of *pater* before that of doctor, the effort to complete a dissertation may be a traumatic experience from which they will never recover, and which will end their careers as productive scholars then and there. The attitude which this uphill struggle may breed in a young scholar's family was brought home to me by a friend whose six year old son was overheard in spirited altercation with the small daughter of a neighboring instructor. As the young lady stalked off in high dudgeon she fired one last Parthian shot: "You—you Ph.D., you!" I have no suggestion to make for the amelioration of this regrettable situation. I am merely taking this opportunity to express a growing alarm at the length of time it seems to take the average student to-day to overcome the hurdle of the doctorate, at the strain it seems to impose on both the candidate and his long-suffering family, and at the irreparable damage it may do to his future career as a productive scholar.

Synthesis in the broadest sense has also been discouraged by the specialization which is the unavoidable corollary of our greatly expanded conception of what is included in history, as well as of the vast accumulation of material that has resulted from a century and a half of research. The problem was simpler when history was simply past politics. To-day the historian is more or less forced to limit the range of his research and writing, not only to a given period, but also very largely to one branch of history — political, economic, cultural or what not. Even within these relatively restricted areas, however, works of interpretation and synthesis are not only possible but indispensable. We are all aware of how much we owe to the men who have attempted this task in our own fields, and the large sale of works of this kind in paper-back editions suggests that they are capable of reaching a wide reading public. Interpretation and synthesis, as I have suggested, are not as a rule for graduate students, who are forced by circumstance to limit their dissertations to clearly defined and manageable subjects. I think, however, that we should encourage them more than we commonly do to look forward to the time when they will be qualified to write more thoughtful and interpretive history on a larger scale, and to feel that to do so is the rewarding climax of a scholar's career, the last of life for which the first was made. We should, I think, persuade them that there is nothing essentially unscholarly about works of synthesis, dependent though they must be on secondary sources. Above all, we should disabuse them of the stultifying conviction that it is the scholar's ultimate goal to leave behind him footnotes on the sands of time.

At this point may I repeat that the academic historian communicates his knowledge and understanding of history not only in writing, but more constantly in lectures to students, and it is in the class-room that he has a golden opportunity to develop a well-organized, interpretive synthesis of a considerable area of history. The exigencies of the curriculum will, indeed, force him to extend his study far beyond the area of his specialized research and his most intensive scholarly interest. This is fortunate, for it furnishes him with an incentive not only to expand his knowledge, but to organize and interpret it; and I venture to suggest that the amount of history the students carry away with them as a permanent acquisition will be measured by the degree to which he has achieved the objective of presenting an interpretive synthesis and not merely a series of lectures. Meanwhile, his own understanding and interpretation of his special field will be immeasurably enriched by being placed in the context of a larger synthesis. Without such a context, indeed, he may lose perspective and his picture of his own special field may slip dangerously out of focus. At the same time, a lecture course may serve the purpose of building up a thoughtful synthesis which, when fully matured, may be presented to a wider audience in published form.

Interpretation and synthesis are always, of course, hazardous, and to present them to a more critical audience than that of your students requires some courage. Those of you who attempt synthesis will always be stumbling around in someone else's china shop. You will be forced to deal in a paragraph with a subject on which some other scholar has spent a lifetime of study. It is almost inevitable that the learned reviewer who will assess your work will be more intimately acquainted with some aspect of the subject than you are and he may, after praising it with faint damns, conclude his review with some such statement as: "It is unfortunate that the author was apparently unaware of the illuminating article by Professor Slawkenbergius in the *Deutsche Vierteljahrsschrift für Literaturwissenschaft und Geistesgeschichte*". Finally, if your synthesis is more than a colorless compilation, if you have ventured to interpret the facts, you may be certain that your interpretation will not be universally accepted. If your work is of sufficient importance it will call forth articles and monographs criticizing it and attacking its thesis in whole or in part. It may even inspire scholars to develop a contrary thesis that might not otherwise have occurred to them. But it is by this dialetic of assertion and rebuttal, of interpretation and reinterpretation, that our understanding of history is broadened and deepened. For a hundred years Burckhardt's *Civilization of the Renaissance in Italy,* to take a famous example, has occupied a central place in the historical writing devoted to that period, not only because it was itself a masterly synthesis, but equally because it has stimulated innumerable scholars to explore areas that he had neglected or to interpret the civilization of the age from different points of view, thereby adding immeasurably to our knowledge and understanding. More recently Huizinga's *The Waning of the Middle Ages* has served the dialectical process of historical thought in a similar way, as have also such seminal works as, for example, Henri Pirenne's *Medieval Cities* or

Turner's essay on the influence of the American frontier. The significance of such works may be measured not only by the number of scholars who have accepted their interpretation and have used it as the basis for further work, but also by the number of those who have found it in some way lacking and have been inspired to work along other lines. If this is the fate of the masters, you should not be discouraged if your interpretation is not greeted with universal acclaim. It should be enough if it presents a mark that other scholars will feel it worth while to shoot at.

I am not suggesting, of course, that all historians who avoid interpretive synthesis do so from lack of courage. Many are fully occupied with more limited but necessary tasks, laying the groundwork of basic research from which a synthesis may be constructed. Some too, I think, tend to shy away from interpretation, because it seems to involve a dangerously subjective element. Enamoured of the scientific ideal, they would like to think of themselves as high fidelity transmitters of historical truth, free from all subjective distortion. This must be a comforting illusion. I have always envied Fustel de Coulanges, who could say when his students applauded him. "Do not applaud me, gentlemen. It is not I who speak, but history that speaks through me." Nevertheless, I do not see how some subjective colouring of the facts can be avoided when once we begin to think about history. If there is one thing that is certain, it is that the truth will not put itself together, and the putting together is a creative act, which, like all creative acts, is conditioned by the mind of the creator. Scientific objectivity is a laudable ideal, but let us not use it as a pretext for the avoidance of thought.

In any case, even the most conscientiously objective historian cannot in fact avoid some element of interpretation when he attempts to do more than report the findings of detailed research. The mere process of selecting certain facts or events out of the mass of material available involves interpretation, since it implies the existence in the author's mind of some standard of values, some conception of what is significant, and the criteria by which significance is judged varies from generation to generation, from group to group. It is for this reason, among others, that history must be continually rewritten. Even the best histories become obsolete in time, not merely because later research has brought new facts to light, but because they no longer tell us what we want to know about the past, or do not tell it with the emphasis and proportion, the attribution of cause and effect, which to us seems reasonable. Since, then, we cannot avoid interpreting the facts, it behoves us to be perpetually conscious that we are doing so, and thus to avoid the perils that accompany a complaisant assurance that the picture of the past that we have created is the only possible one. We should not, in short, be afraid to interpret, but we should not take our interpretation for granted.

Students, I find, are frequently disturbed by the suggestion that in the science of history absolute and demonstrable truth is unobtainable, except in relatively small and unimportant instances. This thought also bothered the tidy and dogmatic mind of Dr. Johnson. "We must consider", he said, "how very little history there is; I mean real authentic history. That certain kings reigned, and certain battles were fought, we can depend upon as true; but all

the colouring, all the philosophy of history is conjecture". Dr. Johnson obviously thought that he had thus disposed of history. I cannot agree. The good
doctor would have been closer to the truth if for "conjecture" he had substi-
tuted "inference"; and inference is a valid form of scientific thought. It is the
peculiarity of the science of history, however, that the validity of our inferences is dependent upon our knowledge of many things apparently
irrelevant to our discipline, and upon the depth and breadth of our experience, whether personal or vicarious, of human emotions and all the infinite
variability of human nature; for the materials with which the historian works
are not merely the acts of men, but the thoughts, emotions and subconscious
drives which motivate these acts. Such are the limitations of the human mind
and personality that we can never hope to bring to the solution of our historical problems the perfect knowledge and experience that would give our
inferences the eternal validity of a Euclidian theorem. What we can hope for
is at best proximate truth, but it is not mere "conjecture".

We may freely admit, then, that history is not an exact science, and that
it can never hope to achieve the kind of knowledge claimed by the
natural sciences. But I submit that it is for that reason in no way inferior
to what are popularly regarded as more scientific disciplines. The sciences
dealing with man need not apologize because the materials with which they
work are frequently of a sort that cannot be measured exactly or verified by experiment. The preeminent importance of their subject matter
guarantees them pride of place. I have tried to think of some other way of
saying that the proper study of mankind is man, and have given up the
struggle. Let it stand. It is trite, but still true. Nor is history in any way a
less arduous discipline than the exact sciences, nor one demanding less of
its practitioners. On the contrary, it demands not only those intellectual
qualities which are required by the natural sciences — rigorous method,
conscientious attention to detail, a wide range of factual knowledge — but
in addition to these, certain qualities that the natural scientist may
conceivably lack without the lack vitiating the results of his work. An
ichthyologist may fulfil the demands of his science without knowing what it
feels like to be a fish. An historian cannot be a good historian without
knowing how men feel under a great variety of circumstances. He must
bring to his task a capacity for empathy, for entering into the minds and
emotions of men, and he must also have the experience that will lend
validity to his imaginative reconstruction of other men's thoughts and
feelings. He must never weary in his search for knowledge, but what he
seeks is not merely knowledge. It is something no less important because
less exact, which Dilthey has called understanding, *Verstehen,* and which the
humanists called wisdom, *sapientia.* Above all, like any man whose profession
requires him to deal with men and to assess human motives, the historian
must be a man of sound judgment. Finally, may I repeat in conclusion
that to fulfil his function the historian must be able to organize and communicate his knowledge, his understanding of the past and such wisdom
as his thoughtful consideration of history has brought him. History, as
I have said, is a science by virtue of being an organized body of knowledge,
but it is a science that can achieve its purpose only with the aid of literary art.

Historiographical Essays

THE REINTERPRETATION
OF THE RENAISSANCE*

Historians of every generation since Petrarch have contributed to the interpretation or reinterpretation of the Renaissance; but it is only in the past half century that it has become an acutely controversial problem in historiography[1]. Bit by bit, generations of humanists, Protestant historians, rationalists, and romantics built up the conception of the revival of art, letters, and learning, until in the mid-nineteenth century Jacob Burckhardt fused the traditional views, with some very significant additions of his own, into a synthetic picture of the Renaissance as a distinct period in the cultural history of western Europe. The historians who followed in Burckhardt's footsteps must have been very happy men. They knew what the Renaissance was. This period of idyllic certainty, however, was not left long undisturbed. Criticism of the master's conception began even before the end of the nineteenth century, though it was generally ignored. Since that time revisionists in increasing numbers, and working from a variety of directions, have collaborated in the task of bringing chaos out of order. And so far as can be discerned at the moment, the end is not yet.

No Renaissance historian today can be unaware of the conflict of interpretations. Most of the historians in this country, whose specialty lies in other fields, however, have tended, at least until very recently, to take the various interpretations of the Renaissance more or less for granted, and have been unconsciously rather than consciously influenced by them. Busy with their own specific tasks, they have not taken the time to study the varying trends of Renaissance historiography nor, perhaps, to consider very definitely their own stand in relation to them. In this country we have been rather wary of definite historical interpretations and philosophies of history. And perhaps rightly so. But however much we may shy away from the *Begriff*-stricken

---

*Reprinted from *Facets of the Renaissance, The Arensberg Lectures* (Los Angeles, 1956).

[1]For an account of the varying interpretations of the Renaissance since the fifteenth century, see W. K. Ferguson, *The Renaissance in Historical Thought, Five Centuries of Interpretation* (Boston, 1948).

Teutonic tendency toward the abstract conception and the *ismus*, we cannot write or teach history without giving it some interpretation, and it may be as well that the interpretation should be a conscious one and that we should be aware of its relation to the historical writing of the past and present. The following brief sketch of the main currents in the history of Renaissance historiography, concluding somewhat rashly with the approach to the interpretation of the Renaissance which I myself have found most satisfactory, is directed primarily to scholars who are not specialists in Renaissance history and is proferred in the hope that it may provoke some thought and discussion, even if it does not, God save the mark, help to clarify the issue.

Looking back over the long evolution of the idea of the Renaissance and its more recent vicissitudes, I am impressed by the fact that the relation of the Renaissance to the Middle Ages is the crucial point. Its relation to modern civilization is a subsidiary problem, dependent on the historian's notion of the extent to which Renaissance culture differed from that of the Middle Ages and the directions in which the deviation occurred. For centuries the conceptions of the Renaissance were shaped by men who disliked what they knew of medieval culture, and the more recent revisions of the traditional interpretation have come, for the most part, from men who for one reason or another felt drawn to some aspect of medieval civilization. In either case Renaissance historiography has fairly bristled with value judgements.

The Italian humanists, who laid the first foundations for the modern periodization of history, as well as for the conception of a rebirth of art and letters after the Middle Ages, were certainly guilty enough in this respect. Their admiration for classical culture led them to draw a clear line of demarcation between antiquity and the period of barbaric darkness that followed the decline of the Roman Empire. Petrarch thought ancient history ended when the emperors became Christian.[2] Flavio Biondo set the date somewhat later and more definitely at the year 410.[3] The humanists thus set up one of the boundaries of the Middle Ages; but their view of the thousand years that were later given that name varied, depending on the aspect of history which occupied them at the moment. As the political historians of the Italian states, they treated the whole period from the first appearance of the communes as one of steady growth down to their own day.[4] But as classical scholars, the products of an urban and secular society, they found much less to value in the culture of the period between the decline of ancient civilization and the recent revival of art and classical learning in Italy. Almost without exception they ignored the whole body of medieval feudal and ecclesiastical literature and leaped straight from the decline of ancient culture to the age of Giotto and Dante or, more commonly, Petrarch. Between those two ages art and

[2]Petrarch, *Epistolae de rebus familiaribus*, VI, 2 ed. F. Fracassetti (Florence, 1859), I, 314.

[3]F. Biondo, *Historiarum ab inclinatione Romanorum imperii decades* (Basel, 1531), p. 4.

[4]See, for example, Leonardo Bruni, *Historiarum Florentini populi libri xii*, in Muratori, XIX, 3 (new ed. by E. Santini, Città di Castello, 1914).

letters were dead, neglected, buried, sleeping, prostrate in the dust—these phrases occur over and over again—until they were revived or restored to the light by the great Italian masters of the fourteenth and fifteenth centuries. For this revival the humanists as a rule suggested no cause except the unexplained phenomenon of individual genius; though Leonardo Bruni, the Florentine historian, found a causal relation in the recovery of freedom by the Italian cities.[5] The Italian humanists, in their capacity as historians, contributed only these ingredients to the full conception of the Renaissance: that art and letters were dead for a period of centuries; that the revival coincided with the restoration of classical literature; and that it was the work of the genius of the Italian masters. But these ideas were to live for centuries among men whose tastes were formed by the classical traditions of education.

Where the Italian humanists had been generally content to pass over medieval culture as though it were nonexistent, the Erasmian humanists of the North added a positive factor to the conception of medieval darkness by a vitriolic attack upon scholasticism. Erasmus was convinced that both religion and learning had declined sadly since the time of the last classical writers and the Fathers of the Church, and that a reform could come only through a return to the sources in their ancient purity. The medieval system of education, he thought, was largely responsible for the deformation of both Christianity and good letters and in his own day it was still the principal barrier to reform.[6]

After the Reformation, the Protestant historians seized eagerly upon the conception of medieval culture thus developed by the humanists and used it as a propagandist weapon against the Roman Church. For two centuries and more, Protestant interpretations of medieval history were oriented by the necessity of proving that the light of the Gospel had been progressively obscured by the malign influence of the popes and their scholastic agents, with the result that Western Christendom had remained for a thousand years sunk in barbaric ignorance, superstition, and spiritual sloth. Philipp Melanchthon described medieval learning as a barbaric mixture of two evils: ignorant yet garrulous philosophy and the cult of idols.[7] And Bishop John Bale, popularly known as "bilious" Bale because of his talent for invective, in one of his milder moments concluded that the mere description of this sordid, obscure, and ignoble kind of writing was enough to move generous and well-born minds to nausea.[8]

---

[5]Bruni, *Vite di Dante e del Petrarca,* in *Autobiografie e vite de' maggiori scrittori italiani,* ed. A. Solerti (Milan, 1903), pp. 115 ff.

[6]See, for example, Erasmus, *Antibarbarorum liber* (Basel, 1520); cf. Ferguson, "Renaissance Tendencies in the Religious Thought of Erasmus," *Journal of the History of Ideas,* XV (1954), 506 ff.

[7]P. Melanchthon, *De Luthero et aetatibus ecclesiae, Opera,* ed. C. G. Brettschneider (Halle, 1834-60), XI, 786.

[8]J. Bale, *Illustrium maioris Britanniae scriptorum summarium* (Ipswich, 1548) f. 4 .

For the Protestant historians the Reformation was the beginning of a new age in the history of the Church, but they also hailed the revival of learning as marking the dawn of the new day. Viewed from this angle the renaissance of letters became a movement inspired by Divine Providence to prepare the way for the acceptance of the Gospel. The genius of the Italian masters dropped into the background as the theologians sought some more evident sign of God's handiwork. John Foxe, the author of the *Book of Martyrs,* found the origins of the movement in that "admirable work of God's Wisdom," the invention of printing, through which by God's grace "good wits" were stirred up "aptly to conceive the light of knowledge and judgment, by which light darkness began to be espied and ignorance to be detected, truth from error, religion from superstition to be discerned."[9] Théodore de Bèze, on the other hand, ascribed the revival to the fall of Constantinople and the flight of the Greek refugees to Italy.[10]

This latter idea took firm root in the following centuries among Northern historians who were but slightly interested in the earlier history of the Italian revival and to whom the cataclysmic cause appealed with all the charm of a theory that made further thought unnecessary. Thanks to Vasari, whose *Lives of the Great Painters, Sculptors and Architects*[11] had made the *rinascita dell' arte* in the age of Giotto and his contemporaries a standard conception, the early history of the revival of art was never forgotten; but through the seventeenth and eighteenth centuries the revival of learning was generally regarded as beginning in the age of the Medici. Meanwhile, the periodization of history implicit in the humanist pattern of cultural history and in the Protestant scheme of church history was reinforced by a growing appreciation of the significance of the explorations and discoveries and of the rise of the national states around 1500. Before the end of the seventeenth century it had hardened into the formal divisions of ancient, medieval, and modern history which still dominate our historical thought. In this scheme of periodization, the Renaissance, in its limited identification with the revival of learning and art, became merely one of the phenomena that marked the beginning of the modern age.

It was thus that the eighteenth century historians treated it, but they gave the revival of learning a new interpretation and a new significance. For them it was the first stage in the modern progress of reason. David Hume regarded it as one of the symptoms of what he called "the dawn of civility and science."[12] Like the Protestant historians, if for different reasons, the his-

---

[9]J. Foxe, *Acts and Monuments of the Christian Martyrs* (London, 1877), III, 718 ff.; IV, 4 ff., 252 ff.

[10]T. de Bèze, *Histoire ecclésiastique des Eglises Réformées au royaume de France* (Paris, 1883-89), I, 5.

[11]G. Vasari, *Le vite de' piu eccelenti architetti, pittori, e scultori italiani da Cimabue insino a tempi nostri* (Florence, 1550).

[12]D. Hume, *History of England from the Invasion of Julius Caesar to the Revolution in 1688* (London, 1864), II, 365.

torians of the Enlightenment condemned both the religion and the learning of the Middle Ages as ignorant, superstitious and barbarous. Like the humanists, too, they judged the literature and art of the past by classical standards, though their classicism was more rigid than that of the humanists and they added to the condemnation of medieval culture a more positive revulsion against its irrationality, eccentricity, and general formlessness. For the eighteenth century, then, the revival of art and learning under classical influences meant both the restoration of good taste and the liberation of human reason. Edward Gibbon summed up this classical-rationalist interpretation of the literary revival with the ponderous authority that only he could achieve:

> Before the revival of classic literature, the barbarians in Europe were immersed in ignorance; and their vulgar tongues were marked with the rudeness and poverty of their manners. The students of the more perfect idioms of Rome and Greece were introduced to a new world of light and science; to the society of the free and polished nations of antiquity; and to a familiar intercourse with the immortal men who spoke the sublime language of eloquence and reason ... As soon as it had been deeply saturated with the celestial dews, the soil was quickened into vegetation and life; the modern idioms were refined; the classics of Athens and Rome inspired a pure taste and a generous emulation; and in Italy, as afterwards in France and England, the pleasing reign of poetry and fiction was succeeded by the light of speculative and experimental philosophy.[13]

But if Gibbon placed the greater emphasis on the influence of the classics, Voltaire laid greater stress on intellectual progress, and on the spontaneous development of Italian genius. He described the history of Western Europe as "l'histoire de l'extinction, de la renaissance, et du progrès de l'esprit humain."[14] And of all the European peoples the Italians were the first to emerge from the *grossièreté* of the Middle Ages. In the fourteenth and fifteenth centuries, barbarism, superstition, and ignorance covered the face of the earth, except in Italy."[15] The Italians had a monopoly of genius. They were the most intelligent people in the world, and only in their rich cities could men live with comfort and enjoy the good things of life. Voltaire gave full value to the independent rebirth of the vernacular literature and the fine arts in the fourteenth century, but described the age of the Medici, which followed the fall of Constantinople and the revival of learning, as one of the four ages in human history that might be counted happy by a man of thought and taste. Voltaire's picture of Renaissance society, however, was not without its dark side. He was the first to stress the moral confusion, the irreligious attitude, and the criminal tendencies which were to become the distinguishing characteristics of the Italian Renaissance in nineteenth century historiography. Apparently assuming that such would be the natural result of the growth of learning and reason, Voltaire concluded that the leading classes in Italy had rejected Christianity. But true philosophy and natural religion, the products

---

[13]E. Gibbon, *The History of the Decline and Fall of the Roman Empire*, ed. J. B. Bury (New York, 1914), VII, 135 f.

[14]Voltaire, *Oeuvres complètes* (Paris, 1883-85), XXIV, 548.

[15]Voltaire, *Essai sur les moeurs et l'esprit des nations, Oeuvres*, XII, 123.

of the age of reason, had not yet been discovered. Hence the moral chaos of the Renaissance. "No century," he declared, "was so prolific in assassinations, poisonings, treason and monstrous debauches."[16]

The tradition of medieval darkness and of the rebirth of art, letters, and reason lasted into the nineteenth century. It was re-echoed by Roscoe, Hallam, and Michelet. True, it was no longer undisputed. The Romantic Movement introduced a rehabilitation of the Middle Ages. In reaction against rationalist values, the romantic historians idealized the chivalry, the religious aspirations, the poetry and art forms of feudal and monastic society. Yet this reversal of values did nothing to minimize the contrast between medieval and Renaissance culture. If anything, the romantic historians heightened the contrast, added color to the rational wickedness of the Renaissance, and regarded the age of the Medici and the Borgias with a kind of fascinated horror.

Thus far the conception of the Renaissance *per se* had been limited to the revival of learning or the *renaissance des lettres et des beaux arts*. Nearly all the ingredients of the Renaissance were already present, but they had not yet been fused together into a comprehensive synthesis, extended to include the whole civilization of the period. The Hegelian philosophy of history with its emphasis on the creative action of the Idea, on the *Volksgeist* and the *Zeitgeist*, pointed the way toward a periodic conception of the Renaissance as a "moment in the life of the spirit," and Michelet had used the term "Renaissance" in a periodic sense.[17] But it was not till the publication of Jacob Burckhardt's *Civilization of the Renaissance in Italy*[18] that the Renaissance was finally established as a separate period in *Kulturgeschichte*.

Burckhardt's Renaissance marked the culmination of the long tradition of medieval darkness and the rebirth of culture. In it the classical and rationalist strains of interpretation were particularly strong, but the whole synthesis would have been impossible before the nineteenth century, and some of its most characteristic features were a direct reflection of Burckhardt's own personality. Burckhardt combined historical insight and a rare capacity for synthesis with the mental and emotional bias of the aesthete and the intellectual aristocrat. Hence his peculiar emphasis on the conscious artistry of Renaissance institutions and on the liberation of individual personality from the corporate bondage of the Middle Ages. His interpretation appealed strongly to the aestheticism and liberalism as well as to the Hegelian idealism of the later nineteenth century. It carried convicion by the consummate artistry with which every aspect of Renaissance life was fitted into its place in an integrated whole, and the perfection of the synthesis helped to conceal the fact that it was a static picture.

But there is little need to dwell upon the Burckhardtian conception of the Renaissance. It is familiar enough. For half a century Renaissance histori-

---

[16]*Ibid.*, XII, 169.

[17]J. Michelet, *Histoire de France*, Vol. VII: *La Renaissance* (Paris, 1855).

[18]J. Burckhardt, *Die Cultur der Renaissance in Italien* (Basel, 1860).

ans did little more than repeat and amplify it, extending it to the Northern countries and appropriating to the Renaissance every indication of new life that they discovered in the Middle Ages. Even when historians began to depart from it in one direction or another, it remained the norm by which the deviations were measured.

The revisions of Burckhardt's formula, which have become increasingly numerous in the past four or five decades, proceeded from a variety of sources; from the religious romanticism of the late nineteenth century, which carried over into the Thomist revival of more recent Catholicism; from the growing nationalism, which in Germany was identified with a Pan-Germanic racial doctrine and in France with a belligerent assertion of French national culture; from a great increase in both the quantity and intensity of medieval studies, which coincided with a general decline in classical education, particularly in this country; and, closely associated with this, the extension of historical research to economic and social fields. Perhaps I might add, too, the natural tendency of historians, most of whom are professors, to think otherwise.

From these and other sources has come an increasing criticism of the following characteristics of the Burckhardtian Renaissance: the causative and determining influence of the revival of classical antiquity; the exclusively Italian origins of Renaissance thought; the unique individualism of Renaissance society; and, finally, the whole conception of the Renaissance as a separate period with a coherent and unchanging character, sharply contrasted with the Middle Ages.

The first notable departure from the classical-rational aspects of Burckhardt's interpretation appeared in the religious romanticism of Henry Thode's *Franz von Assisi und die Anfänge der Kunst der Renaissance in Italien*, first published in 1885. It was Thode's thesis that the individualism of the Renaissance, its subjective energy, and its reconciliation of religion with nature were the results not of the revival of antiquity, but of the religious mysticism and subjectivism of the Middle Ages. The figure of the saint of Assisi occupied the center of his picture. He was represented as both the culmination of one great trend in medieval religion and the inspiration of the Italian culture of the following two centuries, out of which, in turn, grew both humanism and the Reformation. Thode's book made little stir among the historians until his conception of St. Francis was reinforced by Paul Sabatier's unforgettable biography.[19] Since then, however, there has been a growing appreciation of the Christian content in Renaissance thought at the expense of the classical and rational. Emile Gebhardt and Konrad Burdach were directly influenced by Thode, and one might also mention among those who have stressed the continuity of Christian tradition in Italian humanism H. O. Taylor, Alfred von Martin, Ernst Walser, Giuseppe Toffanin, and, more recently, Douglas

---

[19]P. Sabatier, *Vie de St. François d'Assise* (Paris, 1894).

Bush.[20] It was not so necessary to demonstrate the Christian quality of Northern humanism, though Augustin Renaudet[21] and others have done so at great length. The relation between humanism and late medieval mysticism in the North has been pointed out by Paul Mestwerdt and Albert Hyma.[22]

The classical element in Renaissance culture has also suffered from the attacks of the national and racial schools of Northern historians. Early in this century Carl Neumann attempted to prove by the example of Byzantium that classical antiquity could not stimulate a new intellectual life, and asserted the revolutionary thesis that the vigor of Renaissance culture was a natural flowering of the one vital force in the medieval civilization, namely *deutsches Barbarentum*. Since then the Germanic thesis has been carried to the extreme of claiming direct Lombard or Gothic descent for all the geniuses of the Italian Renaissance from Dante to Michelangelo. More commonly, however, the recent German historians have been willing to admit the Italian national character of the Renaissance in Italy, but have insisted on the spontaneous and independent development of German culture. In much the same way, the French art historian Louis Courajod and the Fleming Fierens-Gevaert proclaimed not only the independent development of French and Burgundian art but also its priority to the Italian, thus reversing the stream of influence across the Alps.[24] In the field of literature and learning, too, recent French historians have been at pains to demonstrate the continuity of development from medieval France through the Renaissance. In doing so they have tended either to minimize the influence of the classics and stress that of the medieval French vernacular literature or to claim the revival of antiquity for the twelfth and thirteenth centuries when France still held the cultural hegemony of Western Europe.

The rehabilitation of medieval culture, however, owes most to the scholarly work of recent medievalists who cannot be accused either of undue romanticism or of national or racial bias; and it is from them that has come the most serious attack upon the conception of the Renaissance as a sudden,

---

[20]See, for example, E. Gebhardt, *L'Italie mystique, histoire de la Renaissance religieuse au Moyen Age* (Paris, 1890); K. Burdach, *Vom Mittelalter zur Reformation* (Halle, 1893); H. O. Taylor, *Thought and Expression in the Sixteenth Century* (New York, 1920); A. von Martin, *Mittelalterliche Welt-und Lebensanschauung im Spiegel der Schriften Coluccio Salutatis* (Munich, 1913); E. Walser, *Gesammelte Studien zur Geistesgeschichte der Renaissance* (Basel, 1932); G. Toffanin, *Storia dell'umanesimo* (Naples, 1933); and D. Bush, *The Renaissance and English Humanism* (Toronto, 1939).

[21]A. Renaudet, *Préréforme et humanisme à Paris pendant les premières guerres d'Italie* (Paris, 1916).

[22]P. Mestwerdt, *Die Anfänge des Erasmus: Humanismus und "Devotio Moderna"* (Leipzig, 1917); A. Hyma, *The Christian Renaissance* (New York, 1924).

[23]C. Neumann, "Byzantinische Kultur und Renaissancekultur," *Historische Zeitschrift*, XCI (1903), 215-232.

[24]See L. C. L. Courajod, *Leçons professées à l'Ecole du Louvre* (1887-96), 3 vols. (Paris, 1899-1903); H. Fierens-Gevaert, *La Renaissance septentrionale et les premiers maîtres de Flandres* (Brussels, 1905).

dazzling revival of classical learning, rational thought, and free individualism. Elsewhere I have called this movement "The Revolt of the Medievalists."[25] Charles Homer Haskins, Franz von Bezold, and others demonstrated the extent of the classical revival of the twelfth century.[26] H. O. Taylor insisted on the continuity of both the classical and the Christian traditions.[27] Helen Waddell in her charming book on the wandering scholars has demonstrated a feeling for the beauties of nature and the joys of this world among medieval poets influenced by classical models.[28] Etienne Gilson, the champion of scholastic philosophy, carried his defence of medieval thought still further and asserted the absolute superiority of the schoolmen over the humanists in both the recovery of antiquity and rational thought, and Jacques Maritain has called Scholasticism the true humanism.[29] Lynn Thorndyke and George Sarton have asserted a somewhat similar thesis in relation to science, tending to see in humanism a decline of systematic ratiocination for which the aesthetic interests of the humanists were an insufficient compensation;[30] and James Westfall Thompson has discovered a more extensive lay education in the Middle Ages than had generally been supposed.[31] Art historians, too, have contributed, perhaps more than their share, to the reversal of value judgments about medieval and Renaissance culture. Finally, in a book by no means free from special pleading, the francophile Swedish historian, Johan Nordstrom, has translated all the characteristics of the Burckhardtian Renaissance back into the twelfth and thirteenth centuries.[32] This tendency to discover the Renaissance in the Middle Ages has also been accompanied by a parallel tendency to find much of the Middle Ages in the Renaissance and to view the latter period, in Huizinga's phrase, as the "waning of the Middle Ages"[33] rather than as what Hume called "the dawn of civility and science."

One major result of all this has been a new emphasis on the continuity of historical development. Burckhardt's Italian Renaissance has thus been de-

---

[25]See Ferguson, *Renaissance in Historical Thought,* pp. 329 ff.

[26]C. H. Haskins, *The Renaissance of the Twelfth Century* (Cambridge, 1927); F. von Bezold, *Das Fortleben der antiken Götter im mittlealterlichen Humanismus* (Bonn, 1922); see also R. R. Bolgar, *The Classical Heritage and its Beneficiaries* (Cambridge, 1954), pp. 183 ff.

[27]H. O. Taylor, *The Medieval Mind* (New York, 1911).

[28]H. Waddell, *The Wandering Scholars* (London, 1927).

[29]E. Gilson, "Humanisme médiévale et Renaissance," in his *Les idées et les lettres* (Paris 1932); J. Maritain, *True Humanism* (New York, 1938).

[30]L. Thorndyke, *Science and Thought in the Fifteenth Century* (New York, 1929), pp. 1-10; G. Sarton, "Science in the Renaissance," in J. W. Thompson, G. Rowley, F. Schevill, and G. Sarton, *The Civilization of the Renaissance* (Chicago, 1929), p. 76.

[31]J. W. Thompson, *The Literacy of the Laity in the Middle Ages* (Berkeley, 1939).

[32]J. Nordstrom. *Moyen Age et Renaissance* (Paris, 1933).

[33]See J. Huizinga, *The Waning of the Middle Ages* (London, 1924).

prived of the unique character which differentiated it so clearly from
the contemporary culture of the northern countries. It has also been deprived
of much of its internal integration by the substitution of a dynamic conception for a relatively static portrayal of the spirit of the age.

The recognition of historical continuity is always, I think, a healthy
tendency, and one that was particularly necessary in the interpretation of the
Renaissance because of the deeply rooted tradition of its complete differentia-
tion from, and superiority over, everything medieval. But, granting the corrective value of the recent tendency, is it not possible that the historians who are
influenced by it are in danger of discrediting unduly much that was worth
while in Burckhardt's conception and, above all, of losing sight of the very
real differences between the prevailing tone of Renaissance civilization and
that of the twelfth and thirteenth centuries? To carry the criticism of Burckhardt's Renaissance to the point of abandoning the Renaissance as a period
altogether is, I think, unnecessary and deplorable. The term "Renaissance"
itself may be open to objection. It has unfortunate connotations. But there is
as yet no other recognized term for a period which, I think, requires recognition.

I have been happy to note in the last decade or so a swing of the pendu-
lum back toward appreciation of the originality of Renaissance culture. Some
extremely important contributions to this tendency have been made by the
historians of music, notably Heinrich Besseler, Gustave Reese, Albert Einstein, and Edward Lowinsky.[34] The history of music in the Middle Ages and
the Renaissance has been until recently a much neglected field, but one
capable of furnishing valuable illustrations of the changes in cultural tone
through these two ages. Among art historians, Erwin Panofsky[35] has done
much to rehabilitate the concept of the Renaissance, as Ernst Cassirer and P.
O. Kristeller have done for the history of philosophy[36] and Garrett Mattingly
for that of diplomacy.[37]

It should be understood, of course, that recognition of the Renaissance
as a period in history does not imply that it was completely different from
what preceded and what followed it. Even in a dynamic view of history,
periodization may prove a very useful instrument if properly handled. The
gradual changes brought about by a continuous historical development may
be in large part changes in degree, but when they have progressed far
enough they become for all practical purposes changes in kind. To follow a

---

[34]See, for example, H. Besseler, *Die Musik des Mittelalters und der Renaissance*
(Potsdam, 1931-35); G. Reese, *Music in the Renaissance* (New York, 1954); A.
Einstein, *The Italian Madrigal*, 3 vols. (New York, 1949); E. Lowinsky, "Music in
the Culture of the Renaissance," *American Historical Review*, LIX (1953), 19 ff.,
and numerous other articles.

[35]E. Panofsky, *Early Netherlandish Painting* (Cambridge, 1953), etc.

[36]See especially E. Cassirer, *Individuum und Kosmos in der Philosophie der Renaissance* (Leipzig, 1927); P. O. Kristeller, *The Philosophy of Ficino* (New York,
1943), and numerous articles.

[37]G. Mattingly, *Renaissance Diplomacy* (Boston, 1955).

good humanist precedent and argue from the analogy of the human body, the gradual growth of man from childhood to maturity is an unbroken process, yet there is a recognizable difference between the man and the child he has been. Perhaps the analogy, as applied to the Middle Ages and the Renaissance, is unfortunate in that it suggests a value judgment that might be regarded as invidious. However that may be, it is my contention that by about the beginning of the fourteenth century in Italy and somewhat later in the North those elements in society which had set the tone of medieval culture had perceptibly lost their dominant position and thereafter gradually gave way to more recently developed forces. These, while active in the earlier period, had not been the determining factors in the creation of medieval culture but were to be the most influential in shaping the culture of the Renaissance.

That somewhat involved statement brings me to the hazardous question of what were the fundamental differences between medieval and Renaissance civilization, and to the approach to the problem which I have found most generally satisfactory. It is an approach suggested by the work of the recent economic historians who have called attention to the dynamic influence of the revival of trade, urban life, and money economy in the midst of the agrarian feudal society of the high Middle Ages. Unfortunately, economic historians have seldom spared much thought for the development of intellectual and aesthetic culture, having been content to leave that to the specialists, while, on the other hand, the historians whose special interest was religion, philosophy, literature, science, or art have all too frequently striven to explain the developments in these fields without correlating them with changes in the economic, social, and political structure of society. In the past few years, however, historians have become increasingly aware of the necessity of including all forms of human activity in any general synthesis, an awareness illustrated by Myron Gilmore's recent volume on *The World of Humanism.* Further, there has been a growing tendency to find the original motive forces of historical development in basic alterations of the economic, political, and social system, which in time exert a limiting and directing influence upon intellectual interests, religious attitudes, and cultural forms. As applied to the Renaissance, this tendency has been evident in the work of several historians, notably Edward P. Cheyney, Ferdinand Schevill, Eugenio Garin, Hans Baron and some of the contributors to the *Propyläen Weltgeschichte.*[39]

To state my point as briefly as possible, and therefore more dogmatically than I could wish:[40] let us begin with the axiomatic premise that the two

---

[38]M. Gilmore, *The World of Humanism, 1453-1517* (New York, 1952).

[39]See, for example, E. P. Cheyney, *The Dawn of a New Era, 1250-1453* (New York, 1936); F. Schevill, *History of Florence from the Founding of the City through the Renaissance* (New York, 1936); E. Garin, *L'Umanesimo italiano: Filosofia e vita civile nel Rinascimento* (Bari, 1952); H. Baron, *The Crisis of the Early Italian Renaissance: Civic Humanism and Republican Liberty in an Age of Classicism and Tyranny* (Princeton, 1955); W. Goetz (ed.), *Propyläen Weltgeschichte,* Vol. IV: *Das Zeitalter der Gotik und Renaissance* (Berlin, 1932).

[40]For fuller discussion, see Ferguson, "The Interpretation of the Renaissance: Suggestions for a Synthesis," *Journal of the History of Ideas,* XII (1951), 483-495. See below, pp. 125 ff.

essential elements in medieval civilization were the feudal system and the universal Church. The latter represented an older tradition than feudalism, but in its external structure and in many of its ideals and ways of thought it had been forced to adapt itself to the conditions of feudal society. And feudalism in turn was shaped by the necessity of adapting all forms of social and political life to the limitations of an agrarian and relatively moneyless economy. Into this agrarian feudal society the revival of commerce and industry, accompanied by the growth of towns and money economy, introduced a new and alien element. The first effect of this was to stimulate the existing medieval civilization, freeing it from the economic, social, and cultural restrictions that an almost exclusive dependence upon agriculture had imposed upon it, and making possible a rapid development in every branch of social and cultural activity. That the twelfth and thirteenth centuries were marked by the growth of a very vigorous culture no longer needs to be asserted. They witnessed the recovery of much ancient learning, the creation of scholastic philosophy, the rise of vernacular literatures and of Gothic art, perhaps on the whole a greater advance than was achieved in the two following centuries. Nevertheless, it seems to me that, despite new elements and despite rapid development, the civilization of these two centuries remained in form and spirit predominantly feudal and ecclesiastical.

But medieval civilization, founded as it was upon a basis of land tenure and agriculture, could not continue indefinitely to absorb an expanding urban society and money economy without losing its essential character, without gradually changing into something recognizably different. The changes were most obvious in the political sphere, as feudalism gave way before the rise of city states or centralized territorial states under princes who were learning to utilize the power of money. The effect upon the Church was almost equally great. Its universal authority was shaken by the growing power of the national states, while its internal organization was transformed by the evolution of a monetary fiscal system which had, for a time, disastrous effects upon its moral character and prestige.[41] Meanwhile, within the cities the growth of capital was bringing significant changes in the whole character of urban economic and social organization, of which not the least significant was the appearance of a growing class of urban laymen who had the leisure and means to secure a liberal education and to take an active part in every form of intellectual and aesthetic culture.

Taking all these factors together, the result was an essential change in the character of European civilization. The feudal and ecclesiastical elements, though still strong, no longer dominated, and they were themselves more or less transformed by the changing conditions. The culture of the period we call the Renaissance was predominantly and increasingly the product of the cities, created in major part by urban laymen whose social environment, per-

---

[41]For fuller discussion of this interpretation of the effect of social and economic change on state and church during the Renaissance, see Ferguson, "Toward the Modern State," in *The Renaissance, a Symposium* (New York, 1953), and "The Church in a Changing World: A Contribution to the Interpretation of the Renaissance," *American Historical Review*, LIX (1953), 1-18. See below, pp. 137 ff; 155 ff.

sonal habits, and professional interests were different from those of the feudal and clerical aristocracy who had largely dominated the culture of the Middle Ages. These urban laymen, and with them the churchmen who were recruited from their midst as the medieval clergy had been recruited from the landed classes, did not break suddenly or completely with their inherited traditions, but they introduced new materials and restated the old in ways that reflected a different manner of life. The Renaissance, it seems to me, was essentially an age of transition, containing much that was still medieval, much that was recognizably modern, and, also, much that, because of the mixture of medieval and modern elements, was peculiar to itself and was responsible for its contradictions and contrasts and its amazing vitality.

This interpretation of the Renaissance leaves many of the old controversial points unanswered, though a partial answer to most of them is implied in it. It may be as well not to attempt to answer all questions with a single formula. There was certainly enough variety in the changing culture of Western Europe during both the Middle Ages and the Renaissance to provide historians with material to keep them happily engaged in controversy for some time to come. All that can be claimed for the approach I have suggested is that it seems to offer the broadest basis for periodization, that it points to the most fundamental differences between the civilization of the Renaissance and the Middle Ages, while recognizing the dynamic character of both. At the same time, by suggesting a broad theory of causation in the gradual transformation of the economic and social structure of Western Europe, it tends to reduce the controversial questions regarding the primary influence of the classical revival, of the Italian genius, Germanic blood, medieval French culture, or Franciscan mysticism to a secondary, if not irrelevant, status. Finally, such an approach to the problem might make it possible to take what was genuinely illuminating in Burckhardt, without the exaggerations of the classical-rational-Hegelian tradition, and also without the necessity of attacking the Renaissance *per se* in attacking Burckhardtian orthodoxy.

HUMANIST VIEWS OF THE RENAISSANCE*

The problem of the Renaissance—its character, its causes, and its relation to the Middle Ages—has been one of the most controversial subjects in recent historiography. The relative unanimity of opinion entertained by the followers of Jacob Burckhardt has degenerated during the past generation into chaos. The chronological limits of the Renaissance have been expanded to include the High Middle Ages or have been contracted almost to the vanishing point. The term itself has been used to designate, on the one hand, the entire history of a chronological epoch and, on the other, no more than certain specific developments in literature and the arts. There has been heated debate over the essential character or spirit of Renaissance culture and over the relative causative importance of race, nationality, classical literature, Franciscan mysticism, and economic forces.

Under these circumstances the problem of the Renaissance has become a problem in the field of historiography as well as in the field of history. Numerous articles and monographs, mostly of German origin have been devoted to the historical development of our conceptions of the Renaissance and, incidentally, of the Middle Ages.[1] The subject is, however, too large and too complex for adequate treatment in a single article. The purpose of the present essay is merely to investigate as thoroughly as possible the first chronological period in the history of Renaissance histori-

---

* Reprinted from THE AMERICAN HISTORICAL REVIEW, Vol. XLV, No. 1, October, 1939.

[1] See Walter Goetz, "Mittelalter und Renaissance", *Historische Zeitschrift*, XCVIII (1907), 30-54; Karl Brandi, Das Werden der Renaissance (Göttingen, 1908); Adolf Philippi, *Der Begriff der Renaissance* (Leipzig, 1912); Paul Lehmann, *Vom Mittelalter* (Munich, 1914); Werner Weisbach, "Renaissance als Stilbegriff". *Hist. Zeitsch.*, CXX (1919) 250-80; E. F. Jacob, "The Fifteenth Century: Some Recent Interpretations", *Bulletin of the John Rylands Library*, XIV (1930), 386-409, and "Changing Views of the Renaissance", *History*, XVI (Apr., 1931 - Jan., 1932), 214-29; J. Huizinga, "Das Problem der Renaissance", in his *Wege der Kulturgeschichte* (Munich, 1930); Johan Nordstrom, *Moyen Age et Renaissance* (Paris, 1933); H. W. Eppelsheimer, "Das Renaissance-Problem", *Deutsche Vierteljahrsschrift für Literaturwissenschaft und Geistesgeschichte*, XI (1933), 477-500; G. Weise, "Der doppelte Begriff der Renaissance", *ibid.*, 501-29; C. Neumann, "Ende des Mittelalters?", *ibid.*, XII (1934), 124-71.

ography, that represented by the historical, biographical, and critical work of the Italian humanists.

The conceptions held by the humanists of the course of history from antiquity, through what has since been called the Middle Ages, to their own time have a double significance. In themselves they are an important aspect of Renaissance thought, and they had also a not inconsiderable rôle in shaping the historical ideas of later writers. Yet it is difficult to discover from secondary works what the humanists actually had to say on this interesting subject. There has been much loose generalization from occasional *obiter dicta.* Those modern scholars who have sought the origins of the *Renaissancebegriff* or of the concept of the Middle Ages in the writings of the humanists have limited their research almost entirely to the use of words implying rebirth or the idea of a *medium aevum.*[2] This is notably true of Konrad Burdach and Karl Borinski, who have furnished the most exhaustive investigation into the origins of the word and the idea of rebirth in this period.[3] They have, indeed, made valuable contributions to our knowledge of the pagan and Christian origins and early history of religious, political, and chiliastic conceptions of rebirth and reformation. But Borinski is more interested in the symbolical and philosophical expression of ideas of rebirth of the world than in the historical ideas of the Renaissance writers. Burdach, too, has paid little attention to the historical works of the humanists, and his argument suffers from a tendency to press every obscure reference to rebirth, reformation, or regeneration into the service of his thesis that the Renaissance was essentially the conscious rebirth of the human soul, an *innerliche Bewegung* rising from the subjective religious emotion of the later Middle Ages and reinforced by a growing consciousness of Italian national rebirth in the age of Dante, Petrarch, and Cola da Rienzi.[4] For the present purpose of trying to discover what were the Italian humanists' conceptions of their own and past ages and of the general course and periodization of history, I have felt it better to abandon the search for their use of words meaning rebirth or Middle Ages and to seek instead the fullest and most coherent discussions of the problem to be found in their works.

---

[2]See the articles by Brandi, Lehmann, Weisbach, and Huizinga, cited above. Philippi's monograph is rather an exception but is limited to the history of the fine arts.

[3]Burdach, "Sinn und Ursprung der Worte Renaissance und Reformation", *Sitzungsberichte der Preussischen Akademie der Wissenschaften* (1910), 594-646; Borinski, "Die Weltwiedergeburtsidee in den neueren Zeiten", *Sitzungsberichte der Bayerischen Akademie der Wissenschaften* (1919), I Abh., pp. 1-130.

[4]See also Burdach, *Deutsche Renaissance* (Berlin. 1916), and *Rienzo und die geistige Wandlung seiner Zeit* (2 vols., Berlin, 1913-28). For criticism see Jacob, *History,* XVI, 222, and Paul Joachimsen, "Vom Mittelalter zur Reformation", *Historische Vierteljahrsschrift,* XX (1922), 426-70.

1

The age of the Renaissance saw the birth of modern historiography. Nearly all the leading humanists wrote some history, and the best of them showed an awareness of the essential nature of historical writing that sets their work clearly apart from the chronicles of the preceding centuries. Their historical works, therefore, should naturally form one of the first sources to be examined in any attempt to discover their picture of their own age and its relation to the past. These works, however, have been almost entirely ignored in the search for early conceptions of the Renaissance and the Middle Ages, and, in general, they have been treated very superficially by the historians of Renaissance culture. Much of this neglect has been due, undoubtedly, to the humanists' own very narrow view of the scope of history. For them history was simply past politics. Their histories scarcely mention the economic life of the people and, though many of them commented elsewhere on the history of literature and art, they excluded these subjects from their formal histories as pertaining to a different genre. Still another reason for the comparative neglect of the humanists as historians applies particularly to those who wrote in stylistic Latin under the direct influence of classical models. Since Burckhardt it has been the fashion to dismiss them as sterile imitators of Livy and Sallust and to deplore the lack of definite chronology, local color, and specific realism, which resulted from the use of a rhetorical style and of a vocabulary that was not adapted to post-classical institutions.[5]

Whatever may be the justice of this criticism, and it is at least open to question,[6] it can scarcely be denied that the best of the humanist histories had advanced far beyond the naive and formless medieval chronicle in perspective, coherent organization, and critical sense.[7] Above all, the humanists had taken an essential step in the direction of sound historical thought by abandoning the medieval habit of ascribing all events to supernatural causes. They no longer saw history merely as the working out of Divine Providence but rather as the record of human activity, inspired by human motives. A part of this advance, but only a part, must be ascribed

---

[5]See Jakob Burckhardt, *Die Cultur der Renaissance in Italien* (Basel, 1860), p. 238 ff. (Eng. trans. by S. G. C. Middlemore, 1921, pp. 244 ff.). For more recent expression of the same criticism, though with some modifications, see Eduard Fueter, *Geschichte der neueren Historiographie* (3d ed., enlarged. Munich, 1936), pp. 9 ff., 18 ff.; Vittorio Rossi, *Il Quattrocento* (new ed., Milan, 1933), pp. 169 ff.; Ferdinand Schevill, *History of Florence* (New York, 1936), p. xvii.

[6]Emilio Santini, *Leonardo Bruni Aretino e i suoi "Historiarum Florentini populi libri XII"* (Pisa, 1910), p. 88; Walter Goetz, "Renaissance und Antike", *Hist. Zeitsch,* CXIII, (1914), 254 f.

[7]See an illuminating discussion of the advances made in historiography during the fifteenth century in Hans Baron, "Das Erwachen des historischen Denkens im Humanismus des Quattrocento", in *Hist. Zeitsch.,* CXLVII (1932), 5-20; see also Paul Joachimsen, *Geschichtsauffassung und Geschichtschreibung in Deutschland unter dem Einfluss des Humanismus* (Leipzig, 1910), pp. 19 ff. Even Fueter admits the advance in the use of criticism (p. 17).

to the advantages of a classical education. More important than the fact that they were classical scholars was the fact that most of them were laymen who had had wide experience in business, law, government, or diplomacy. Even those whose connection with the papal curia or whose search for benefices had given them a nominal status as clergy had a thoroughly lay point of view. They represented at once the secular attitude of the now dominating class of educated urban laity and the practical politics and diplomacy of the newly developed states. The humanists brought to the writing of history an appreciation of the part played by individuals, parties, and states that was far beyond the range of the monastic chroniclers and also a knowledge of the past and a breadth of political experience far greater than had been enjoyed by the medieval burghers whose chronicles were devoted exclusively to the interests of their own self-centered communes. They wrote a different kind of history from that of the Middle Ages not only because they had a different kind of education but because they lived in a different economic, social, and political environment. And it was just because they expressed the ideas and interests of the most influential classes of their day that their work is significant for the history of Renaissance culture and that their picture of their own and past ages, despite their unfortunate limitation to political history, is too important to be ignored.

It cannot be denied, however, that exclusive preoccupation with politics did rob the humanist histories of much of the interest they might otherwise have possessed. This is particularly true of those that dealt only with the military, diplomatic, and political history of their own time. There is little of value in them for our purpose. Those that included a large section of the past are much more significant. Even purely political history, when extended far enough into the past, provides an opportunity for the development of historical perspective and makes almost inevitable the creation of some time scheme or periodization that will fit the purposes of the narrative. It also opens the way to rational speculation, if on very limited grounds, as to the reasons for the rise and decline of states and the nature of historical change. Finally, political history provides a medium for the expression and development of patriotic or national sentiments which may color the historian's whole picture of the past and its relation to the present.

Indeed, it was the very fact that they were writing the political history of states that forced the humanists to adopt an organization and periodization of history and a method of interpretation radically different from that common in the Middle Ages. The world chronicles of the medieval churchmen were constructed on a basis of theology and were shaped by concepts of a divinely ordained universal church with its secular counterpart in a universal empire. They divided human history into six ages, corresponding to the six days of creation, or, more frequently, into the four monarchies mentioned in the prophecy of Daniel. The fourth and last of these monarchies had been definitely identified by St. Jerome with the Roman Empire.[8] Under the influence of Augustine and Orosius the idea of the Roman Empire as the last

---

[8]Borinski, *Sitz. Bayerischen Akad.*, I, 35.

of the world monarchies, which should continue until the beginning of the reign of Antichrist, was transferred from the pagan to the Christian empire, and the belief in the necessary continuity of the Roman Empire was maintained throughout the Middle Ages by the fiction of the *translatio imperii ad Francos* or *ad Teutonicos*.[9] As long as historical thought remained within this framework of supernatural teleology there could be no idea of a distinction between ancient Roman civilization and that of the age following the breakup of the empire, nor of a rising civilization after the darkest period was passed. Many of the medieval historians, as Otto of Freising, were aware of the decline of the Roman Empire, but only as a symptom of the general senescence of a world approaching its end. In any case it was regarded as the continuous decline of a universal empire still existing in their own day.[10] This view of the empire was still accepted in Dante's time and formed the basis of his political theories in the *De monarchia.* Such an organization of world history was perfectly adapted to the needs of medieval theologians and fitted the conception of the unity and universal character of the Respublica Christiana. It could not satisfy the humanist historians, who were primarily interested in the secular history of individual Italian states.

The transition from medieval to Renaissance modes of thought was in this as in all other respects a gradual one. The changing mental attitudes that came with the growth of the cities and the appearance of an educated urban laity were expressed first in the practical fields of business and politics. It was only after considerable delay and by slow degrees that they began to operate in the fields of more abstract thought and speculation which had so long been dominated by theology and scholastic philosophy. Among the historians the figure of Giovanni Villani marks one of the early stages in this transition. Like so many of his humanist successors, he was a practical man of affairs. His discussion of contemporary economic and political life in Florence is based on acute and independent observation. But, as Professor Schevill has noted, "on the reflective and speculative side of his mind he remained contentedly a medieval man."[11]

Though his interests were in many respects different from those of the medieval world chroniclers, Villani accepted their supernaturalistic interpretation of world history. He begins his *Cronica* with the Tower of Babel, recounts with complete credence the mythological stories of the founding of his city, and observes at every turn the workings of Divine Providence. Yet he does not mention the Six Ages or the Four Monarchies, and toward the end of his book he makes an effort to work out a new scheme of periodization together with what he probably regarded as a more

---

[9]Walther Rehm, *Der Untergang Roms im abendländischen Denken* (Leipzig, 1930), pp. 27 f.

[10]*Ibid.*, pp. 33-41.

[11]*History of Florence*, p. 227.   See a similar judgment in Ernst Mehl, *Die Weltanschauung des Giovanni Villani* (Leipzig, 1927), p. 181.

natural theory of causation. With the aid of current astrology he developed a historical scheme based on the conjunctions of certain planets, occurring at approximately twenty-year intervals, which were invariably accompanied by great changes in the course of history, such as the conquest of Sicily by Robert Guiscard or the defeat of Manfred by Charles of Anjou.[12] Modern historians may regard this as no great improvement over the lore of the Four Monarchies, but it had, at least, the incidental value of making the decline of the Roman Empire, because of the barbarian invasions, the starting point for a new historical epoch, for the first and most powerful of the forty-eight conjunctions was that which marked the invasion of Italy by the Goths and Vandals, some 960 or 953 years prior to the last conjunction of 1345.[13]

A generation later, Petrarch, with his romantic admiration for ancient Roman literature and republican virtue, emphasized the distinction between the period of purely Roman history and the Christian-barbarian era that followed.[14] He rejected the *translatio imperii* as an actual impossibility, for the Roman *imperium* belonged to Rome alone, having sprung from the *virtus* of the Roman people, and could not be alienated. "Si imperium Romanum Rome non est, ubi, queso, est?"[15] But if Petrarch did not share Dante's teleological belief in the continuation of the Roman Empire, he had an equally unhistorical faith in the mystical continuation of the *virtus Romana* among the degenerate Roman populace of his own day and in the possibility of a political rebirth of the ancient republic, whence his enthusiastic approval of Cola di Rienzi's fantastic revolution.[16] This identification of virtuous republican Rome with the papal city as it was in the fourteenth century bore so little relation to reality that it made no great impression on the later humanists. Nevertheless, Petrarch's literary devotion to the ancient republic, his ascription of its greatness to human causes, and his clear distinction between what was Roman and what was barbarian or Teutonic were all to bear fruit. It was left for the humanist historians of the Quattrocento, however, to adapt these ideas to the political interests and realities of their own age and to fashion a coherent scheme of secular Italian history.

One of the prime motives inspiring all humanist historiography was

---

[12]Giovanni Villani, *Cronica*, xii, 41, in *Croniche di Giovanni, Matteo, e Filippo Villani, secondo le migliori stampe* (Trieste, 1857), I, 469. See Mehl, pp. 169 ff. for a fuller explanation of Villani's astrological periodization.

[13]"E in novecentosessanta, ovvero in novecentocinquantatrè anni fornite le quarantotto congiunzioni; e tornando alla prima, ch' è la più poderosa di tutte, chi cercherà indietro troverà il cominciamento del calo della potenzia del romano imperio alla venuta de' Goti e de' Vandali in Italia, e molte turbazioni a Santa Chiesa, et caetera." *Cronica*, xii, 41 (ed. 1857, I, 469).

[14]H. W. Eppelsheimer, *Petrarca* (Bonn, 1926), p. 82.

[15]Petrarch, *Liber sine nomine*, letter 4, in Paul Piur, *Petrarcas 'Buch ohne Namen' und die päpstliche Kurie* (Halle, 1925), p. 176.

[16]Eppelsheimer, *Petrarca*, pp. 78, 100 ff.; Baron, *Hist. Zeitsch.*, CXLVII, 8.

patriotic sentiment. This was certainly true of Petrarch and true also of the historians of the following century; but the latter wore their patriotism with a difference. The argument, so frequently repeated as to be a historical commonplace, that the Italians of the Renaissance recognized in ancient Rome the glory of their own national past and that their enthusiasm for Roman antiquity was reinforced by national sentiment applies more truly to Petrarch than to the majority of his successors. His life in exile from his paternal city had given him a romantic national patriotism that was rare in Renaissance Italy, while his psychological shrinking from the realities of the present led him to seek compensation in the ancient glories of his native land.

The later humanists, for the most part, lived in more contented harmony with present reality. Like Petrarch, they showed a certain degree of national consciousness in their pride in the achievements of modern Italy and in their dislike and contempt for the barbarians of the north; but the most fervid patriotism of nearly all fifteenth century Italians was concentrated on their own particular states. To celebrate the history of one of the Italian states was the patriotic motive that inspired the majority of humanist historians or was imposed upon them by their official patrons. And since these city-states arose only after the collapse of the Roman Empire, those historians who did not limit their work to purely contemporary events naturally began their story with the decline of the empire and carried it through the medieval period in which the cities grew great.[17] The result was a new periodization of history, with the decline of the empire marking the end of one epoch and the beginning of another.[18]

Leonardo Bruni, called Aretino, was the founder and one of the most profound exponents of the new school of humanist historiography. In his *Historiarum Florentini populi libri xii,*[19] begun about 1415 and still not quite completed at his death in 1444, he set a standard for the critical use of sources, for the rejection of legend, and for the interpretation of political history according to human and natural causes. This work had a very wide influence, though one of its most striking characteristics, the strongly republican interpretation of history, could not be followed very far by the wandering humanists who wrote at the command of princely despots. In this respect Bruni's thought was more in harmony with Florentine burgher humanism

---

[17]The idea, originating with Georg Voigt (*Enea Silvio,* II [Berlin, 1862], pp. 309 f.) and since frequently repeated (as in Lehmann, p. 4) that the humanists wrote only ancient and contemporary history and ignored the Middle Ages is far from the truth. Few wrote ancient history, but many wrote on the Middle Ages. See Fueter, pp. 16, 28 f.

[18]This, of course, applies only to the fifteenth century historians who wrote in the humanist tradition. An occasional friar whose training had been more scholastic than humanistic still wrote world chronicles of the old type, *e.g.,* Antonio Pierozzi, whose *Chronicon universale* (completed in 1459) was based on the old scheme of the six ages and four monarchies. See Joachimsen, pp. 80 ff.

[19]Recently republished in the new edition of L. A. Muratori, *Rerum Italicarum scriptores,* Vol. XIX, pt. 3, ed. by Emilio Santini, 1914.

than with that of the despotic courts. His own thought, too, had been profoundly influenced by Aristotle's *Politics,* with its emphasis on the connection between virtue and the public life of the city-state.[20] More than any historian of his generation he perceived the vitally important rôle of the free Italian communes in the evolution of modern Italy. Consequently he regarded the dissolution of the Roman Empire less as an unrelieved disaster than as a prelude to the rise of the communes, thus providing, as Santini observes, the first historical justification of the Middle Ages.[21]

Bruni's feeling for political liberty colors his whole interpretation of the problem of the decline and fall of the Roman Empire. Rome reached the apex of her power in the days of the republic; the decline began with the loss of political freedom under the despotism of the emperors.[22] He admits that Augustus and Trajan accomplished some good things and that there were others worthy of praise; but, he argues, if one considers the number of excellent men put to death by Augustus, the savage cruelty of Tiberius, the madness of Caligula, and so on through a long list of "such monsters", it cannot be denied that the Roman *imperium* began to go to ruin when first the name of Caesar fell like a disaster upon the city.[23] Freedom ended with the appearance of the imperial title, "et post libertatem virtus abivit."

This conception of the decline of Rome as beginning with the creation of the imperial monarchy was not entirely new, though it was foreign to the thought of the Middle Ages. Petrarch, with his literary passion for the Roman republic, had already suggested it.[24] There is a hint of it, too, in Orosius,[25] but it is unlikely that this was the source of Bruni's theory,[26] for the latter based his conclusions on entirely different grounds. Bruni saw the fundamental cause of the empire's decline in the moral effects of despotism, just as the greatness of the republic had been due to the moral qualities engendered by freedom. In the old days, he says, virtue had opened the road to honors, and those who surpassed their fellows in greatness of soul *(magnitudine animi),* virtue and industry easily achieved the highest offices.

---

[20]Introduction to Leonardo Bruni Aretino, *Humanistisch-philosophische Schriften,* ed. by Hans Baron (Leipzig, 1928), pp. XVIII ff.

[21]*L. Bruni e i suoi Hist.,* pp. 41 ff.

[22]"Declinationem autem romani imperii ab eo fere tempore ponendam reor quo, amissa libertate, imperatoribus servire Roma incepit", *Hist. Flor. pop.,* p. 14.

[23]*Ibid.:* "negare non poterit tunc romanum imperium ruere coepisse, cum primo caesareum nomen, tanquam clades aliqua, civitati incubuit".

[24]Eppelsheimer, *Petrarca,* p. 93.

[25]Paulus Orosius, *Historiarum adversum paganos libri vii,* vi, 14: "Caesar Galliam perdomuit Romanumque imperium usque ad extremos propemodum terrae terminos propagatum est. Hanc nunc amplissimam dilatationem vastissima ruina consequitur." *Corpus scriptorum ecclesiasticorum latinorum,* V (1882), 393.

[26]As suggested by Rossi, p. 171. See Santini, *L. Bruni e i suoi Hist.,* page 39, and his note to page 14 of the *Hist. Flor. pop.* for an argument to the contrary.

But as soon as the republic fell under the power of one man, virtue and magnanimity began to be suspect, and only those pleased the emperors who had not that *vis ingenii* which love of liberty stimulates. Thus weaklings took the place of the strong; instead of the industrious, sycophants filled the court; and the government, having been given over to the worst element, brought ruin on the empire. Bruni gives a long list of crimes and revolutions that were the inevitable result of this situation. At first the strength of Rome enabled her to keep her enemies at bay despite these internal ills, but after Constantine had moved the capital to Byzantium, Italy and the other parts of the empire in the West were neglected and left open to the invasions of the barbarians, "qui ceu in vacuam possessionem ruentes, variis temporibus, tanquam diluvia quaedam, has terras inundarunt".[27]

The last vivid picture leaves no doubt in the reader's mind that the Roman Empire in the West was no more. If there remain any doubts as to Bruni's conviction on that score, they are set at rest by his later discussion of the coronation of Charlemagne and the "usurpation" of the imperial title in Germany down to his own day.[28] To make his point clear he reviews the whole history of the empire and the imperial title. He insists on the purely Roman character of the empire, which was the creation of the Roman people, and finally on the fact that it ceased to exist in the West after the barbarian invasions—after Augustulus no ruler of the West bore the title of emperor until Charlemagne.[29] This new empire, revived after more than three hundred years, was not a part of the united Roman Empire as the earlier Western Empire had been. Charlemagne and his successors did not co-operate with the Eastern emperor and did not consider the two rulers colleagues. The insignia of the empire, the method of election, everything was different.

Having broken with the theory of the continuation of the Roman Empire, Bruni was free to break also with the tradition of continuous decline. That he saw an end to the decline and a decided turning point in the history of Italy after the breakup of the Carolingian Empire is made clear by a significant passage following his discussion of Charlemagne. Here he notes that after the *imperium* departed into Germany and when few of the emperors kept a permanent residence in Italy, visiting the country only for brief campaigns, the cities of Italy gradually began to be mindful of their freedom and to think less of the imperial authority. Thereupon such cities throughout Italy as had survived the various barbarian floods began to grow

[27]*Hist. Flor. pop.*, p. 15.

[28]*Ibid.*, p. 22.

[29]"Romanum imperium a populo romano institutum atque perfectum est" (*ibid.*, p. 22). "Occupantibus deinde Italiam barbaris, occidentale cessavit imperium: nec post Augustulum illum, quem ab Odoacre deiectum ostendimus, quisquam, ne tirannice quidem, per Italiam et Occidentem id nomen suscepit usque ad Carolum Magnum, quem a Leone pontifice imperatorem diximus appellatum" (*ibid.*, p. 23).

and flourish and return to their original power.[30] He then goes on to note the Tuscan cities that had survived or were now refounded. The dark period during which many great cities had perished was now past, and for Tuscany he evidently felt that that unhappy period extended back to the very beginning of the Roman domination, an idea that would have shocked Petrarch's Roman patriotism.[31] From this point on Bruni's history is the story of the growth of the Italian cities and their struggle for freedom until, with the collapse of the Hohenstaufen empire, he returns more specifically to the history of the Florentine state. His interpretation of the struggle between the papal and imperial factions, which divided the Italian cities, carries out his major thesis. The Guelf faction was made up of those who loved liberty and regarded the domination of Italy by German barbarians, "sub praetextu romani nominis", as shameful, while the Ghibellines were those who were so attached to the imperial name and so forgetful of the liberties and glories of their ancestors that they preferred to bow to the foreigner.[32]

Bruni's general conception of the Middle Ages was strongly reinforced and given much more definite chronological limits in the *Historiarum ab inclinatione Romanorum imperii decades* of Flavio Biondo of Forlì, written between the years 1439 and 1453.[33] Though it contains decided evidence of Bruni's influence,[34] the *Decades* represents a distinct departure from the popular type of state history that originated with the *Historiarum Florentini populi libri xii* and is the only history written during the fifteenth century that can compare with it in originality or influence. It is a careful, critical work, based on the best and oldest sources obtainable, covering the history of all Italy with a running commentary on the Eastern Empire, and as such it was the first, though by no means the last, of its kind. Indeed, with its plenitude of definite dates, its factual treatment of events, and its incredibly heavy style, it is unhappily reminiscent of innumerable history texts "from the fall of Rome to the present". The humanists damned Biondo with faint praise because of his hopelessly unclassical style, but they paid him the sincere compliment of plagiarizing his work more extensively than that of any other

---

[30]"Postquam igitur in Germaniam imperium abiit, ac pauci ex iis in Italia statione continua, plurimi vero adventiciis, cum erat opus, exercitibus ad tempus morabantur, civitates Italiae paulatim ad libertatem respicere, ac imperium verbo magis quam facto confiteri coeperunt, Romamque ipsam et romanum nomen, veneratione potius antiquae potentiae quam presenti metu recognoscere; denique quotcumque ex variis barbarorum diluviis superfuerant urbes per Italiam, crescere atque florere et in pristinam auctoritatem sese attollere". *Ibid.,* p. 23.

[31]"Sed in Etruria quidem, a primis illis Romanorum bellis usque ad haec tempora, civitates multae, oppidaque magna, quorum prius fuerat auctoritas, interierant." *Ibid.,* pp. 23 f.

[32]*Ibid.,* p. 25.

[33]First printed at Venice in 1483. The following quotations are from the Froben edition of Biondo's works (Basel, 1531). For an excellent life of Biondo and a discussion of his writings see *Scritti inediti e rari di Biondo Flavio,* with an introduction by Bartolomeo Nogara (Rome, 1927).

[34]Joachimsen, p. 22.

historian.[35] "Procul Blondus ab eloquentia prisca fuit", wrote Aeneas Silvius at the time of Biondo's death, and could think of no more to say of his history than that it was "opus certe laboriosum et utile, verum expolitore emendatoreque dignum".[36] Nevertheless, the humanist pope thought it worth his while to assume the rôle of "expolitor emendatorque" and wrote a full résumé of a large part of the *Decades*.[37]

Biondo's work, unlike the state histories written by the majority of the humanists, was not instigated by official patronage. He was led to undertake it by a sincere, if somewhat antiquarian, love of all evidences of the Italian past. He had a profound admiration for the ancient Roman civilization and a stronger feeling for the empire than had the republican Bruni, but he had also a genuine affection for the later centuries, as is amply demonstrated in his *Italia illustrata* and *Roma instaurata*. Moreover, the Middle Ages presented the irresistible appeal of a virgin field. As he explains in the opening sentences of the *Decades,* the period of Rome's growth and power have been celebrated by many good historians, but the age that followed the beginning of her decline is shrouded in darkness. It is his purpose, therefore, to restore to the light the history of the thousand and thirty years following the sack of Rome by the Goths in 412 (*recte* 410). When he wrote this introduction he had, as a matter of fact, already completed the history of the final thirty years (1412-42) in twelve books, which in the finished work form the third decade and the beginning of a fourth.[38] The first two decades, then, are devoted to the even thousand years between the decline of Rome and what he regarded as contemporary history, *i.e.,* to the Middle Ages, though he did not of course, use that term. The first decade ends with the war of Pepin against the Lombards in 752, a well-chosen turning point in Italian history.

This definite chronological scheme is one of the most significant features of Biondo's history. His insistence on the date 412 for the beginning of Rome's decline drew a sharp line between the period of ancient history and that which followed. Throughout the first decade he dates events from that year, and in the introduction he justifies his position in a lengthy argument against the opinion of those who, like Bruni, thought that the decline of Rome began with the emperors, and those who would date it from the removal of the capital to Constantinople. The empire, he argues, continued to grow in power or, at least, to hold its own till the time of Theodosius the Great. Whatever the underlying causes of weakness, the actual decline began

---

[35]Fueter, pp. 16, 109.

[36]Quoted by Nogara from the *Commentarii* of Aeneas Silvius (Frankfurt, 1614), p. 310, in *Scritti rari e inediti di Biondo Flavio*, p. cxi.

[37]*Aeneae Sylvii Pii Pontificis Max. supra Decades Bl. ab inclinatione imperii usque ad tempora Joannis vicesimi tertii Pont. Max. Epitome,* in the Basel edition of Aeneas Silvius's *Opera* (1551), pp. 144-281.

[38]The second book of the fourth decade remained in manuscript and was first published in the *Scritti inediti e rari* (pp. 1-28).

with the sack of Rome.[39] This emphasis on an external, if dramatic, event may indicate a more superficial view of history than that of Bruni, but it made a lasting impression simply because it was definite and hence memorable.

The continued decline and the desolation of Italy through the barbarian invasions is the major theme of the first decade. But Biondo's picture of the whole medieval period is not one of "Verfall bis nahe an die Gegenwart", as Karl Brandi described it.[40] With the coming of Charlemagne and the end of the Lombard wars, at the beginning of the second decade, the tone gradually changes.[41] The lamentations over the destruction of Rome's grandeur disappear, and he begins to date events by the conventional *anno salutis* rather than the *anno inclinationis Romanorum imperii* commonly used in the first decade.

Save for the significant division between the first two decades at the year 752, the turning point in medieval history at which the period of decline ends and the rise of modern Italy begins is indicated only in the general tenor of the narrative, without benefit of editorial comment. But that Biondo was aware of new developments that would in time compensate for the destruction of the Roman Empire had already been clearly shown in one of his rare bits of theoretical generalization at the beginning of Decade I, Book 3. This passage is the clearest statement of his view of Italian history, though it has apparently been missed by all the critics who have analyzed his historical thought. The preceding book had ended with the abdication of Romulus Augustulus, the last emperor of Roman race. This "abominable" event, he says, recalls the memory of those indignities which had long restrained him from writing, for shame had almost deterred him when he contemplated beginning his history with the decline, or rather the destruction, of the Roman Empire. It galled him to repeat the injuries to his country and ancestors. But the hope held before him of narrating the origin of new cities and most distinguished peoples, whose excellence has restored the Roman dignity of Italy, gave him heart so that he could write without any feeling of shame. He then lists the cities that grew great through God's special kindness to Italy, by whose wealth and the vigor of their inhabitants the dignity and glory of Italy exist once more. And this, he felt, resulted directly from the decline of the city of Rome. For, he continues, it is clear that, as Rome diminished, the strength of Italy in cities increased, since the neighboring greatness of the capital had prevented older cities from growing and new ones from being founded. The burden of his argument is that Rome had monopolized the wealth and energy of Italy. But when it ceased to dominate, its decline permit-

---

[39] "Ipsam itaque imperii inclinationem, sive ob praedictas omnes causas, sive ob earum aliquam sit facta, dicimus principium habuisse a Gothorum in urbem Romam irruptione." *Decades*, p. 4.

[40] P. 6; see Joachimsen, p. 24, for similar comment.

[41] Borinski, *Sitz. Bayerischen Akad.*, I, 107, notes that in the *Roma instaurata* he seems to end the idea of decline with the end of the Lombard wars.

ted the growth of other cities which its rising power had prevented.[42] One is reminded of Bruni's thesis. Again the implication that the fall of Rome was not an unrelieved disaster and the proud awareness of the rising power of Italy through her cities, once they were free to work out their own salvation. Biondo was in full agreement with his Florentine friend on these points, though he departed from his interpretation of the causes of Rome's decline and blamed the city rather than the empire for the subservience of the old Italian cities.

In Biondo's view, then, the revival of Italy began far back in the medieval period. He gives no indication of seeing a Renaissance at the end of the Middle Ages. There is, however, in the neat chronological organization of his work and in the introduction to the third decade, where he rejoices at having completed the history of the thousand years from 412 to 1412 and looks forward to an easier course through the events of his own times, a faint suggestion that he regarded those thousand years as forming a historical epoch in some way distinct from contemporary history.[43] It is difficult to say how much of this was the result of a preconceived historical pattern. The work on the thirty years from 1412 to 1442 was written first, so that the introduction to Decade III must have been an afterthought. And so far as that thousand-year period is given any definite characterization, it is only as the period following the decline of Rome, during which there was no good history written. In the contemporary period the author does not have to depend in the same way on unsatisfactory histories since the events fall within the memory of living man. This is an obvious distinction and one that made little impression on his contemporaries, though it may have helped to set the idea of a thousand-year Middle Age for later historians at a time when the year 1412 no longer introduced contemporary history.

Bruni and Biondo were, each in his own way, the pioneers of humanist historiography. The other humanist historians of Italy followed faithfully in their footsteps, imitating the style and method of Bruni and borrowing material, often without acknowledgement, from Biondo. Even Machiavelli followed the traditional pattern fairly closely in his *Istorie fiorentine*, completed in 1525, adding to the earlier interpretation of the Middle Ages only his keen analysis of the part played by political factions, the papacy, and the *condottieri* in dividing and weakening Italy.[44] The great majority of the

---

[42]"Quamprimum vero inclinare et cessare coepit dominae urbis potentia, dedit permisitque eius imminutio, quod abstulerat prohibueratque incrementum." *Decades,* pp. 30 f.

[43]"Laetanti iam mihi et exultanti non obscuram magis quam sepultam mille annorum historiam viginti librorum voluminibus in lucem, certumque ordinem reduxisse, et faciliore cursu per notissima aetatis nostrae gesta procedere meditanti ..." *Decades,* p. 393. This is perhaps worth noting in view of the positive statements of Lehmann (p. 5) and Joachimsen (pp. 24 f.) that he gives no suggestion of a periodic break between contemporary and earlier history.

[44]He begins with the barbarian invasions, devoting four of the eight books to the period "from the decline of the Roman Empire" (see preface) to the accession of the Medici in 1434. The first book, which deals with general Italian history, leans heavily on Biondo. See Fueter, pp. 62 and 69.

humanists outside of Florence wrote at the command of state governments
and had a more personal interest in the literary style of their work than in its
content. But if they were not the most thoughtful of historians, their work as
a whole served to reinforce the patriotic interpretation and untheological
periodization of history set forth by Bruni and Biondo. The task of glorifying
the history of the Italian states forced upon them the necessity of beginning
with the early Middle Ages. Consciously or unconsciously, they treated the
period after the decline of Rome as a new historical epoch and one not of unbroken decline but of active growth from the time when the Italian cities
began to recover from Roman domination and barbarian invasion.

The extent, however, to which the new view of history was accepted by
the humanists as an independent theory and not merely as a necessary
attribute of Italian state histories is demonstrated most clearly in the
*Rapsodie historiarum enneadum ab orbe condito ad annum salutis humane
1504* of Marcantonio Coccio, called Sabellicus.[45] It is the one essay on
universal history arising from Italian humanism and as such is the exception
that proves the rule. Sabellicus wrote under the patronage of the Venetian
government and had previously published a history of the republic entitled
Rerum Venetarum ab urbe condita libri xxxiii. Here he followed the customary pattern of state history, imitating Bruni in style and treatment and for his
material borrowing from Biondo to the point of plagiarism.[46] In the
Rapsodie he undertook the more original and ambitious task of applying the
method of humanist historiography to the history of the world since the
creation, a field hitherto monopolized by the theologians. Though distinctly
pious, Sabellicus broke completely with the traditions of the ecclesiastical
world chronicle. His treatment of ancient history, whether sacred or profane,
is free from theological interpretation. He follows a strictly chronological
sequence throughout, completely ignoring the doctrine of the Four
Monarchies.[47]

The whole work is divided, rather arbitrarily, into eleven *enneades*
(groups of nine books), but with some reason wherever possible for the
division. The sixth ennead, for example, ends with the establishment of peace
by Augustus, the seventh opening with the birth of Christ. The most decisive
periodic break, however, comes between the seventh and eighth enneads, the
former ending with the sack of Rome in 412 (following Biondo's date), the
latter beginning with the foundation of Venice. Having completed the
seventh ennead, and with it ancient history, Sabellicus decided to publish,
leaving the second part of the work dealing with more modern history to be
written and published later, "si tamdiu superesset vita." That he regarded this

---

[45]First published in Venice in 1498-1504, later by Badius Ascensius, in Paris, in
three volumes in 1509 and again 1516-17; also in Lyons in 1535. I have used the
1509 edition.

[46]For his dependence on Biondo's *Decades* see R. Bersi in *Nuovo Archivio Veneto,*
XIX (1910), 435-60; XX (1910), 151-62; for his general adherence to Bruni's
school see Fueter, p. 32.

[47]*Rapsodie, Enn.* II, *lib.* 5, f. CI^v ff.

as an obvious place to break off the work is indicated in both the dedicatory letter to the Venetian government and the added *epistola apologetica,* in which he explains his reasons for publishing before the work was finished. In both he emphasizes the fact that the part he is publishing separately includes the whole period from the creation of the world to the decline of the Roman Empire.[48] There is a further indication that he regarded the second part of his work as dealing with a new historical period in the fact, duly noted in his dedication to the Venetian government, that it begins with the founding of Venice. The central theme of this second part, which in the 1509 edition is published as Tom. III with the title, *Enneadum ... ab inclinatione romani imperii usque ad annum 1504,* is the rising power of Venice and other Italian cities. Biondo's *Decades* are obviously his chief source. In the preface to Ennead VIII he presents an interesting little essay on the causes of the decline of Rome, which is in effect a summary of Bruni's theory of the fatal results of the imperial despotism.[49] But though his republican sympathies led him to accept Bruni's theory, convenience or custom or Venetian patriotism dictated his adoption of Biondo's chronological scheme.

II

As has been illustrated in the foregoing discussion, the Italian humanists created a fairly definite pattern for the history of Italy and the Italian states from the decline of Rome to their own time. It was a pattern admirably designed to serve the secular, political interests, the state patriotism and embryonic national consciousness of the Renaissance Italian, but it suffered from one serious weakness. It excluded from consideration the developments in literature, learning and art, which so keenly interested the men of the Quattrocento and which contributed in no small degree to both local and national patriotic pride. The omission of these from their formal histories was the price paid by the humanist historians for the otherwise valuable guidance of their classical models, the purely political historians of antiquity. For the history of literature and art they were forced to utilize other forms, less well adapted to the purpose. One of the most common was the biography or collection of biographies of writers and artists.[50] These were satisfactory in individual instances, but they provided little opportunity for connected narrative or treatment of development over a long period. For coherent accounts of the humanist conception of cultural history from antiquity to their own age we are forced to depend on brief essays, inserted into the midst of biographies, prefaces, or works on allied subjects.

[48]"Sunt quae nunc vestro nomini inscribuntur, Enneades septem . . . .quibus a prima mundi origine ad Romanorum imperii inclinationem, in quae tempora auspicatissimus vestrae urbis ortus incidit." *Rapsodie,* Tom. I, *Praefatio;* compare his description of the work to this point in the *epistola apologetica,* at the end of Tom. II in the 1509 ed.: "quibus sum omnium res gentium complexus, a primordio mundi ad Arcadii et Honorii tempora. His enim imperantibus, Roma direpta a Gothis et incensa, labefactari coepit Ro. Imperium. . . ." Tom. II, CCXXV[v].

[49]*Rapsodie,* Tom. III, f. I.

[50]Fueter, pp. **93** ff.

The general picture of the past and present that these historical essays present is in many respects similar to that portrayed in the political histories, but there are also significant differences. As in the political histories, the decline of Rome is an epoch-making event, marking the end of the period of antiquity. Italian cultural history, as distinct from the Roman, begins after the decline. There is first an age of degradation under the barbarians, then a great revival culminating in the writer's own generation. But in the history of culture the period of darkness appears to be much longer than in the political story, and the revival more recent and more sudden, also more clearly the work of certain individual men. Both forms presented those aspects of Italian history which interested the educated class in Italy and appealed to their patriotic pride. The political history of the medieval communes appealed to both secular interest and local patriotism. The fact that the history of medieval culture was so largely ignored suggests that it appealed neither to the interest of the educated laymen in the secular and urban society of Renaissance Italy nor to their national or local patriotism. The best of medieval culture was either feudal or ecclesiastical, and in neither case Italian. It came mostly from north of the Alps and was, therefore, barbarous by definition.

The humanists' conception of a comparatively recent and rapid rise in Italian culture contains a suggestion of the modern Renaissance idea, which was lacking in their political history. The metaphor of rebirth in the literal sense of the word is rare, but there is general agreement that for a long period letters and art had been dead and had since taken on a new and vigorous life. In the case of Latin and Greek literature, and to a much lesser degree of art, the excellence of the new forms is judged by the standard of resemblance to the ancient style. But the chief emphasis is placed on the creative activity of modern Italians. The general tone of all accounts is markedly similar, though there is a good deal of variation within the general scheme, depending on the subject discussed, the author's interests, and the date of composition. Both the prevailing tone and the individual variations may best be shown by summaries or quotations.

The pioneer essay on the decline of ancient culture, the medieval *lacuna,* and the recent revival is to be found in the first of those collections of biographies of writers and artists that served the humanists as a substitute for cultural history. The *Liber de civitatis Florentine famosis civibus* of Filippo Villani, 1382 (?),[51] contains the biographies of thirty-five famous Florentines, mostly poets, scholars, and painters. It opens with the poets, first Claudian, then Dante, followed by Petrarch, Boccaccio, and others. To explain the absence of representatives from the nine centuries between Claudian and Dante, the author inserts as a preface to the life of Dante a brief but illuminating sketch of literary history from the decline of Rome. Since he is writing about famous Florentine citizens, it is natural that Villani should

---

[51]So in Fueter, p. 94; for the suggestion that it may have been composed as much as twenty years later see Philippi, p. 12.

exclude those medieval writers who had not the good fortune to be born in
Florence. However, that is not the reason he gives. His argument is simply
that after Claudian, who was almost the last poet of the ancient times, all
poetry decayed, due to the weakness and avarice of the emperors, and also
because it was no longer prized, since the Catholic faith began to hold the
product of poetic imagination in abhorrence as a pernicious and a vain thing.
So poetry lay dead, without honor or dignity, until Dante recalled it as from
an abyss of shadows to the light and, giving the fallen art his hand, set it upon
its feet.[52] This vivid if somewhat mixed metaphor indicates a sudden and
recent revival of letters but certainly not a rebirth of the antique literature.
The emphasis on Christian antagonism to poetic imagination as a cause of the
decline is interesting. Villani returns to it again in explaining Dante's success
in reviving poetry. Dante, he says, had reconciled poetry with moral and
natural philosophy and with Christian literature and had shown that the
ancient poets were divinely inspired to prophesy the Christian mysteries, thus
making poetry pleasing not only to the learned but also to the common and
uneducated, of whom, he adds, the number is infinite.

In a later chapter Villani turns to the Florentine painters, "qui artem
exanguem et pene extinctam suscitaverunt".[53] He gives credit for the first
step in the revival of painting to Cimabue, and it is significant that he makes
Cimabue's service consist not in imitating the ancients but in the skill and intelligence with which he recalled painting to natural similitude, from which
it had long departed because of the childish ignorance of the older painters.[54]
Before Cimabue, Greek (i.e., Byzantine) and Latin painting had lain dead
for many centuries because of the crude technique of the artists, as is plainly
shown by the pictures in the churches. After him, Villani continues, the road
to a new art was open, and Giotto, who not only can be compared to the illustrious painters of antiquity but surpassed them in skill and genius, restored
painting to its ancient dignity and greatest fame.[55] Here again the great
advance made by Giotto is ascribed to the closer resemblance to nature of his
pictures, "ut vivere et anhelitum spirare contuentibus viderentur". It is clear
that for Villani the revival of both poetry and painting after centuries of
ignorance and neglect was an independent, spontaneous development, in
which the sole motivating force was the genius of the great Florentine
masters.

Villani's account of the revival of painting established a tradition that

---

[52]"Ea igitur iacente sine cultu, sine decore, vit maximus Dante Allagherii, quasi
ex abysso tenebrarum eruptam revocavit in lucem, dataque manu, iacentem erexit in
pedes."   G. C. Galletti, ed. (Florence, 1847), p. 8.

[53]*Ibid.*, p. 35.

[54]"Inter quos primus . . . Cimabue antiquatam picturam, et a naturae similitudine,
pictorum inscitia pueriliter discrepantem, coepit ad naturae similtudinem, quasi lascivam
et vagantem longius, arte et ingenio revocare."   *Ibid.*

[55]"Post hunc, strata iam in novis via, Giottus non solum illustris famae decore
antiquis pictoribus comparandus, sed art et ingenio praeferendus, in pristinam digni-
tatem nomenque maximum picturam restituit."   *Ibid.*

was followed, *mutatis mutandis,* for two centuries or more. The conception of literary history, however, was soon modified by the growing enthusiasm of the humanists for the ancient tongues to the prejudice of the *volgare.* This tendency is clearly visible in Leonardo Bruni's essay on the history of letters from Cicero to Petrarch, inserted in the second part of his *Vite di Dante e del Petrarca,* 1436.[56] Bruni admired Dante and took a patriotic satisfaction in the fame he had brought to Florence,[57] but his admiration was tempered by the fact that Dante excelled only in *rima volgare,* for no one in his generation could write good Latin prose or verse, "ma furono rozzi e grossi e senza perizia di lettere."[58] The true literary revival, that of classical Latin, he ascribed to Petrarch, who was the first to recall it to the light of knowledge after it had long been buried and ignored, after which it continued to rise ever higher.[59] It is to explain this situation that he turns to the history of Latin letters since the age of Cicero.

Bruni's story of the decline and revival of good literature runs closely parallel with his history of the decline of Rome and the later revival of the Italian free cities, as told in the *Historiarum Florentini populi libri xii.* Latin letters reached their highest peak of perfection, the result of a gradual development, in the time of Cicero, that is, at the end of the republic. Thereafter both Rome and her literature began to decline for the same reason, because the Roman people had lost their freedom under the tyrannous emperors. After a definite statement of this thesis,[60] he continues with a lengthy discussion of the decline as due to the oppressive acts of the individual emperors, which is almost a paraphrase of that in the *History.* It ends with a reiteration of his belief that Rome was destroyed by the tyrannous emperors and that letters declined with it until there was no one who understood Latin with any grace.[61] Then came the Goths and Lombards, "nazioni barbare e strane", and completed the destruction of Latin literature.

[56]Published in Angelo Soletri, ed., *Autobiografie e vite de' maggiori scrittori italiani* (Milan, 1903), pp. 93-123.

[57]He gives this as his reason for writing the lives of Dante and Petrarch (*"perocchè la notizia e la fama di questi due poeti grandemente riputo appartenere all gloria della nostra città"*), *ibid.,* p. 94.

[58]*Ibid.,* pp. 109 and 123.

[59]"Ed ebbe tanta grazia d'intelletto che fu il primo che questi sublimi studi lungo tempo caduti ed ignorati rivocò a luce di cognizione: i quali dapoi crescendo montati sono nella presente altezza." *Ibid.,* p. 115.

[60]"E puossi dire che le lettere e gli studi della lingua latina andassero parimente con lo stato della Repubblica di Roma, perocchè infino all' età di Tullio ebbe accrescimento; di poi, perduta la libertà del popolo romano per la signoria degl' imperadori, i quali non restarono d'uccidere e di disfare gli uomini di pregio, insieme col buono stato della città di Roma peri la buona disposizione degli studi e delle lettere." *Ibid.,* pp. 115 f.

[61]"A che proposito si dice questo da me? Solo per dimostrare che come la città di Roma fu annichilata da gl' imperadori perversi tiranni, così gli studi e le lettere latine riceverono simile ruina e diminuzione, intanto che all' estremo quasi non si trovava chi lettere latine con alcuna gentilezza sapesse." *Ibid.,* p. 116.

The story of the literary revival in Italy, too, is almost a repetition of his account of the political revival, though the former is represented as being, at first, a more gradual movement. When the Italian people recovered their freedom after the expulsion of the Lombards, the cities of Tuscany and other parts of Italy began to revive and to pay attention to learning and the refinement of their gross style, and so gradually recovered literary vigor. But this was a feeble development. The men of that age were without true taste, for they were given more to writing in Italian verse than in Latin, so that even in Dante's time there were few who understood the "literary" style, and they but poorly. Petrarch, he repeats, was the first "che riconobbe e rivoco in luce l'antica leggiadria dello stilo perduto e spento". And even Petrarch did not attain perfection, though he did accomplish enough through his study of Cicero to point the way for later writers.[62] Here Bruni demonstrates again his awareness of the rise of Itailan civilization through the rise of the cities from the early Middle Ages; but his appreciation of the literary aspects of the early development is dimmed, though not destroyed, by his classical prejudices. The evolution of the *rima volgare* and of learning "al modo fratesco scolastico"[63] could not altogether compensate for the lack of classical style. Later he added an appendix, as it were, to this sketch of the literary revival in his *Rerum suo tempore gestarum commentarius,* where he tells with vast enthusiasm how Chrysoloras brought back Greek to Italy after it had been forgotten there for seven hundred years.[64]

The general conception of the relative cultural darkness of a large part of the Middle Ages and of a fairly recent revival owing to the genius of certain great Italian masters was by this time pretty well fixed. There was still, however, some variation as to the date and the authors of the new movement. At just about the time that Bruni was writing the *Vite di Dante e del Petrarca,* another Florentine humanist, Matteo Palmieri, included a little essay on the cultural revival in Italy in his treatise *Della vita civile.* Here he asserts that the neglect of letters and all liberal studies had lasted for eight hundred years, and he credits the revival of good Latin not to Petrarch, but to his friend Bruni, whom he describes as the father and ornament of letters, called into the world "come splendido lume della eleganzia latina, per rendere a gli uomini la dolcezza della latina lingua".[65] This is obvious flattery of a famous fellow citizen, but we have Vespasiano's evidence (see below) that the crediting of the classical revival to the work of contemporary Florentines was not unusual in Palmieri's circle. In his discussion of the fine arts, however, Pal-

---

[62]*Ibid.,* p. 117.

[63]*Ibid.,* p. 110.

[64]*Commentarius,* ed. by Carmine di Pierro, in Muratori, Vol. XIX, pt. 3 (1926), p. 431.   See also Bruni's preface to his translation of Plato's *Phaedrus:* "Chrysoloras Byzantinus, vir magnus quidem ac prope singularis, disciplinam Graecarum litterarum in Italiam rettulit, quarum cognitio, quae quidem liberaliter erudita foret, septingentos iam annos nulla nostros apud homines habebatur . . ." Baron, ed., *Brunis humanistisch-philosophische Schriften,* p. 125.

[65](Milan, 1825), p. 47.

mieri returns to the more conventional chronology, though with an
interestingly original approach. He attributes the lack of progress in the
earlier period to the weight of tradition, which caused men to be satisfied to
do just as their fathers had done, so that the noble arts fell into a dis-
honored and sterile condition for many centuries. But later, whether through
grace or industry or continuous diligence, the lost art was raised up
again.[66] The reason for this, he continues, was that good masters began to
teach, and their disciples profited by good teaching to become better, just as
before the revival of art ("innanzi il rilevare dell'arti") those badly taught
became worse. Thus, before Giotto, painting was dead but since has become excellent through his work and that of his disciples.[67] The same
holds for architecture and sculpture, which were backward for a long time,
but "in our time" have been raised up, returned to the light, and made
perfect by good masters.[68]

The most complete historical account of the classical revival,
together with a sketch of literary history since antiquity, appeared a few
years after this in Biondo's *Italia illustrata,* written between the years 1448
and 1453. In accordance with ancient tradition Biondo had ignored the
history of culture in his *Decades* save as the necessity of discussing his sources suggested it. Thus, in his introduction to the *Decades,* he
bewailed the lack of good histories from the age of Orosius to his own time
and attributed that lack to the general cultural decadence which accompanied
the political decline of the Roman people.[69] Later he noted the medieval
ignorance of Greek, which prevented writers of that period from using the
Greek sources.[70] In the *Italia illustrata,* however, he felt free to include the
literary revival in his general celebration of Italy and her achievements. The
subject was suggested, in the midst of his description of Ravenna, by the fame
of John of Ravenna (Giovanni Malpaghini, 1346-1417), whom he cites on
the authority of Bruni as the first to restore the present flourishing study of
eloquence to Italy.[71]

Biondo follows the general consensus of humanist opinion in connecting
the literary with the political decline of Rome, but here, as in the *Decades,*
he departs from Bruni's chronology by dating both from the early fifth century rather than from the fall of the republic. There were few or almost none,

---

[66]*Ibid.,* p. 46: "poi, o per grazia, o per industria, o per continuata diligenza, nascere
chi l'arte perduta rileva."

[67]"Di quinci veggiamo innanzi a Giotto la pittura morta." *Ibid.*

[68]*Ibid.,* p. 47: "nella età nostra si sono rilevate, tornate in luce, e da più maestri
pulitesi e fatte perfette."

[69]*Decades* (Basel, 1531), p. 4: "cum praepotentis populi gloriae ruina factus est,
bonarum artium interitu . . ." See a similar discussion in the preface to *Italia
illustrata* (Basel, 1531), p. 293.

[70]*Decades,* I, *lib.* 4.

[71]P. 346.

he says, who wrote Latin with any elegance whatsoever after the doctors of the
church, Ambrose, Jerome, and Augustine, who lived in the time of the decline
of the Roman Empire, unless one might include among the writers St. Gregory and the Venerable Bede, who were near that same time, and, much later,
the blessed Bernard.[72] The inclusion of the Fathers among the ancient writers
and the honorable mention accorded to Bede and St. Bernard is interesting,
as is his failure to mention Dante and the rise of Italian poetry. From
Bernard he goes straight to Petrarch, who, he says, was the first to begin the
awakening of poetry and eloquence. Like Bruni, however, he refuses to credit
Petrarch with attaining the full flower of Ciceronian eloquence, and he adds
the shrewd observation that for this we must blame Petrarch's lack of books
rather than of intelligence. After discussing the limited number and poor
quality of the Ciceronian works at Petrarch's disposal, Biondo continues the
story of the revival of ancient literature with the teaching of John of Ravenna
and Emanuel Chrysoloras and an imposing list of the men who gained from
these two masters a love of Ciceronian style and of Greek letters. Then follows
an account, too long for summary here, of the search for old manuscripts at the
Council of Constance and elsewhere, of the founding of new classical schools
like those of Vittorino and Guarino, and of the work of a fairly complete list
of the more distinguished Italian humanists of the first half of the fifteenth
century. It is a remarkable survey of the contemporary humanist movement,
showing a proud consciousness of the advances made since the generation of
Petrarch.

Biondo was almost unique in his feeling for Italy as a whole. Most of the
fifteenth century writers tended rather to stress achievements of their own
native cities. Thus Jacopo Filippo Foresti of Bergamo in his *Supplementum
chronicarum* hails Gasparino da Barzizza, also of Bergamo, as one of the
principal founders of the revival of letters, though he follows Biondo in
ascribing the original initiative to Petrarch.[73] The Florentines were especially
inclined, and with good reason, to this form of civic patriotism. We have
already noted it in Villani, Bruni and Palmieri. We may observe it again in
the comments of Vespasiano da Bisticci. He was not himself a distinguished
humanist, but he knew many who were, and his opinions may be taken as a
fairly accurate echo of the learned world of fifteenth century Florence. In his
Vite di uomini illustri del secolo xv he presents the lives of distinguished men
from all parts of Italy, but the position of leadership in the revival of letters
is invariably ascribed to his fellow citizens. Of the writers
prior to the fifteenth century he mentions Dante, whom he describes as the
first writer in Florence since the foundation of the city, and also Petrarch and
Boccaccio, but these are noted only in passing as outside the province of his
book.[74] The contemporary writers with whom he deals are the classical

---

[72]*Ibid.*, p. 346.

[73]Venice, 1483, pt. 1, f. 80ᵛ and 143ᵛ; see Joachimsen, p. 84.

[74]*The Vespasiano Memoirs,* trans. by William George and Emily Waters (New
York, 1926), p. 14.

humanists. And the founders of humanism are all Florentine. Writing of
Fra Ambrogio Traverari, he recalls that "it was firmly held by all men of
learning that Fra Ambrogio and Messer Lionardo (Bruni) had revived the
Latin tongue which had been dead and buried for a thousand years or more,
and he adds that "although Petrarch did much to revive Latin he never
approached these two".[75] Later he includes Poggio among the founders. "The
city itself and all who had the Latin tongue were under great obligation to
him, to Messer Lionardo, and Fra Ambrogio, the first exponents of Latin,
which had lain obscure and neglected for many centuries. Thus Florence
found itself, in this golden age, full of learned men."[76] Even the philosophers
were not exempt from the conviction that their own city was the exclusive
creator of the new cultural life. Marsilio Ficino wrote: "It is undoubtedly a
golden age which has restored to the light the liberal arts that had almost been
destroyed: grammar, poetry, eloquence, painting, architecture, sculpture,
music. And that all in Florence."[77]   Again a few years later this sentiment
was echoed by Machiavelli in the conclusion to his treatise Dell'arte della
guerra, addressed to the youth of Florence: "And let me conjure you not to
despair of success, since this province seems destined to revive arts which
seemed long since dead, as we see it has already raised poetry, painting, and
sculpture, as it were, from the grave."[78]

Expressions of pride in the literary accomplishments of their own generation and in the new cultural life of their age in general, as contrasted
with the darkness and inactivity of the Middle Ages, could be culled from
the works of many of the Quattrocento humanists. For the most part they are
merely statements of the humanist credo that literature and the arts were dead
and now live again, offered without the qualifications or the feeling for
historical continuity that characterized the essays of men like Bruni and
Biondo, who had worked in medieval history. We may let one example suffice, that in Lorenzo Valla's preface to his De linguae Latinae elegantia
(1444), which has justly been called a manifesto of humanism.[79] His description of the complete ignorance of Latin since the decline of Rome is absolutely unqualified.[80] It is presented as an article of faith with no attempt at historical justification. He refuses, indeed, to venture any explanation of why it
should have happened any more than why the kindred arts of painting, sculp-

[75]Ibid., p. 211.

[76]Ibid., p. 356.

[77]Quoted from Nordstrom, p. 18.

[8]Engl. trans. (Albany, 1815), p. 284.

[79]Huizinga, p. 92.

[80]"Siquidem multis iam seculis non modo Latine nemo locutus est, sed ne Latina
quidem legens intellexit: non philosophiae studiosi philosophos, non causidici oratores,
non legulei iureconsultos, non caeteri lectores veterum libros perceptos habuerunt, aut
habent: quasi amisso Romano imperio, non deceat Romane aut loqui aut sapere,
fulgorem illum Latinitatis situ, ac rubigine passi obolescere." De linguae Latinae
elegantia (Lyons, 1538), p. 8.

ture, and architecture, like letters, degenerated and died, nor why they are now raised up and live again.[81] But, he concludes, the more unhappy those earlier times were, the more to be congratulated is the present age in which, he believes, the Roman tongue will live again and with it all disciplines will be restored.

The humanists, as men of letters, naturally have more to say about the revival of literature, and particularly of the ancient languages, than about the fine arts. As the foregoing references show, however, they were not unaware of the great development of the arts in their age. But for more detailed and critical history of the artistic revival one must turn to the artists themselves, many of whom left records of their own activity and that of their predecessors and contemporaries. A survey of their conceptions of the course of the arts through the Middle Ages and the recent revival can be found in the first seven chapters of Adolf Philippi's monograph, *Der Begriff der Renaissance*. It need not be duplicated in detail here.

In the main the Quattrocentist view of the history of art follows the same broad outlines as that of literature. Knowing little and caring less about the work of medieval artists beyond the Alps, it concentrates on the arts as practised in Italy and especially in Florence. Ghiberti amplified the brief account of Filippo Villani[83]: ancient art declined in the age of Constantine; then followed six hundred years devoid of all art until the Byzantines introduced the awkward *maniera Greca;* finally came the revival of natural painting with the masterly work of Cimabue and Giotto. But, as in the history of letters, there were those who regarded the revival of the arts as dating only from their own generation. Leo Battista Alberti ascribed the founding of the new arts to his contemporaries, Brunelleschi, Donatello, Ghiberti, Luca della Robbia, and others.[84] These he thought equal to the ancients, if not greater in genius, since they had produced so much beauty without teachers or models. Alberti evidently regarded the revival as the independent work of modern Italians rather than as a mere imitation of antiquity.[85] The place of Brunelleschi as the originator of a new style of architecture in contrast to the Gothic was reaffirmed by Filarete and others, though Cimabue and Giotto remained the conventional founders of the new painting.

The men of the Quattrocento, however, were too close to the new movement to see it in its entirety. The first complete and rationalized history of

---

[81]"Non magis quam cur illae artes quae proxime ad liberales accedunt, pingendi, sculpendi, fingendi, architectandi, aut tamdiu tantoque opere degeneraverint ac paene cum literis ipsis demortuae fuerint, aut hoc tempore excitentur ac reviviscant: tantusque tum bonorum opificium, tum bene literatorum proventus efflorescat." *Ibid.*

[82](Leipzig, 1912), pp. 1-64.

[83]*Commentarii*, II, sec. 1, 1452-55; see Philippi, pp. 15 ff.

[84]"Trattato della pittura", 1436, in *Kleinere kunsttheoretische Schriften,* ed. by Hubert Janitschek (Vienna, 1877), p. 49; see Philippi, pp. 25 ff.

[85]Brandi, p. 10, where he notes the significance of Alberti's phrase, "sanza praeceptori sanza exemplo alchuni", giving greater weight to it than does Philippi.

Italian art was written only after the Renaissance had passed its peak. In
Giorgio Vasari's *Le vite de' più eccellenti architetti, pittori e scultori italiani
da Cimabue insino a' tempi nostri* the revival of the fine arts in the age of
Cimabue and Giotto was for the first time referred to as "the Renaissance"
(*rinascita*), and the periodization of medieval and Renaissance art by schools
was first given a definite historical form.[86] Vasari was a thorough classicist in
taste but conscious also of the existence of medieval art, inferior though it was.
He noted the beginning of an improvement after the period of Lombard
domination and a still greater improvement in the early eleventh century.[87]
But this early art was crude and stiff. Vasari classifies it under the derogatory
names of *maniera Greca* (Byzantine) and *maniera Tedesca* (Gothic). The
rinascita began with Cimabue and Giotto as the recovery of a more living
likeness to nature. From the rebirth of the arts to his own time he discerned
three periods or manners, the first that of the founders, the second a greatly
improved school in the fifteenth century, and finally the perfected style
(*maniera moderna*), which began with Leonardo da Vinci.[88]

The temptation to generalize in conclusion is irresistible, although
there are dangers in any attempt to force the various individual opinions of
the humanists into a single coherent scheme. Still, certain general tendencies
have been noted and may be recapitulated with profit. The humanists whose
works we have examined are in fairly general agreement that there was a
decline of ancient civilization with the decline of Rome and that this
decline led to a period of barbaric darkness, which in turn was followed by a
revival of the Italian cities and, later, of Italian literature and art. Further,
they are of one mind in ignoring almost all cultural and political development
outside of Italy, as well as the most characteristic institutions and cultural
contributions of the Middle Ages, such as the medieval empire, scholastic
learning, feudal and ecclesiastical literature, and Gothic art. These things apparently held little interest for them. On the other hand, though they speak
of revival in specific fields of political or cultural activity, there is no
general agreement as to when these revivals occurred, nor is there in any account, save possibly in the most brief and vague statements concerning the
new cultural life of contemporary Italy, the suggestion of a definite chronological period of general rebirth as contrasted with the preceding period.
Individual writers assign different dates to the revival in different fields, the
widest variation being, as a rule, that between the political and the literary or
artistic revival. Moreover, there is little suggestion that the revival in general
or in particular aspects of culture was a rebirth of antiquity, although the
ancient classics were accepted as models for Latin and Greek style, and, in
greatly diminishing degree, the ancient works of art set standards for
architecture, sculpture, and painting. The Italian humanists thought of the
civilization of their own day as a new and original creation, in many respects
like that of antiquity but distinctly their own. It was, in all aspects, the work
of the Italian cities and their men of genius.

---

[86](Torrentine, 1550); the most convenient English translation is in Everyman's
Library.

[87]I, preface, pp. 14-15.

[88]Preface to Part II, *ibid.*, I, 202 ff.; see Philippi, pp. 53 ff.

RECENT TRENDS IN THE ECONOMIC
HISTORIOGRAPHY OF THE RENAISSANCE*

First of all, may I express my pleasure at having been invited to partici-
pate in this twentieth anniversary of the New England Renaissance Conference. I would also like to take this opportunity to congratulate Professor
Bradner and his colleagues on the part they played in originating the
idea of a regional conference on the Renaissance—an idea that has since
spread from coast to coast and has in no small degree been responsible for the
growing interest in Renaissance studies in this country during the past two
decades. Few of us who took part in the first conference here could have
realized that we were assisting at the birth of a movement with such a bril-
liant future. Had we done so we might have echoed the words erroneously
attributed to Sir Walter Raleigh when he saw the smoke rise from his first
pipe of tobacco: 'We have this day lighted such a fire as by God's grace will
never be put out.'

At that first conference, I read a paper rather ambitiously entitled 'The
Historian's View of the Renaissance'. It still reposes peacefully in my desk
drawer. Its chief value was that it gave me an opportunity to crystalize in a
brief statement my current thoughts about the Renaissance, and I was grateful
for the occasion which forced me to do so. Now, twenty years older, if not
appreciably wiser, I am once more grateful for an occasion which forces me to
think back over the scholarly writing on one important aspect of Renaissance
history and to try to assess its significance for the interpretation of the Renaissance as a whole. In scarcely any other field of study dealing with the Renaissance—the history of music and philosophy are the principal exceptions—has
there been so much new material brought to light or so much signifcant reinterpretation as in economic history. That this should be so ought not to
seem surprising, for economic history is one of the newer disciplines. So
far as it touches the period of the Renaissance, its beginnings can be dated

*Read at the New England Renaissance Conference at Brown University, 17 October
1959. Reprinted from *Studies in the Renaissance*, VII, 1960.

back scarcely more than half a century. By the 1930's the pioneer work was
fairly well completed. The initial hypotheses had been worked out, fought
over, and in part abandoned. The main outlines of the picture had been
sketched in, with a fair amount of detail, but much work still remained to be
done. What has been achieved in the past two or three decades is largely the
result of the application of new methods, new interests, or new frames of
reference. It is the purpose of this paper to trace some of these changing
trends, and to venture an assessment of their value.

An initial difficulty confronts us in dealing with the contribution of
economic historians to the study of the Renaissance. With few exceptions,
they have entirely ignored it as an epoch in the history of European civilization. For them it can scarcely be said to exist. The *Economic History Review* and other journals customarily observe the time-honored dividing line
at about 1500 between 'late medieval' and 'early modern', listing works dealing with the economic history of the Renaissance under one heading or the
other. Even when the economic historians acknowledge the term 'Renaissance' in a periodic sense, they merely add to the confusion by the wide
variety in the chronological range they assign to it.[1]

We can hardly blame them for this chronological confusion, however,
since they were merely following in the footsteps of the historians of art,
literature, philosophy, and learning, who were chiefly responsible for developing the periodic concept of the Renaissance and from whom the economic
historians took it over without giving the matter very much thought. F. L.
Nussbaum has summed up this aspect of the situation in words that are
almost as applicable today as they were when he wrote them twenty years ago:
"The general development of historiography with an economic intention has
made less space than almost any other specialization for the conceptual pattern
for which we use the symbol "Renaissance".' Then, a few lines further on he
added: 'Broadly speaking, the equivalent category in economic history is "early
capitalism" or sometimes "the commercial revolution'.[2] This last comment',

---

[1] A few examples will suffice to demonstrate the variety. One of the earliest
economic histories to use the term 'Renaissance', R. Ehrenberg, *Capital and Finance
in the Age of the Renaissance* (London, 1928), dealt with the late fifteenth and sixteenth centuries. G. Luzzatto in 'Piccoli e grandi mercanti nella città del Rinascimento', *Studi in onore di G. Prato* (Turin, 1931), was thinking of the period from
the late thirteenth to the early sixteenth. A review article by F. L. Nussbaum, 'The
Economic History of Renaissance Europe', *Journal of Modern History* XIII (1941),
527-545, covered the literature on the sixteenth and seventeenth centuries. More
recently A. Sapori in *Il Rinascimento: significato e limiti: Atti del III Convegno
Internazionale sul Rinascimento, 1952,* (Florence, 1953); 'I primi viaggi di Levante
e di Ponente delle galere Fiorentine', *Archivio Storico Italiano* CXIV (1956), 87 ff.;
'Medioevo e Rinascimento: spunti per una diversa periodizzazione', *Archivio Storico
Italiano* CXV (1957), 135-164, and in other articles has argued that the economic Renaissance began as early as the beginning of the twelfth century and that it had passed
its peak by the time the Burckhardtian Renaissance began. M. Mollat, in 'Y a-t-il
une économie de la Renaissance?' *Actes du Colloque sur la Renaissance, 1956* (Paris,
1958), argues for an economic Renaissance from the middle of the fifteenth century
to the early years of the seventeenth.

[2] Nussbaum, *op. cit.,* p. 527.

may furnish us a clue through the chronological maze, although there have also been wide variations in the chronological limits assigned to early capitalism and there has been more than one commercial revolution.[3] At the same time, since in many respects the Renaissance was a transitional period, the disintegration of such medieval forms of economic activity as the manorial system must concern us as well as the rise of such characteristically modern phenomena as capitalism. While recognizing that any scheme of periodization must be abitrary and open to objection, for the purpose of the present discussion I will consider the term 'Renaissance economic history' as applying to Western Europe during the period from roughly 1300 to 1600.

Before discussing the new developments in economic historiography during the last two decades or so, it might be well to take a brief glance at the work of the preceding generation and the problems which interested it. It is always easier to assess the significance of change if one has first established a point of departure.

In the early decades of this century, students of medieval and Renaissance economic history generally followed one of two distinct, though not altogether mutually exclusive, methods. Those whose interest was primarily in what might be called pure economic history were busy establishing the structure—the external form—of commerce, industry, agriculture and finance. This group—the more numerous, if less spectacular—may be classified roughly as institutionalists. Their work was of basic importance, and it retains its value despite later additions and modifications. A second group, which might be termed idealist and which owed its inspiration in part to Marx and Hegel, in part to the school of sociological *Geisteswissenschaften* founded by Wilhelm Dilthey, was concerned primarily with the spirit—the Geist—of capitalism. Of the exponents of this tendency, the most influential—and controversial—figures were Werner Sombart and Max Weber. Their theories are too complex to be summarized here, and are still too familiar to need retelling. Briefly, Sombart regarded the capitalist spirit as the creative force responsible for the evolution of modern capitalism, a spirit which made its first appearance toward the end of the fifteenth century and which was radically different from the spirit of the artisan or craftsman which characterized the pre-capitalist economy of the Middle Ages. Working more closely in the Diltheyan tradition, Weber sought to find the origins of the capitalist spirit or type of *Weltanschauung,* which he also regarded as essentially a new phenomenon in the sixteenh century, and he found them primarily in Calvinist or Puritan worldly asceticism and the religiously motivated concept of the calling. About these two theories the storms of controversy raged until the

---

[3]Nussbaum was following the prevailing opinion in making the 'commercial revolution' date from the beginning of the sixteenth century; but R. Lopez in *The Cambridge Economic History,* II (Cambridge, 1952), 289, uses the term for the period from the late eleventh to the early fourteenth century, and R. de Roover, *Money, Banking and Credit in Medieval Bruges* (Cambridge, Mass., 1948), p. 11, speaks of a 'Commercial Revolution' around the year 1300.

early thirties,[4] by which time they were largely discredited, the origins of capitalism having by that time been traced by historians of the institutionalist school back to the fourteenth century and beyond.

Meanwhile, the emphasis placed upon the spirit of capitalism by Sombart and Weber, together with the discovery of the early development of capitalist economy, especially in Italy and the Netherlands, had encouraged a number of historians to note a relation between the economic individualism characteristic of capitalist enterprise and the spirit of individualism which the Burckhardtian tradition had established as the essential trait of Renaissance civilization from the fourteenth century.

As early as 1907, Henri Pirenne, a pioneer here as elsewhere, noted that capitalism 'impregnated the economic world with that character of individualism which was manifesting itself equally at that time in the domain of thought and art'. And he concluded: 'In short, the Renaissance manifested itself in the order of exchange and production as in all the other manifestations of human activity.'[5] Some twenty years later Jakob Strieder called attention forcibly to the same parallel between the two types of individualism.[6] But by that time the more common tendency, as illustrated for example by Ferdinand Schevill,[7] was to give priority to the individualistic spirit of the capitalist entrepreneur and to find in it the original causal force. In 1924 Halvdan Koht argued at some length that the emancipation of the individual, which, following Burckhardt, he accepted as the dominant characteristic of the Renaissance, had originated not in the peculiar political situation of Italy but in the economic individualism that was the essential characteristic of capitalism.[8] A somewhat similar thesis was later worked out with infinite ramifications by Alfred von Martin.[9] As a variation on this theme, Edgar Zilsel, too, ascribed the motive force behind the growth of modern science to the rational method and calculating spirit of capitalistic economy.[10]

---

[4]For discussion of this controversy and the relevant literature see the article by Nussbaum cited above and F. H. Knight, 'Historical and Theoretical Issues in the Problem of Medieval Capitalism', *Journal of Economic and Business History* I (1928), 119-136; Talcott Parsons, 'Capitalism in Recent German Literature: Sombart and Weber', *Journal of Political Economy* XXXVI (1928), 641-661; M. M. Postan, 'Studies in Bibliography: Medieval Capitalism', *Economic History Review* IV (1932-1933), 212-227; E. Fischoff, 'The Protestant Ethic and the Spirit of Capitalism: the History of a Controversy', *Social Research* XI (1944), 53-77; and H. M. Robertson, *Aspects of the Rise of Economic Individualism* (Cambridge, 1933).

[5]H. Pirenne, *Histoire de Belgique,* III (Brussels, 1907), 219.

[6]*Propyläen Weltgeschichte,* IV (Berlin, 1932), 5 f.

[7]J. W. Thompson, G. Rowley, F. Schevill, and G. Sarton, *The Civilization of the Renaissance* (Chicago, 1929), pp. 55 f.

[8]H. Koht, "Le problème des origines de la Renaissance', *Revue de synthèse historique* XXXVII (1924), 107-116

[9]A von Martin, *Soziologie der Renaissance* (Tübingen, 1932).

[10]E. Zilsel, 'The Sociological Roots of Science', *American Journal of Sociology* XLVII (1942), 544-560.

Meanwhile, too, the solid researches of an increasing number of economic historians, mostly of the institutionalist type, had been piling up masses of detailed information which had not been available to the pioneers who had formed large hypotheses on the basis of inadequate data. By the 1930s the time was ripe for attempts at synthesis. In the decade before the second World War a distinguished group of historians—I need mention only the names of Henri Pirenne, Henri Laurent, Marc Bloch, Henri Sée, Joseph Kulischer, Alfred Doren, M. M. Knight, Herbert Heaton, and J. W. Thompson— had made available the results of detailed research in general economic histories. The major outlines of the formal structure of medieval and Renaissance economy were now established. What remained was to fill in further detail or to modify the resultant picture by regarding the data from a new point of view or in the context of a new frame of reference.

The outbreak of the second World War slowed up research and writing in economic history, as in all other branches of scholarship, and eventually it brought them almost to a standstill in the countries most deeply engaged. Even where scholars continued to work, they were cut off from fruitful intercourse with their colleagues on the other side of the belligerent line. When the restoration of peace of a sort once more released the flow of scholarly work, the atmosphere had in many respects changed.

There was, of course, a very large element of continuity. Many economic historians continued to work along the lines already laid out, or resumed their work at the conclusion of hostilities where they had been forced to leave it. Works outlining the structure and tracing the development of particular industries or branches of commerce continued to appear,[11] although not in such volume as in the preceding two decades. Regional studies of the kind that Gino Luzzatto had noted as among the most important contributions to the economic history of Italy in the early part of the century[12] also continued, and in ever-increasing proportion. This seems to be particularly true of France, where lists of recent publications on the economic history of our period show a preponderant majority of such studies,[13] a fact possibly explained in part by the immense influence of the late Marc Bloch.

---

[11]See, for example, E. Power, *The Wool Trade in English Medieval History* (London, 1941); D. Burwash, *English Merchant Shipping, 1460-1540* (Toronto, 1947); G. D. Ramsey, *The Wiltshire Woollen Industry in the Sixteenth and Seventeenth Centuries* (Oxford, 1943); E. Sabbe, *Histoire de l'industrie linière en Belgique* (Brussels, 1945); and K. Pagel, *Die Hanse* (Brunswick, 1952).

[12]G. Luzzatto, 'The Study of Medieval Economic History in Italy: Recent Literature and Tendencies', *Journal of Economic and Business History* IV (1931-1932), 708-727.

[13]See, for example, R. Boutruche, 'Histoire de France au Moyen Age: Publications des années 1904-46', *Revue Historique* CCVII (1949), 235-272; 'Histoire de France au Moyen Age: Publications des années 1947-53', *ibid.* CCXIII (1955),47-80; Ph. Wolff, 'List of Books and Articles on Medieval Economic History of France published in France, 1950-52', *Economic History Review,* 2nd Series VI (1953-1954), 339-343.

On the other hand, certain problems seem to have dropped out of the picture. I find in the economic history written since the war little interest in the spirit of capitalism in the sense in which Sombart and Weber had made it a subject of controversy. I also find fewer references to the relation between economic individualism and Renaissance individualism, although it has been recently reasserted by Armando Sapori,[14] while Yves Renouard and others[15] have called attention to the influence of business men on the shaping of Renaissance culture. Perhaps the apparent lack of interest since the war in the *geisteswissenschaftlich* approach is a symptom of the decline of German leadership in historical thought and scholarship since the early thirties. But it is also noticeable that there have been fewer general economic histories devoted to our period in the past twenty years than in the single decade before the war. I can think of only three significant works of that kind as compared to the dozen or so published in the thirties: the two volumes of *The Cambridge Economic History*, published in 1942 and 1952, but both planned before the war; Gino Luzzatto's *Storia economica d'Italia* (1949); and F. Lütge's *Deutsche Sozial- und Wirtschaftsgeschichte* (1952). The predominant characteristics of the economic history written during the past twenty years, as compared to that of the preceding period, seem to be the collecting of factual information, the empirical testing of accepted ideas, and the interpretation of the data in terms of economic theory, rather than making extensive surveys or formulating the sociological hypotheses of the early pioneers.

One important tendency in the past two decades has been the greatly accelerated interest in business history as a distinct discipline. This is one of the newer branches of economic history. As described by N. S. B. Gras, one of its early protagonists, business history is not the history of commerce, industry, banking, agriculture, and so forth, but that of individual units of business enterprise.[16] Its source material is to be found, not in guild regulations, city ordinances, state legislation, or treatises on the conduct of business, but in the records of individual business men, partnerships, and firms — in account books, diaries, partnership agreements, notarial records, correspondence, and all the detailed evidence of the way in which a particular business actually operated. The value of this kind of study is that it sees commerce and industry as it were from the inside and thus frequently serves as a corrective to the generalizations of those institutionalist historians who were primarily concerned with the external structure of the various forms of economic activity. The range of focus is narrow, but the details seen thus have a realistic clarity lacking in the broader view. Above all, it concentrates attention on the practical problems of management and control of business enterprise, problems for which guild statutes and economic legislation in general offer little evidence.

---

[14] A. Sapori, *L'età della Rinascita: secoli XIII-XVI* (Milan, 1958), pp. 250 ff.

[15] Y. Renouard, *Les Hommes d'affaires italiens du Moyen Age* (Paris, 1949), p. 246; and A. Sapori in *Il Rinascimento: significato e limiti*, p 130.

[16] N. S. B. Gras, 'Business History', *Economic History Review* IV (1934), 385-398.

Studies of individual businesses or firms were not, it is true, entirely unprecedented. The Fuggers early attracted the attention of scholars, largely because of the great influence they exerted on political events in the reign of Charles V, and the preservation of their records and news letters led to a series of extensive studies early in the century. The flamboyant career of Jacques Coeur as merchant and royal minister also attracted numerous biographers. The scholars whose attention was drawn to such unusual personalities as Jacques Coeur and Jacob Fugger, however, were not primarily interested in business history in the sense in which Professor Gras envisaged it. The true pioneer in that field was Armando Sapori, whose studies of the Bardi and Peruzzi firms (1926) and of the firm of del Bene (1932) were models of their kind.[17] He has since furnished material for further such studies by publishing the account books of several fourteenth- and fifteenth-century firms.[18] The influence of Professors Gras and Usher has also led to a considerable interest among American historians in the history of Renaissance business, and there is evidence in other countries of a growing interest in this field. Some of the most fruitful research has been devoted to merchants who were not politically important and who did not operate on an unusually large scale, but whose records for that very reason furnish us with a clearer picture of the activity of the average business man of that period. The degree to which studies of this kind can lend concrete reality to the economic history of the Renaissance has been demonstrated, for example, by Raymond de Roover's study of a firm of Florentine cloth manufacturers (1941),[19] which corrected Alfred Doren's classic account of the industry in many particulars, by Frederick Lane's monograph on Andrea Barbarigo (1941),[20] and by Iris Origo's more recent biography of Francesco di Marco Datini of Prato (1957).[21] Such studies may also give us a more accurate description of the capitalist spirit in action than we could get from more general and theoretical works.

Research based on business records has been especially fruitful in clarifying the early history of banking and exchange procedures. This was

---

[17]A. Sapori, *La crisi delle compagnie mercantili dei Bardi e dei Peruzzi* (Florence, 1926); *Una compagnia di Calimala ai primi del Trecento* (Florence, 1932). See also the articles collected in his *Studi di storia economica medioevale* (Florence, 1946).

[18]A. Sapori, *I libri di commercio dei Peruzzi* (Milan, 1934); *I libri della ragione bancaria dei Gianfigliazzi* (Milan, 1943); *Liber tercius Friscorubaldorum* (Florence, 1947); and *I libri degli Alberti del Giudice* (Milan, 1952).

[19]R. de Roover, 'A Florentine Firm of Cloth Manufacturers: Management and Organization of a Sixteenth-Century Business', *Speculum* XVI (1941), 3-33; see also his 'The Story of the Alberti Company of Florence, 1302-1348, as revealed in its Account Books', *Business History Review* XXXIII (1958), 14-59.

[20]F. C. Lane, *Andrea Barbarigo, Merchant of Venice, 1418-1449* (Baltimore, 1944); see also his 'Family Partnerships and Joint Ventures in the Venetian Republic', *Journal of Economic History* IV (1944), 178-196.

[21]I. Origo, *The Merchant of Prato: the Life and Papers of Francesco di Marco Datini* (London, 1957).

one of the last aspects of early capitalism to receive adequate analysis and interpretation. The technical problems involved here were unusually forbidding, and the fact that the great banking firms combined traffic in goods with handling foreign exchange and commercial loans, and that they operated in part on capital deposited with them on which they paid interest, made it difficult to isolate and define their activity as bankers. In the early work on the economic history of this period, too, there was a good deal of confusion regarding the distinction between the activity of moneychangers who handled actual coins and that of dealers in bills of exchange, between banks of international scope and local banks of deposit, as well as the important distinction between the great Italian banking firms who made commercial loans or loans to governments and the Lombards or Cahorsins who were merely petty usurers and pawnbrokers.

Work of basic importance for the early history of banks of deposit and the technique of making transfers of credit on the books of local banks was done by A. P. Usher[22] and F. C. Lane[23] in the thirties and forties. The most important recent contributions to the whole problem of banking and exchange, however, have been made by Raymond de Roover, whose training, first as an expert accountant for some ten years in his native Belgium and then as a graduate student with Usher and Gras at Harvard and J. U. Nef at Chicago, made him peculiarly fitted to unravel and interpret the records of the early banking concerns. Choosing Bruges as a center where the activity of both Italian and Flemish financiers—the most advanced in that period— could be studied and compared, he analyzed the whole range of financial procedure during the fourteenth and fifteenth centuries in a book entitled *Money, Banking and Credit in Medieval Bruges* (1948). Here he clarified much earlier confusion by dealing separately with three distinct types of dealers in money: the Italian merchant-bankers, the Lombards or Italian pawnbrokers, and the native money-changers. In this book and in a number of supplementary monographs and articles[24] he also worked out in detail the technique of transferring money from one country to another by bills of exchange, and established the fact that the bill of exchange was also an instrument of credit, by means of which short-term loans could be made without running afoul of the ecclesiastical prohibition of usury. In the same year,

---

[22]A. P. Usher, 'Deposit Banking in Barcelona, 1300-1700', *Journal of Economic and Business History* IV (1931), 121-155; 'The Origins of Banking: the Primitive Bank of Deposit, 1200-1600', *Economic History Review* IV (1934), 399-428; *The Early History of Deposit Banking in Mediterranean Europe* (Cambridge, Mass., 1943).

[23]F. C. Lane, 'Venetian Bankers, 1496-1533: a Study in the Early Stages of Deposit Banking', *Journal of Political Economy* XCV (1937), 187-206.

[24]R. de Roover, *L'Evolution de la lettre de change, XIVe-XVIIIe siècles* (Paris, 1953); 'Appunti sulla storia della cambiale e del contratto di cambio', *Studi in onore di Gino Luzzatto* (Milan, 1950) pp. 193-219; 'Le Contrat de change depuis la fin du treizième siècle jusqu'au début du dix-septième', *Revue belge de philologie et d'histoire* XXV (1946-1947), 111-128; 'Cambium ad Venetias: Contribution to the History of Foreign Exchange', *Studi in onore di Armando Sapori* (Milan, 1957), pp. 629-648.

1948, de Roover also published a second major contribution to the history of
early banking in his study of *The Medici Bank, its Organization, Management, Operation and Decline.* There had been earlier studies of the Medici
bank. The pioneer work was done by Heinrich Sieveking in 1905.[25] But
the political and cultural importance of the Medici has so far overshadowed
their purely business activity that the operation of their bank has been largely
neglected or taken for granted in the voluminous literature devoted to the
family. De Roover's study, on the contrary, deals with the Medici bank exclusively as a business concern, drawing its material almost entirely from the
firm's account books and other records. As he himself notes in the preface:
'this study is an attempt to show how the wheels turned around in the business
world of the Renaissance. The method is the same as that which would be
used in the analysis of the structure, the policies and the history of a modern
business concern.' In the process he not only illustrates the business life of
the fifteenth century but also rounds out our picture of its most illustrious
family.

The recent school of business history has, by the very nature of its
methods, contributed more to the establishment of concrete information than
to general interpretation, but it has served to correct many misapprehensions
and it has furnished the basis for some important generalizations. One result
of its concentration upon the problems of business management has been a
growing awareness of the change in the methods of conducting business in
Italy and the Netherlands around the end of the thirteenth century and the
beginning of the fourteenth, a change so decisive that it has been termed a
'commercial revolution'[26] and has been hailed as marking a definite stage in
the evolution of capitalist enterprise. The change may not, indeed, be sufficiently revolutionary to warrant our drawing a clear line between medieval
and Renaissance capitalism at about the year 1300, but it seems significant
enough to be taken into consideration when we attempt to establish the
chronological boundaries between the two periods. What was involved in
the change was the gradual passing of the type of itinerant merchant who
traveled with his goods and whose activity centered around the Champagne
fairs , and the appearance in his place of a new type of entrepreneur, the
sedentary merchant who remained at home in his counting house and conducted his business abroad by means of correspondence with partners, factors,
or commission agents. The basic distinction in character, methods, and
activity of these two types was outlined by N. S. B. Gras in his *Business and
Capitalism* in 1939.[27] It has since been generally accepted, although there is
still debate as to whether the change was caused by the decline of the
Champagne fairs, the opening of a direct sea route from Italy to the Netherlands and the resultant migration of Italian business men to Bruges, or

---

[25]H. Sieveking, *Die Handlungsbücher der Medici* (Vienna, 1905).

[26]See note 4 above.

[27]See also N. S. B. Gras, 'Stages in Business History', in *Studi in onore di Armando
Sapori,* pp. 5-27; and R. Grousset, *Villes marchandes aux XIVe et XVe siècles* (Paris,
1948), pp. 25 ff.

whether it was simply the result of shrinking profits as commerce became safer and competition keener. The latter argument, at any rate, has been advanced by Robert Lopez in the second volume of *The Cambridge Economic History*.[28]

A second noticeable tendency in the economic historiography of the past two or three decades has been the accumulation of statistical data and the introduction of quantitative criteria in place of the earlier preoccupation with the institutional structure of commerce, industry, and finance or the still earlier qualitative criteria of those scholars whose primary concern was the capitalist spirit. In place of description or sociological analysis, the new tendency is to concentrate attention upon the discovery of secular or long-term trends and upon the measurement of the rate of change in population, prices, and the volume of production and exchange, concepts susceptible of interpretation in terms of pure economic theory.[29] The quantitative approach is basically empirical, but it can also lead to the formation of hypotheses. In a programmatic article in 1932, entitled 'The Application of the Quantitative Method to Economic History',[30] A. P. Usher called attention to the potential usefulness of this method for the correction of institutionalist or idealist constructions of economic history. It has since become increasingly prevalent in studies of late medieval and Renaissance economy. The combination of statistical research with economic theory has been particularly fruitful in elucidating the problems presented by the relation of money to the general economy: the fluctuating values of the monetary metals, their shifting relation to one another and to money of account, the relative rapidity of monetary circulation and the effect of governmental devaluation of coinage.[31] E. J. Hamilton's massive study of *American Treasure and the Price Revolution in Spain* (1932), based on a vast accumulation of statistics and a quantity theory of money, was an early example and has influenced all later discussion of the economic trends of the sixteenth century.[32] Since the early thirties English economic historians have also devoted a great deal of attention to the statistical study of trends in English foreign trade from the fourteenth to the sixteenth centuries, a study for which the preservation of the customs accounts offers unusual opportunities; but continental scholars, too, have been increasingly preoccupied with the search for such statistical data as are available. In 1955 Armando Sapori was able to hail with satisfaction the immense progress

---

[28]*The Cambridge Economic History*, II, 335.

[29]See, for example, H. and P. Chaunu, 'A la recherche des fluctuations cycliques dans l'économie des XVIe et XVIIe siècles', in *Homage à L. Febvre*, II (Paris, 1953), 389-407.

[30]*Journal of Political Economy* XL (1932), 186-209.

[31]For a recent survey of the literature on this subject, see F. Braudel and F. C. Spooner, 'Les métaux monétaires et l'économie du XVIe siècle', in *Relazioni del X Congresso Internazionale di Scienze Storiche, 1955*, IV (Florence, 1957), 233-264.

[32]The general accuracy of Hamilton's statistical curves has recently been confirmed by H. and P. Chaunu, *Séville et l'Atlantique, 1504-1650* (Paris, 1955-1957).

that had been made in the collection of quantitative data on production, circulation, and prices of goods since he had urged the need for such research at the International Congress held at Zurich in 1938.[33]

Now the value to the specialist in economic history of quantitative data, as of any other form of pertinent information, is incontestable, although it is obvious that it furnishes only one of the ingredients from which he may reconstruct the complex economic life of any period, and too exclusive reliance upon it on the part of recent historians has aroused apprehension in the minds of some thoughtful scholars.[34] But historians of culture in general also must be interested to know whether the period they are attempting to interpret was one of rising or declining prosperity. The accumulated evidence of a great quantitative expansion of the European economy in the sixteenth century will cause no one to change his views. It has long been taken for granted. On the other hand, Fernand Braudel's study of the Mediterranean world in the age of Philip II,[35] with its argument, supported by masses of statistical evidence, that the balance of financial and commercial preponderance did not shift from the Mediterranean to the north until well into the seventeenth century, may cause historians to reconsider some of their assumptions regarding the economic background of the decline of the Italian Renaissance in the sixteenth century, although it remains true that Italy was not the economic center of Braudel's Mediterranean world as it had been in earlier centuries.

A more serious problem for historians of the Renaissance, however, and particularly of the Renaissance in Italy, it seems to me, is that posed by a number of recent scholars whose statistical research has led them to depict the fourteenth and fifteenth centuries as, on the whole, a period of economic stagnation or decline. As Delio Cantimori pointed out in a recent article,[36] students of the Italian Renaissance have found it disturbing to discover that the period which they think of as the Renaissance in literature, learning, and art is now depicted as one of economic decadence. English, French, and German cultural historians, accustomed to thinking of their national renaissance as beginning toward the end of the fifteenth century or in the early sixteenth, may be less concerned, as also may be those who accept Huizinga's characterization of the fourteenth and fifteenth centuries as the waning of the Middle Ages. There may even be some medievalists who would welcome the idea with a feeling that an economic depression served the Renaissance right and was no more than could be expected. The thesis of economic stagnation or decline in the fourteenth and fifteenth centuries cannot, however, be so lightly dismissed by historians who, like myself, regard these centuries as marking

[33]A. Sapori, 'I beni del commercio internazionale nel medioevo', *Archivio Storico Italiano* CXIII (1955), 3.

[34]Cf. Sapori, *ibid.*, pp. 4-11; and G. Luzzatto, 'Tendenze nuove negli studi di storia economica', *Nuova Revista Storica* XXXV (1951), fasc. 3-4, p. 13.

[35]F. Braudel, *La Méditerranée et le monde méditerranéen à l'époque de Philippe II* (Paris, 1949).

[36]D. Cantimori, 'Il problema rinascimentale proposto da Armando Sapori', in *Studi in onori di A. Sapori*, pp. 935-947.

one of the most important stages in the transition from medieval to modern
civilization, not only in Italy but throughout Western Europe. Whether we
accept all the conclusions of the most enthusiastic proponents of this thesis or
not, we must, I think, pause to reconsider the assumptions upon which our interpretation has in part been based, and to this subject I would like to devote
the remainder of my paper.

A generation ago the assumption taken for granted by most historians
was that the transformation of European civilization during this period was
accompanied by—if not founded upon—a steadily rising prosperity, increasing wealth, and expanding commercial and industrial activity. As stated by
E. P. Cheyney in 1936 in the opening chapter of his book, *The Dawn of a
New Era,* 1250-1453, 'the most fundamental of the changes that marked the
passage from medieval to modern times was the increase of wealth, and the
principal cause of the increase of wealth was the extension of commerce.'[37]
An assumption of constantly increasing wealth during this period formed
part of my own conception of the Renaissance twenty years ago.[38]   It was
obvious, of course, that the mortality caused by the Black Death must for a
time have reduced the number of both consumers and producers, and that the
devastation which accompanied the Hundred Years' War must have materially reduced the wealth of a large part of France. But I think that there was
a general assumption that the development of more efficient forms of capitalist organization of commerce, industry, and finance soon made good the
losses caused by the Black Death in most parts of Europe. In any case, the
predominantly institutionalist approach of the majority of economic historians in the prewar period focussed attention on changes in economic organization rather than upon quantitative variations or trends in the volume of production and exchange.

Now, the first serious suggestion of which I am aware that this conception was open to question appeared in Henri Pirenne's *Economic and Social
History of Medieval Europe* (1937). Here he noted that the beginning of
the fourteenth century marked the end of the period of medieval economic
expansion, that 'during the early years of the fourteenth century there is
observable in all these directions [of economic activity] not perhaps a decline but a cessation of all advance. Europe lived, so to speak, on what had
been acquired; the economic front was stabilized.'[39] During the next few
years this revisionist thesis was echoed in scattered articles[40] which stated it

---

[37] (New York, 1936), p. 2.

[38] W. K. Ferguson, *The Renaissance* (New York, 1940), p. 46.

[39] H. Pirenne, *Economic and Social History of Medieval Europe* (New York, 1937),
p. 192 f.

[40] See, for example, M. M. Postan, 'Revisions in Economic History: the Fifteenth
Century', *Economic History Review* IX (1938-1939), 160-167; J. U. Nef, 'Industrial
Europe on the Eve of the Reformation', *Journal of Political Economy* XLIX (1941),
1-40, 183-224; J. Saltmarsh, 'Plague and Economic Decline in the Later Middle
Ages', *Cambridge Historical Journal* VII (1940), 23-40.

more strongly and translated stability into decline, but it did not attract general attention until after the war, when scholars were once more able to establish contact with the work of their colleagues in other countries and when the volume of scholarly research, dammed up by the war, once more flowed freely into print. It dominated the debates of the section on late medieval economy at the Ninth International Congress of Historical Sciences at Paris in 1950 and again at the Tenth Congress held in Rome in 1955, and it was given the official sanction of those august bodies in the cooperative reports subsequently published.[41] It also formed the central theme of the second volume of *The Cambridge Economic History* (1952). The effort to revise the traditional conception of the Renaissance as a period of expanding wealth has been international in scope. Among the most prominent contributors to it are M. M. Postan in England, Renée Doehaerd in Belgium, Edouard Perroy in France, W. Abel in Germany, Armando Sapori and Carlo Cipolla in Italy, and J. U. Nef and Robert Lopez in the United States.

The first question we have to ask in relation to their thesis, it seems to me, is: has it been proven? There have been some dissenting voices,[42] and even its protagonists are not agreed as to either the intensity or the duration of the recession. Carlo Cipolla, for example, notes a rising secular trend in Italy, beginning toward the end of the fourteenth century and continuing through the fifteenth,[43] while Robert Lopez states flatly that the period from about 1330 to 1530, with perhaps an additional decade or two at either end, was 'one of deep depression followed by moderate and incomplete recovery', and that Italy 'felt the impact of the economic recession most heavily'.[44] Masses of statistical evidence have been produced, but the available statistics seldom form a continuous series or are sufficiently homogeneous to serve as a basis for accurate comparison. It is difficult to determine whether the decline of some old industries, like the manufacture of fine woolen cloth in Florence and the Netherlands, was not adequately compensated by the growth of newer industries like the making of silks, light woolens, linens, and fustians; or whether the decline of some old cities was not compensated by growth in others. To what extent did the growth of rural industry in England and the Netherlands make up for the losses suffered by the old industrial cities? These and other similar questions still call for further research.

---

[41]M. M. Postan, 'Rapport: Histoire économique: Moyen Age', in *IXe Congrès International des Sciences Historiques, Paris, 1950*, I (Paris, 1950), 225-241; and discussion, II, 110-114; M. Mollat, P. Johansen, M. Postan, A. Sapori and C. Verlinden, 'L'économie européen aux deux derniers siècles du Moyen Age', *Relazioni del X Congresso Internazionale di Scienze Storiche, Roma, 1955*, III (Florence, 1957), 655-811.

[42]See E. A. Kosminsky, 'Peut-on considérer le XIVe et le XVe siècles comme l'époque de la décadence de l'économie européen?' *Studi in onore di A. Sapori* pp. 551-570; and H. Baron in *American Historical Review* LXI (1956), 1087 ff.

[43]C. M. Cipolla, 'The Trends in Italian Economic History in the Later Middle Ages', *Economic History Review*, 2nd Series, II (1949), 181-184.

[44]R. Lopez, 'Hard Times and Investment in Culture', in *The Renaissance: a Symposium* (New York, Metropolitan Museum of Art, 1953), pp. 19-34.

Nevertheless, the weight of the evidence does seem to justify the conclusion that, taking Western Europe as a whole, there was a general cessation of economic growth in the early years of the fourteenth century, and that this was followed by a long period of contraction in the volume of production and exchange. There seems to be especially convincing evidence of a prolonged agricultural depression in England, France, and parts of Germany. Land prices fell and not only did the clearing of land for cultivation cease, but much marginal land that had been cleared during the thirteenth century was now abandoned, either because worked out or no longer needed. The demographic curve, which had been rising for two or three hundred years, apparently began to drop in the early fourteenth century, then fell drastically with the Black Death, while normal recovery was checked for a century or more by recurrences of the plague and by the devastation caused by war.[45] It seems reasonable to assume, too, that commerce and industry suffered quantitatively from the reduction in population and hence in both labor supply and markets. And, meanwhile, the European economy had ceased to expand geographically. The eastward drive of German colonization came to a halt, while the frontiers of European trade in the Near East were beginning to shrink. The medieval frontier was closing, as A. R. Lewis argued in an article in *Speculum* in 1958,[46] with results comparable to those which followed the closing of the American frontier at the end of the last century. The fourteenth century and the first half of the fifteenth, in short, were plagued throughout by catastrophes and crises. But did not these very crises hasten rather than retard the transition from medieval to modern civilization?

With that question in mind, let us grant for the moment the thesis of the economic revisionists, and ask what effect it may have upon our interpretation of this period. In the first place, one of the major elements in the transition from medieval to modern civilization seems to me to be a shift in the center of gravity of economic, social, and cultural life from the country to the city,[47] and this may well have been accelerated by the relatively more severe impact of the depression upon the land-holding classes—the nobles and the higher clergy—although, because of falling rents and rising wages, the peasants were in most places apparently better off than they had been. A second, and related, element, the disintegration of feudalism and the rise of centralized state governments, was undoubtedly hastened by the impoverishment of the nobility and by the disruption of the manorial system, the economic basis of feudalism, which accompanied the economic and demographic crisis of the fourteenth century and the first half of the fifteenth. Despite any possible reduction in total wealth, this period saw a rapid increase in governmental income through taxation, which enabled kings and princes to

---

[45]See J. C. Russell, *Late Ancient and Medieval Populations* (Philadelphia, 1958), pp. 99, ff., 113 ff.

[46]A. R. Lewis, 'The Closing of the Medieval Frontier, 1250-1350', *Speculum* XXXIII (1958), 475-483.

[47]W. K. Ferguson, 'The Interpretation of the Renaissance: Suggestions for a Synthesis', *Journal of the History of Ideas* XII (1951), 483-495. See below, pp. 125 ff.

extend their military and administrative authority at the expense of feudal particularism, even though it aggravated the economic crisis, as Lopez has pointed out,[4b] by imposing a crushing burden on the economy of the state. In these centuries the Church, which represented the universal principle in medieval civilization, also passed through a crisis that shook it to its foundations, but this crisis seems to have been caused less by economic recession than by the intrusion of too much money into the fabric of church government. When we turn to the economic and social development within the cities, we may admit as a reasonable hypothesis that there was a reduction in total wealth corresponding to the reduction in population. But was the *per capita* wealth reduced thereby? In any case most of the exponents of the thesis of recession are agreed that shrinking markets, smaller profits, and keener competition accelerated the development of more rational and efficient technique of business enterprise, resulting in a qualitative advance in the evolution of capitalism much greater than that which took place during the rapid quantitative expansion of the European economy in the sixteenth century.[49] And if, as has been suggested,[50] one result of the crisis was that the rich got richer while the poor got poorer, we must remember that it was concentrated wealth rather than widely distributed prosperity that was responsible for the patronage of art, letters, music, and all the higher forms of intellectual and aesthetic culture. Nor, in this regard, should we forget the unprecedented concentration of wealth during this period in the hands of kings and princes which accompanied the growth of central government in territorial and national states. It was the wealth of the Burgundian court as well as of the Flemish cities that furnished the material basis for the flourishing art of the Netherlands in the fifteenth century. And if, as Huizinga has so brilliantly demonstrated, an air of decadence hangs over the literature of northern France and the Netherlands in this period, this was not the result of poverty but rather of the fact that under the influence of the Burgundian and royal courts literary tradition still expressed, with increasing aridity, the ideals and conventional attitudes of a noble class whose economic, social, and political roots had been cut off from the soil in which they had grown during the Middle Ages.

But it is in Italy rather than the north that the relation of economic to cultural growth poses the most serious problem for the historian, for it was here that the culture we think of as specifically Renaissance grew in the midst of what is now portrayed as a period of economic depression. So far as patronage is concerned, I think the fruits of those years are ample proof that there was still enough to go around. In Italy, earlier than elsewhere, the concentration of wealth based on taxation furnished princes with the means of patronage. If, moreover, there was any reduction in total wealth, it was more than compensated by the growth of a tradition of culture which, more than any quantitative variation in wealth, differentiates the world of the Medici from

---

[48]Lopez, 'Hard Times', p. 22 f.

[49]Cf. Braudel and Spooner, *op. cit.*, pp. 245 f.; and Mollat, *op. cit.*, pp. 45 f.

[50]*The Cambridge Economic History*, II, 343 ff.

that of the Bardi and Peruzzi. But the economic factors which helped to condition the culture of the Italian Renaissance were by no means limited to the mere existence of surplus wealth or the direct economic stimulus of patronage. The culture of the Italian Renaissance was different from that of the Middle Ages—though not, of course, completely different—because it was produced by and for a different kind of society from that characteristic of the greater part of medieval Europe. It was a society formed in large part by the early expansion of commerce and industry and the resultant growth of a wealthy urban society. One distinguishing characteristic of this society was the increasing participation in cultural activity of urban laymen, which broke the clerical monopoly of learning and the chivalric tradition in vernacular literature and which found expression in an increasingly urban and secular tone in literature, learning, art, and music. Now the growth of capitalism was, it seems to me, an important factor in stimulating this development of lay culture, first, by requiring literacy of every one engaged in business and, second, by offering opportunities for the passive investment of inherited income, which made it possible for a growing number of the upper classes in the cities to seek higher education, to qualify for the lay learned professions, and to form an appreciative public for the work of artists and writers. It seems to me, then, that the influence of capitalism upon the culture of the Renaissance depended rather more upon the evolution of its forms of business organization than upon the production of absolute wealth.

In conclusion, it seems to me that the recent tendency to concentrate attention upon the quantitative analysis of long-term trends in economic production and exchange, while undoubtedly important, tells us less that is of value in explaining and intepreting the civilization of this period than did the earlier studies of the structure of economic life, amplified as they have been by the more recent studies of individual business enterprises. It might be well to heed the warning of Armando Sapori not to ask of statistical data more than they can offer.[51] Perhaps it is time now, with our increased knowledge, to return to the kind of question posed earlier in the century by Sombart, Weber, Pirenne, and others and to analyze once more the spirit which motivated Renaissance business men, to reconsider the relation between religion and business ethics,[52] and to reassess the possible relation between economic individualism and the culture of the Renaissance. If we are to understand a civilization in which business men played an active part, it seems more important to know how they conducted their business, how they felt about it, what manner of men they were, and what were their aims and interests than to know whether the long-term trend of production and exchange was rising or falling. There may, indeed, be a point in asking whether the men of that

[51]Sapori, 'I beni del commercio', *Archivio Storico Italiano* CXIII, 6 f.

[52]Some important work has been done recently on the subject of usury as one aspect of the relation between religion and business ethics. See, for example, B. Nelson, *The Idea of Usury* (Princeton, 1949); Florence Edler de Roover, 'Restitution in Renaissance Florence', *Studi in onore di Armando Sapori* (Milan, 1947), pp. 773-789; R. de Roover, 'Cambium ad Venetias', *ibid.*, pp. 632 ff.

age *thought* that things were getting better or worse, whether the psychological atmosphere was basically optimistic or pessimistic, but such subjective reactions are not susceptible of statistical analysis. Francesco di Marco Datini may have lived in an era of economic depression, but it is illuminating to know that he hopefully headed each of his ledgers with the inscription 'in the name of God and of profit'.[58] Perhaps this was, after all, the spirit of capitalism.

---

[58]Origo, *op. cit.*, p. 114.

Studies in Renaissance Humanism

THE ATTITUDE OF ERASMUS TOWARD TOLERATION*

Though hailed with adulation from one end of Europe to the other as Prince of the Humanists, Erasmus of Rotterdam was often to find himself in the lonely position of one crying in the wilderness. His services to scholarship excited an almost extravagant admiration; his attempts to revive an enlightened and spiritual Christianity attracted a wide following in the days before the Lutheran schism; but for all his popularity, many of his most humane teachings were appreciated by none but the high-minded few in his own day, and were to meet with full recognition only after centuries had passed. As examples we may cite his courageous pacifism in an age when warfare was man's most honored occupation, and with it his broad-minded tolerance in an age of passionate dogmatism. In the latter he found more followers than in the former; for there was a fairly powerful group of men who, under his influence, labored to restore peace to the schism-torn Church through a policy of mediation. There were also other and more thorough-going apostles of toleration in that century; but on the whole, Erasmus stood far above his age as the champion of intellectual freedom and the opponent of persecution. Later historians have recognized his tolerance; yet as he asserted no doctrine of absolute or unqualified toleration, and indeed wrote relatively little directly on the subject, they have for the most part been content to mention him as one of the most tolerant men of his century, or to assume that he was, with little attempt at analysis or definition of his attitude. The task, indeed, presents some difficulties. There are no carefully planned works like *The Complaint of Peace* to guide one, as there are in studying his pacifism. On the contrary, his attitude toward toleration was expressed directly only in scattered *obiter dicta,* and in isolated passages from various *apologia* and from his correspondence. These of course are important. But more important, for their influence on the growth of religious tolerance and hence on the development of legal toleration, were the implications of his whole attitude toward life, religion, morals and ethics—and it is in estimating these that the

---

*Read before the American Historical Association, December, 1930. Reprinted from *Persecution and Liberty, Essays in Honor of George Lincoln Burr,* 1931.

difficulty lies. Only the most exhaustive study of his works would show all the ways in which he taught tolerance. It was an integral and perhaps largely unconscious part of his Christian humanism. To a greater or less degree it was implicit in every book he wrote, from the *Enchiridion* to the *Praise of Folly,* from the *Adages* to the *Familiar Colloquies.* To trace its full expression in his works, however, would be a task beyond the scope of a short paper. Here I can attempt merely a brief analysis of the sources and nature of Erasmus's tolerance, in connection with his character, interests and beliefs, and then try to define as clearly as possible his actual position with regard to the toleration of dissent.

In our search for the sources of Erasmus's tolerance we must turn first to the consideration of the character and temperament of the amiable sage himself. One cannot read far in any of his works without realizing that his mind was too finely balanced ever to fall a prey to that dogmatism which is the greatest enemy of tolerance. He saw the other side of every argument far too clearly to believe that he had achieved the absolute truth, or indeed that it was possible of attainment. To believe that one is absolutely right, and hence that others who disagree are absolutely wrong, requires at once an egotism and a passionate conviction that were alike foreign to his nature. His instinctive aversion to dogmatism showed itself in every line he wrote and became the most characteristic element of the Erasmian style. He had, too, a nice sense of humor and no very deep conviction of sin. Thorough humanist that he was, he had faith in human nature, and regarded the world with the eye of the kindly satirist who sees the follies rather than the sins of men. Never depressed by the utter depravity of man's inherent nature, he refused to recognize anyone, with the possible exception of the obscurantist monks who attacked his beloved *bonae litterae,* as hopelessly unregenerate. He shared the Renaissance faith in the potentialities of the human mind, and had himself never suffered the soul-torture of the devout sinner who has despaired of salvation. As a result he saw men as essentially free—free to fall into error, but free also to return under the influence of rational persuasion to the right path. In the meantime for him the erring man had other human characteristics than error, and he was always interested in humanity. In the days when the feeling aroused on both sides by the Lutheran controversy had become very bitter, he wrote to his friend Botzheim: "I have never renounced the friendship of anyone either because he was inclined to Luther or because he was against him. For I am of such a nature that I could love even a Jew, were he only a pleasant companion and friend, and did not blaspheme in my presence."[1]

A man "of such a nature" must have possessed a tolerant temper in any age and under any circumstances. In the case of Erasmus, however, the development of his thought was conditioned by powerful influences which turned his mind toward a more positive tolerance, affording a basis of rational theory for what might otherwise have been a mere matter of temperament. One of

---

[1]Allen, P. S., *Opus Epistolarum Des. Erasmi Roterodami* (7 vols., Oxford, 1906-28), I, p. 17.

the most important of these was the absorbing interest in the classics, which
filled all his early years and continued to hold a large share of his attention
throughout life. From the first he read the ancient authors with passionate
devotion and with an admiration that included their thought as well as their
style. The clear sanity and dispassionate rationalism of the great pagan
writers found an echo in his own character, broadened his interests and
strengthened his natural aversion to dogmatism. Above all, he owed to the
classics something of the preoccupation with the ethical and moral aspects of
life that was so significant a part of his religious attitude. His admiration
for the Roman moralists was so great that he was almost prepared to include
them among the Christian saints. In one of the *Colloquies* he wrote:

> One should not call anything profane that leads to piety...And it
> may be that the spirit of Christ is more widely found than we would credit.
> There are many to be found among the saints who are not listed in our
> catalogue. I confess my own feeling among my friends: I cannot read
> Cicero's *De senectute, De amicitia, De officiis, De tusculanis quaestionibus*
> without covering the parchment with kisses and bowing in veneration to
> that saintly mind.[2]

This admiration for men whose works made for piety, whatever their religious beliefs, might be extended to heretics as well as to the great pagans.

The classics were Erasmus's first love. When later, whether under the
influence of Colet or as a natural development, religion began to assume a
predominating place in his thought, his methods and interests still bore the
stamp of his classical training. There was the same scholarly study of the
original texts, the same contempt for the medieval scholastic theologians, the
same enthusiasm for enlightened education, and the same predominant emphasis on ethics and morals. His religious teaching, beginning with the
Enchiridion, had little to do with dogma, but concerned itself almost entirely
with the Christian way of life. His attacks on the Church were levelled
against practical abuses and unchristian ideals rather than against forms of
belief. He himself summed up his whole doctrine in the significant phrase,
"the Philosophy of Christ." He had first become interested in the critical
work of re-editing the New Testament and the Fathers through a desire to
restore the teaching of Christ in its pristine purity and to free it from the en-
crustations of centuries of dogmatic argument. If men could be made to
understand the spirit of Christ in an enlightened manner, and to live as He
lived, nothing else was of serious import. This emphasis on the way of life
rather than on the form of belief led inevitably to a tolerant attitude toward
varying opinions. Dogmatic differences were relegated to a position of secondary importance. Erasmus had little sympathy with heresy, which seemed
to him rather unnecessary and perverse; but on the other hand, he had no
conviction of the guilt of error. In his own defence he frequently asserted
that even the Fathers had erred.[3] That was after all a matter of opinion. The

---

[2]*Desiderii Erasmi Roterodami Opera omnia,* ed. J. Clericus (10 vols., Lugduni
Batavorum, 1703-06), I., col. 682A.

[3]Cf. *Opera omnia,* IX, col. 900 B.

implication of his whole religious attitude was that if a man lived a good Christian life he need not worry over-much about the exact form of his belief. Time and again he defended Luther on the ground that, though he did not agree with all the reformer's doctrines, everyone said he led a good life.[4]

It must not be imagined, however, that Erasmus's conception of the *Philosophia Christi* implied the merely negative tolerance that springs from indifference to dogma. On the contrary, it led him to a very positive feeling in favor of the toleration of heresy. The great humanist had always a sincere hatred of persecution. Partly this was natural to him, a result of his temperamental horror of violence and cruelty; but still more it was an essential part of his enlightened Christianity. To his mind, persecution for purely religious reasons was above all unchristian, a direct contravention of the spirit and example of Christ. Moreover, it was both useless and stupid. Coercion can touch nothing but the unimportant externals of the religious life, and men cannot be made truly Christian by the use of unchristian force. If, on the other hand, those who have fallen into error are at the same time leading good Christ-like lives, there is no sufficient reason for persecution. Rather, they should be taught with all possible gentleness and so be won back to the true belief. This is the course he invariably recommended, as not only the most Christian but also the most effective means of coping with error; for he was sufficiently clear-sighted to realize that persecution may make men more stubborn in their opinions, and by creating martyrs to heresy merely aggravate the evil. To Duke George of Saxony he wrote in December 1524: "Now I fear greatly lest these vulgar remedies, that is, recantations, imprisonments and burnings, do nothing but exasperate. Two were recently burned at Brussels: since then the whole city begins to favor Luther."[5] And again in the same letter: "The terrible papal edict, the more terrible imperial edict, the imprisonments, the confiscations, the recantations, the fagots and burnings, all these things I can see accomplish nothing except to make the evil more wide-spread."[6]

Yet despite his tolerant attitude toward unorthodox opinion and his steady opposition to persecution, we find, as we examine more closely his position on the question of legal toleration, certain limitations and reservations, which, though apparently inconsistent, are nevertheless characteristic of the man and in harmony with his philosophy and his plans for a religious reformation. The key-note to Erasmus's thought on the treatment of heretics is struck in his own definition of heresy: "By heresy I mean, not error of any sort, but the wilful malice of those who for their own profit by perverse dogmas disturb the tranquillity of the Church."[7] This sentence from the *De ratione concionandi* concludes a list of impieties in which are included perjury, lawsuits for frivolous causes, slander of one's enemies, forgetfulness of

---

[4]Cf. Allen, Epp. 939, 69-73; 947, 33-4; 967, 85-6; 1167, 132-5.

[5]Allen, Ep. 1526, 165 ff.; cf. also Ep. 1983.

[6]*Ibid.*, 102 ff.

[7] *Opera omnia*, V, col. 1081 B.

God in time of prosperity, and finally heresy. The implication is clear. His condemnation of heresy was based on ethical rather than on theological grounds. Whenever Erasmus refers to the dangers of heresy, one may safely read for heresy not mere error in belief, but obstinate and aggressive error, expressed in open revolt against the established church or state, and threatening the peace and unity of the Christian Republic. Indeed, in such references heresy is most always coupled with sedition and schism.[8] The Donatists, as murderers, rebels and schismatics, he considered the worst type of heretic, and most meriting suppression by the state. He cited them repeatedly in his arguments,[9] in one place adding the illuminating comment: "But against the Pelagians there was never any suggestion of an appeal to the power of Caesar, because they did not in the same way disturb the tranquility of the state."[10]

Erasmus, the peaceful scholar, had always hated violence and tumult. He was prepared to approve almost any means of suppressing it and of preserving order and tranquility in the body politic. This feeling was particularly strong with regard to religious dissension; for in the days before the Lutheran schism he had entertained high hopes of a reformation within the Church under the inspiration of an enlightened, undogmatic and evangelical Christian spirit. It would take time—for such a reformation could be accomplished only through a gradual evolution in Christian thought and practice— and its success, he believed, depended on the continued peace and unity of the Church. Anything that provoked violent dogmatic argument or fired partisan passions would be detrimental if not ruinous to his cause. If Erasmus had little patience with the aggressive dogmatism of the orthodox, he was not likely to have much more sympathy with the equally violent dogmatism of heretics. Schism, he felt, was almost the worst possible fate that could befall the Christian Church. "Summa nostrae religionis pax est et unanimitas."[11]

From his various comments on the subject, then, this point emerges clearly: that though heresy which is mere error should be combated with spiritual weapons only, the secular rulers have the right, in cases of extreme danger, to suppress heresy that shows itself in sedition leading to riots, revolt and schism, by legal means and by imposing the penalties prescribed in the law of the land. In a well-known passage, later condemned by the University of Paris, he implied this distinction: "Nor did he [Augustine] condemn if God inspired the minds of princes to coerce those who disturbed the tranquility of the Church. But whoever heard of orthodox bishops inciting kings to the slaughter of heretics who were nothing but heretics?"[12] A little further on in the same argument he wrote: "But if the affair develops into seditious tumult and both sides cry that they are defending the Catholic Church . . . then the princes on both sides ought to suppress them. For what is there to forbid a

---

[8]Cf. *De amabile Ecclesiae concordia* (*Opera omnia,* V, col. 474 D).

[9]Cf. *Opera omnia,* IX, cols. 580 ff.; 904 ff.; Allen, Epp. 1033, 104-6; 1167, 308-12; 1983, 25.

[10]*Opera omnia,* IX, col. 908 D.

[11]Allen, Ep , 1334, 217, to Carondelet, 5 Jan. 1523.

[12]*Opera omnia,* IX, col. 581 A.

prince from putting out of the way heretics who are disturbing the public peace, when the same right is accorded even to heathen princes, and also to our own princes in dealing with the orthodox?"[13] Again he drew the distinction clearly in the letter to George of Saxony already quoted: "It is not right that any error should be punished by fire, unless sedition is added to it, or some other crime that the laws punish by death."[14]

Later, in a letter of uncertain date, he emphasized still more strongly the importance of enforcing obedience to the law: "The Anabaptists are by no means to be tolerated; for the Apostles command us to obey the magistrates, and these men object to obeying Christian princes."[15] Yet while recognizing the right of rulers to keep the peace and to enforce the laws, the humanist urged them to use their power only as a last resort, after all other means had failed, and then as far as possible to moderate the severity of the penalties, according to Christian charity. He concluded his discussion of the treatment of heretics in the Reply to the Spanish Monks with the solemn warning:

> But Christian princes should be warned that not until everything else has been tried, not except in the most necessary cases and then only with fear and trembling should they resort to the sword, whether for war or for the capital punishment of men, as they must be prepared to render an account for each instance to the King of Kings[16]

This distinction between the two types of heresy was carried over into his attitude toward the respective rights of church and state in dealing with heretics. The heresy which merited legal suppression was a civil offence against the peace, and he insisted that it should be left entirely to the secular rulers, acting independently of the ecclesiastical authorities and according to established forms of law and justice. The duty of the Church, on the contrary, was to teach, not to coerce—to combat heresy of opinion by the use of spiritual weapons and persuasion. It offended his whole conception of the spirit of Christianity that the ministers of Christ should take part in active persecution. Rather they should follow the example of "the great Pastor, who came not to destroy souls but to save them."[17] "Whatever may be the severity of the laws, which are perhaps necessary (he wrote), certainly priests and monks should strive to heal rather than to destroy."[18] And again: "It is the duty of bishops, so far as in them lies, to teach, correct and mediate. For what kind of bishop is he who can do nothing but oppress, torture and drag to the flames?"[19]

This argument he developed at some length in three separate apologiae. In his Paraphrase of St. Matthew, he had interpreted the parable of the tares and wheat as follows: "The servants who wished to gather up the tares before

---

[13]Ibid., col. 581 B.

[14]Allen, Ep. 1526, 157-8.

[15]Epistolarum Des. Erasmi libri xxxi (London, 1642), XXX, Ep. 77, col. 1963 D; cf. Preserved, Smith, Erasmus (New York, 1923), p. 324.

[16]Opera omnia, IX, col. 1059 E.

[17]Ibid., col. 1056 D.

[18]Ibid., col. 1056 B.

[19]Ibid., col. 581 B.

it was time are those who think that pseudo-apostles and heretics should be destroyed by the sword and put to death; whereas the Master did not wish them destroyed, but rather tolerated so that perchance they might repent and from tares become wheat." This passage was condemned with other articles by Noel Beda in 1526, and also by representatives of the chief religious orders of Spain in the following year.. Erasmus replied to both, and again in 1528 defended himself against a more comprehensive censure, issued by the Faculty of Theology of Paris, which condemned along with the original articles several sentences from his reply to Beda.[20] Though in form a justification of his own position, the sections dealing with the censured paraphrase were in reality powerful polemics against the persecution of heretics by the ecclesiastical authorities, and especially against the use of the death penalty. His reluctant admission of the right of secular princes to enforce law and order in extreme cases has already been quoted, but with regard to the Church his attitude was uncompromising. He appealed to the spirit of Christ, to the sacred obligation of giving time for repentance—"for who can teach the dead, or convert those who are slain?"[21]—and finally to the authority of the Fathers and the tradition of the early Church. He showed that until the time of Augustine there was never any appeal to the civil power for the suppression of heresy, and that even in dealing with the Donatists Augustine was opposed to the death penalty. He cited the authority of the Bishop of Hippo, who was so often quoted as justifying persecution, in support of his assertion, often repeated here and elsewhere,[22] that excommunication was the severest measure used by the Church against heretics in those days. He insisted that nothing could be found, either in the writings of Augustine or in the laws of the emperors as preserved in the Justinian Code, to justify the slaughter of heretics, no matter how terrible their offence against God or man. "Whereas now, men are dragged to the flames for doubting whether the Roman pontiff has jurisdiction in purgatory."[23] Finally, "Would Augustine, who wished to spare the murderous Donatists, who felt that the glory of the servants of God would be tarnished by the blood of their enemies, have tolerated that simple heretics, however obstinate, should be devoured by the flames?"[24]

Thus the Christian humanist, in a time when to most churchmen heresy was a crime worse than murder or patricide. But few there were to accept his teaching. Had he been able to stamp his personality and impose his thought upon the men of his age as did Luther, Calvin or Loyola, the world might have been spared a century of torture, pillage and bloodshed. But that he failed to do so is no reproach to him. It is the fate commonly accorded to those men born out of due time, who do not think as the majority think, and who stand alone against the spirit of their age.

[20]*Supputatio errorum in censuris Beddae, Opera omnia,* IX., cols. 515 ff.; *Declarationes ad censuras Lutetiae vulgatas sub nomine Facultatis Theologiae Parisiensis, Ibid.,* cols. 813 ff.; *Apologia adversus articulos aliquot per Monachos quosdam in Hispaniis exhibitos, Ibid.,* cols. .1015 ff.

[21]*Ibid.,* col. 582 B.

[22]Cf. Allen, Ep. 1167, 315.

[23]*Opera omnia,* IX, col. 1057 D.

[24]*Ibid.,* col. 582 D.

RENAISSANCE TENDENCIES IN THE RELIGIOUS THOUGHT OF ERASMUS*

To define Renaissance tendencies in religious thought may seem a rash undertaking, as hazardous as the attempt to define the Renaissance itself, for in that transitional age the most varied tendencies were manifest on every hand. There can be no general formula for the piety or theology of a period that contained such exponents of the worldly authority of the Church as were the majority of the popes from John XXII to Julius II, such orthodox reformers as Gerson and Cusa, such heretical reformers as Wycliff and Huss, such sceptical critics as Lorenzo Valla, such humanists in the Vatican as Pius II, such practical mystics as the Brethren of the Common Life, and, in the generation immediately preceding the Reformation, such diverse religious types as Savonarola, Pico della Mirandola, John Colet, Noel Beda and Cardinal Ximenes. Yet, within this mixture of the medieval and the modern, there are, I think, certain tendencies that were peculiar to the age itself, however firmly their roots might be fixed in the past and however far their branches might reach into the future. And these were to a remarkable degree gathered together and welded into a coherent, if unsystematic, synthesis in the thought of Erasmus. In the words of Imbart de la Tour: "If it is true that in all the great epochs of thought there arises a man who summarizes the tendencies of his age, such a man was Erasmus."[1]

So many tendencies, indeed, entered into the religious thought of Erasmus that it seems at times fraught with inconsistencies, especially to those who regard it retroactively from the viewpoint of either Wittenberg or Trent. He was, in fact, the most unsystematic of philosophers, both by natural inclination and by conscious design. If his religious *Weltanschauung* achieves in the end a coherent unity, it is only through the integrating force of his personality. However derivative the ideas expressed—and his alert mind was open to every wind that blew—they were transformed through the alchemy of his spirit into something peculiarly Erasmian. But, while recognizing the

---

*The following paper was read at the New England Renaissance Conference at Smith College, Oct. 30, 1953. Reprinted from *Journal of the History of Ideas XV*, 1954.

[1] P. Imbart de la Tour, *Les Origines de la Réforme* II (2nd ed. Melun, 1946), 345.

strongly personal quality of Erasmus's religious thought, the historian whose
instinct it is to seek origins cannot but be interested in discovering the seeds
of inspiration that bore fruit in what was not merely a personal phenomenon,
but was also to a unique degree representative of a crucial age in the history
of civilization.

The difficulties inherent in analyzing the thought of so unsystematic a
thinker as Erasmus are rendered more acute by the fact that it was expressed
most commonly in isolated *obiter dicta* or in little gems of satire scattered
throughout works ostensibly designed for other purposes. Moreover, he
trusted to wit rather than to logical exposition to make his points, and his
constitutional inability to reject a good phrase once it had occurred to him
sometimes drove him to make comments that a sober second thought might
have suppressed. In two places only, with the possible exception of the *Praise
of Folly,* did he attempt a formal and reasonably systematic presentation of
his religious thought. In the *Enchiridion Militis Christiani* (first published
in 1503 and reissued with a notable prefatory espistle in 1518) he offered a
comprehensive guide to Christian piety. And in the prefatory materials published in 1516 and 1519 with the first two editions of the Greek New Testament, he presented the clearest statement of his conception of the nature of
Christian theology. These included a *Paraclesis ad Lectorem Pium,* the
Methodus, which in the second edition was expanded into a lengthy essay sig-
nificantly entitled *Ratio seu Methodus compendio perveniendi ad veram
theologiam,* and finally an *Apologia* defending his presentation of a critical
edition of the New Testament in its original tongue together with a new Latin
translation.[2] We may take these works as the principle evidence for the positive religious thought and emotion which formed the solid kernel of Erasmus's
philosophy, but which elsewhere was usually expressed in the more negative
form of criticism of the abuses and absurdities that he saw about him in the
Church, the theological faculties and the society of his day.

There is actually very little in these works that can be regarded as original, except as the whole bears the unmistakable imprint of an original mind.
Innumerable scholars have traced the intellectual antecedents of almost all of
his most characteristic ideas, finding them in varying degree in the influence
of Colet and his other English friends, of the Belgian theologian Jean Vitrier,
of Lorenzo Valla, of Pico and the other Florentine Platonists, of Thomas à
Kempis and the Brethren of the Common Life or simply in the teaching of
Jesus Christ. It is not, however, my intention to reassess once more the intellectual sources of Erasmus's piety and theology, though the fact that parallels
to his ideas may be found in so many diverse places is in itself significant,
whether the parallelism was the result of direct borrowing or of independent
progress toward similar conclusions. Rather I should like to note the cor-

---

[2]The *Enchiridion* and the prefatory material to the ʼNew Testament are to be
found in the *Opera Omnia,* edited by J. Clericus (Leyden, 1703-1706) vols. V and
VI; they are, however, more conveniently found in the fine critical edition of
Erasmus ausgewählte Werke by Hajo Holborn (Munich, 1933). The following
citations are to this edition. The translations are my own.

respondence of certain dominant tendencies in his religious thought to certain basic tendencies in the social and cultural evolution of the Renaissance period, and to suggest that it is in noting these that we will approach most closely to an understanding of the degree to which Erasmus was the representative figure of his age. For Erasmus, though incurably literate, was a man who learned not only from books. Throughout his adult life he wandered constantly over the face of the earth, observing and talking to men everywhere, drawing his own independent and frequently caustic conclusions, but also absorbing ideas and attitudes from the social atmosphere he breathed.

As a basis for this discussion I would like to lay down, perhaps somewhat dogmatically, certain premises which I have argued elsewhere at length and with some necessary qualifications that must here be omitted.[3] Briefly, I would say that the Renaissance was in essence a transitional age, one of the basic characteristics of which was that the economic, social and cultural balance was in process of shifting from the clerical and feudal elements that had dominated the Middle Ages to the lay and urban elements that have so largely dominated the modern world. And in that process one of the decisive factors was the increasing participation of laymen, and especially of urban laymen, in intellectual, religious and other forms of cultural activity. From this resulted an irreparable breach in the clerical monopoly of learning, a more questioning attitude toward ecclesiastical authority and a gradual laicization of religion and culture. From the growing complexities and expanding opportunities of this age of social dislocation, there also emerged a stronger awareness of individual personality and the rights of the individual. And this individualism found expression in equal degree in the religious and cultural life of the age.

For the religious life of the Renaissance it was of primary importance that the preponderant mass of the middle and upper classes was learning to read and was no longer solely dependent on the clergy for religious instruction and inspiration. This, of course, was to become increasingly true in the following centuries. What was peculiar to the Renaissance was the coincidence of this new phenomenon with a crisis in the history of the Church, as the medieval Church strove to adjust to the new forces of money economy and nationalism, while still retaining all its accustomed claims to secular power. Within the Church the administrative authority of the papacy was strengthened during the fourteenth and fifteenth centuries by increasing centralization of government, but the preoccupation with fiscal concerns that was a necessary concomitant to this development seriously weakened the moral authority of the clergy and bred a tendency to place a more materialistic emphasis upon the mere mechanics of salvation.[4] And in reaction to these tendencies there grew throughout Europe, but especially in the northern coun-

---

[3]See my article, "The Interpretation of the Renaissance: Suggestions for a Synthesis," *of the History of Ideas Journal*, XII (1951), 483-495. See below, pp. 125 ff.

[4]For further discussion of this theme, see my article, "The Church in a Changing World: A Contribution to the Interpretation of the Renaissance," *The American Historical Review*, LIX (1953), 1-18. See below, pp. 155 ff.

tries, a specifically lay piety, orthodox in the main, but tending to shift the emphasis from the means of salvation to the individual's direct relation to God, and from theological dogma to the Christian conduct of daily life. It is this specifically lay piety that found its clearest expression in the *Enchiridion Militis Christiani.*

This guide to Christian living was addressed to a layman, we are told, a courtier friend of the author, who was apparently much in need of it. It was obviously written for laymen and written, moreover, by one who in his manner of life and point of view was as nearly a layman as was possible at that time for anyone who had once entered a monastic order. The lay quality of its piety is as notable in what is omitted as in what is included. There is almost no reference to dogma save for those basic Christian doctrines that Erasmus loved to call the Philosophy of Christ; and such incidental references as there are to the services of the Church place them in a category of secondary importance.

Four major themes run through the entire work. The first is a persistent emphasis on the inner life of the spirit in contrast to all external observances, ceremonies and what were technically termed good works. This theme is founded upon a lengthy discussion of the distinction between soul and body,[5] the inner and the outer man, and an identification of the former with things visible, that might have been inspired as much by Neoplatonism as by Christianity.[6] Without making the connection quite clear, he seems to make this distinction one of the bases for his perpetual contention that all external acts and visible symbols are of secondary importance and may degenerate into superstition.

> Consider perfect piety to be constituted in this one thing only, [he writes] that thou attemptest always to progress from things visible, which are for the most part imperfect or indifferent, toward things invisible, according to the division of man already discussed. This precept, indeed, pertains to the matter, since through neglect or ignorance of it most Christians are superstitious rather than pious and, except for the name of Christian, are not far removed from the superstitions of the gentiles.[7]

True, he asserts repeatedly that he does not condemn formal observances as harmful, provided they are merely adjuncts to the Christian life. They may even be very helpful to those who are immature and infirm of spirit, and they should be practised by the more perfect lest they cause their weaker brethren to offend.[8]

> These things ought not to be omitted, but other things it is necessary to do. Corporeal works are not to be condemned, but the invisible are to be preferred. The visible cult is not to be condemned, but God is not pleased save by invisible piety. God is a spirit and is moved by spiritual sacrifices.[9]

---

[5] Cf. *Enchiridion, Holborn,* 41ff.

[6] Cf. *ibid.,* 67ff.

[7] *Ibid.,* p. 67, lines 23-28.

[8] *Ibid.,* p. 76. ll. 32-35; cf. p. 85, ll 22-24.

[9] *Ibid.,* p. 85, ll. 25-28.

He does make it clear, however, that if pursued as an end in themselves, or regarded as the whole duty of a Christian man, formal observances may become pernicious.[10]

The kernel of Erasmus's thought is an abiding faith that piety is a matter of the spirit, and all else is secondary. "It is the spirit that quickeneth; the flesh profiteth nothing." And he illustrates this theme with some pointed observations on the inadequacy of such practices as being buried in a religious garb, fasting, pilgrimages, veneration of relics, indulgences and even confession without full participation of the spirit.[11] A couple of quotations may suffice as examples.

> Thou dost embrace the ashes of Paul with the utmost veneration; this I do not condemn, if thy religion is in accord with it. But if thou dost venerate the mute and dead ashes and neglect the living, speaking and, as it were, breathing image of him which still survives in his letters, is not thy religion distorted? Dost thou adore the bones of Paul preserved in a shrine and not adore the mind of Paul made manifest in his writings?[12]

Again, urging upon the sinner a profound abhorrence of his sins as essential to true repentance, he uses terms that a careless or biased reading might interpret as a more positive denial of the efficacy of confession and other elements of the penitential system than was intended.

> Thou dost deplore thy sins in the presence of a priest, a man; consider how thou mayest deplore them in the presence of God. For to deplore them in His presence is to hate them inwardly. Perchance thou dost believe that with a wax seal or a little money or a minor pilgrimage thy sins are once and for all washed away. Thou art altogether on the wrong road.[13]

Here, as in his eloquent plea, too long to be quoted here, for full inward realization of the spiritual significance of the sacrifice of the Mass, a realization that must result in the spiritual regeneration of the participant, his condemnation of those who merely observe the outward forms and are content therewith is designed to throw into stronger relief his positive appeal for a deeply experienced inner piety.[14]

This is the first theme. The second is like unto it. True piety consists in the application to daily life of Christian virtues and the spirit of Christ.[15] The obligation so to live, moreover, is laid upon all men, not only upon the professionally religious.

[10]Cf. *ibid.*, p. 83, ll. 25-30; 85, ll. 1-2 and 16, ll. 4-13.

[11]Cf. *ibid.*, 86f., *et passim*.

[12]*Ibid.*, p. 75, ll. 3-8.

[13]*Ibid.*, p. 87, ll. 7-10. The wording of the original here may be worth noting: "Accusas apud sacerdotem hominem tua peccata, vide quomodo accuses apud deum. Nam apud illum accusare intus odisse est."

[14]*Ibid.*, 73f.

[15]See especially *ibid.*, 63ff., and the concluding chapters, 99ff.

It is a hard thing indeed and known to very few men, even of monks, to die to sin, to die to carnal desires, to die to this world. And yet this is the common profession of all Christians. This thou didst swear long since in thy baptism, than which vow what could be more sacred or religious. Either we must perish or we must without exception take this road to salvation, whether we be kings or poor plowmen. For as it falls not to everyman's lot to achieve perfect imitation of Christ, yet all must toil hand and foot to ascend thither. He hath a good part of Christian piety who with a sure mind desires to be a Christian.[16]

It is a call to the pious layman to practise his religion in practical deeds, not in external observances. "The uses of the spiritual life lie not in ceremonies, but in charity to thy neighbor."[17]

It is also in essence an appeal to the individual conscience. That is where the emphasis lies. This is, indeed, a third theme, which runs throughout the book, but is developed especially in the early chapters where he enlarges on the theme: "know thyself," and stresses the need for constant examination of one's motives. The battle of the Christian knight is an inward and personal one, a matter primarily concerning the individual man. There is a distinct Renaissance note, too, in his suggestion that an efficacious remedy against falling into sin may be found in contemplating how unworthy it is of the dignity of man,[18] as there is also in his confident assertion of the freedom of man's will. "The human mind never willed anything vehemently that it could not accomplish. The great part of Christianity is to will with the whole heart to be a Christian."[19]

A fourth theme that runs implicitly or explicitly throughout the *Enchiridion* is that the only pure source of the Christian religion is to be found in antiquity, in the teaching of Christ and the apostles as set forth in the New Testament, interpreted when necessary by the earliest Fathers who were themselves close to the ancient sources, and supported by the wisdom of the ancient pagans, especially Plato and the Stoics, whose philosophy he found in many ways conformable to that of Christ. But this brings us to consideration of another of the major tendencies which we have noted in Renaissance culture: the laicization of learning, the most characteristic aspect of which was classical humanism. In their passionate desire to recover the literary treasures of antiquity, a desire inspired, as I have suggested elsewhere,[20] by the needs of a rising class of educated urban laymen, the humanists developed a science of their own, that of philology. It was, as distinguished from the clerically dominated learning of the medieval universities, a layman's science, and what they drew from the philosophy of the ancients was essentially a layman's philosophy, dealing largely with moral problems rather than with metaphysics, unsystematic, and expressed in cultivated prose rather than in syllogisms or the technical jargon of the

---

[16]*Ibid.*, p. 59, ll. 32-60; cf. p. 12.

[17]*Ibid.*, p. 85, ll. 9-11; cf. p. 82.

[18]*Ibid.*, p. 118.

[19]*Ibid.*, p. 46, l. 37-p. 47, l. 1.

[20]See the article cited above, *Journal of the History of Ideas,* XII, 493f.

schoolmen. Whether actually a layman or technically a cleric, the typical humanist was a professional scholar and man of letters but an amateur philosopher and theologian. And it was thus that Erasmus, with a depth of religious feeling drawn from the contemporary currents of lay piety, undertook to place the fruits of classical scholarship at the service of Christian theology.

The Greek New Testament and the critical editions of the Fathers are the measure of his practical contribution to that end. And in the *Ratio seu methodus* he outlined his conception of how a theologian should be trained and by what methods he could attain to true theology. In the first place, the theologian should have a competent knowledge of the three ancient languages—Latin, Greek and Hebrew. This should be a first consideration: "citra controversiam prima cura debetur."[21] There is no possibility of knowing what is written if you do not understand the language in which it is written.[22] Next he argues the desirability of a general education, from which—and he mentions especially historical books—one may acquire a useful knowledge of the words and things mentioned in the Bible as well as the geography of the places and the history, manners and institutions of the people referred to there.[23] The youth destined for theology should also be trained in the rules of grammar and rhetoric.[24] The methods of dialectic and sophistical disputations, on the other hand, merely chill comprehension of the sacred Scriptures.[25] Paul and the early Fathers did not despise poetry, rhetoric or profane learning. "But where," he asks, "in these is there any mention of first and second intentions, syllogistic forms, or formalities or quiddities or even haecceities?"[26] And again: "What could be more different from the style of the prophets, Christ and the Apostles than that in which those who follow Thomas and Scotus now dispute about sacred matters?"[27] This is the deeply-rooted prejudice of the humanist man of letters against the rigid logic and barbarous jargon of the schools, the amateur theologian's protest against the wilful obscurities propagated by the professionals. But this is merely the negative side of his program. The positive side appears again in his insistence that the budding theologian should draw his knowledge of Christian doctrine as far as possible directly from the evangelical sources.[28] These he should study with the utmost care, giving due consideration to the time, place and circumstance of each saying,[29] collecting and comparing passages on all subjects,[30] and learning to cite the Scriptures appositely, not distorted out of context.[31] If he follows this method he will need no commentaries, for those who first wrote commentaries had none to follow, and others can do the same.[32] Nor will he need the learning

---

[21]*Ratio*, Holborn, p. 181, ll. 15-18.

[22]*Ibid.*, p. 182, ll. 14-16.

[23]*Ibid.*, p. 185, ll. 6-10.

[24]*Ibid.*, p. 187.

[25]*Ibid.*, p. 188.

[26]*Ibid.*, p. 191, ll. 4-6.

[27]*Ibid.*, p. 191, ll. 23-25.

[28]*Ibid.*, p. 193ff.

[29]*Ib.*, 196ff.

[30]209ff., 291ff.

[31]284ff.

[32]*Ibid.*, p. 295, ll. 1-13.

of the schools. At any rate, "It is better to be ignorant of the dogmas of Aristotle than not to know the decrees of Christ .... He is an abundantly great doctor who teaches Christ purely. If it is shameful not to know what Scotus defines, it is more shameful not to know what Christ has ordained."[33]

This layman's declaration of independence is characteristic of Erasmus's whole approach to theology, for what he thought most essential in it were those simple doctrines and ethical teachings set forth by Christ and the Apostles in the New Testament so plainly that the wayfaring man though a fool might not err therein. True, he was not always consistent in this, for there was an inherent conflict between what might be called the democratic tendency of lay piety and the aristocratic tendency of lay learning as represented by the humanists. But it was a conflict that, like other inconsistencies in his thought, did not seriously trouble Erasmus, for the conflict was more apparent than real. As a classical scholar and serious student he could assert that a knowledge of Latin, Greek and Hebrew was essential to the understanding of sacred Scriptures. As an exponent of lay piety he could assert with equal conviction that nothing was needed but "a pious and alert mind, provided above all with simple and pure faith."[34] In both instances he echoes the layman's protest against dependence on the clergy for religious instruction and against the clerical monopoly of the interpretation of the Bible. The essential matter was to get at the words of Christ directly, not through glosses and commentaries, and it was to this end that he devoted his philological labors. If he railed against the ignorance of those who did not know the biblical languages, it was the ignorance of the theologians—those ancient parrots[35]—rather than that of the laymen that he had in mind. The theologian should read the Bible only in its original tongue, but the Scriptures should also be available to laymen who could not even read Latin. Nowhere is the right of every layman to independent access to the Scriptures more clearly stated than in Erasmus's preface to the Greek New Testament.

> I dissent most vehemently from those who would not have the divine Scriptures read by the unlearned, translated into the vulgar tongue, as though Christ taught in such an involved fashion that he would be but barely understood by a few theologians, as though the safeguard of the Christian religion lay only in its being unknown .... I would desire that all little women (omnes mulierculae) should read the Evangel, should read the Pauline epistles. And would that these might be translated in all languages so that they might be read and known, not only by Scots and Irishmen, but even by Turks and Saracens .... Would that from these the ploughman might sing at his plow, and that with something from these the weaver might keep time to his loom; would that with stories from these the traveller should while away the tedium of his voyage.[36]

[33]*Ibid.*, p. 304, ll. 12-15; p. 305, ll. 10-12.

[34]*Paraclesis ad lectorem pium, ibid.*, p. 141, ll. 29-30.

[35]"Vetuli psitaci quibus mutandae linguae spes non sit." Ep. to Antony of Bergen, Jan. 14, 1518, in P. S. Allen, ed., *Opus Epistolarum Des. Erasmi Roterodami* (Oxford, 1906ff.), III, 200.

[36]*Paraclesis*, Holborn, p. 142, ll. 10-22.

Just as in the *Enchiridion* he maintained that the religious life is not limited to the formally religious, but is open to all, so here he argues that "since baptism and the other sacraments and finally the reward of immortality are equally common to all Christians, it is not to be tolerated that dogma alone should be relegated to the few who are known today as theologians or monks."[37]   On the contrary, he who teaches the simple piety of Christ and exhorts and inspires thereto, "he, indeed, is a true theologian though he be a digger or a weaver."[38]   I will add one final quotation that sums up Erasmus' approach to both theology and Christian piety.

> This kind of philosophy [the philosophy of Christ], which lies in the state of mind more truly than in syllogisms, is a way of life rather than a disputation, inspiration rather than erudition, *transformatio magis quam ratio.* To be learned falls to the lot of but few, but there is no one who cannot be a Christian, no one who cannot be pious; I may add this boldly: no one who cannot be a theologian.[39]

---

[37]*Ibid.*, p. 142, ll. 29-34.

[38]*Ibid.*, p. 143, ll. 3-16.

[39]*Ibid.*, p. 144, l. 35-p. 145, l. 3.

THE REVIVAL OF CLASSICAL ANTIQUITY OR THE FIRST CENTURY OF HUMANISM: A REAPPRAISAL*

It is almost a hundred years since Georg Voigt published *The Revival of Classical Antiquity or the First Century of Humanism* (1859)[1] and Jacob Burckhardt published *The Civilization of the Renaissance in Italy* (1860).[2] Together these two books set a pattern for the interpretation of humanism and the Renaissance which went almost unchallenged for half a century and which still exercises a pervasive influence upon our conceptions of the period. During the past fifty years or so, however, that interpretation has been not only challenged but profoundly modified in a variety of directions, some of them mutually exclusive. The learned controversy has focussed primarily upon the interpretation of the Renaissance as a whole; but humanism was such an integral part of Renaissance culture that its interpretation has shared all the vicissitudes that have characterized recent Renaissance historiography. Almost every aspect of the humanist movement has become problematical. It has been looked at from new points of view and set in new frames of reference. It is not my intention, however, to discuss here the various trends in recent interpretation of the Renaissance and of humanism, nor to outline once more the familiar picture drawn by Voigt and Burckhardt. I have done so at some length elsewhere.[3] But it seems to me that the time has come to ask what has emerged from a hundred years of research and interpretation. Specifically, I would like to try, as briefly as possible, to reappraise "the revival of classical antiquity or the first century of humanism," to quote Voigt's title, as it appears to me in this year of grace 1957. With the scope of Voigt's work in

---

*Read before the Canadian Historical Association, June 1957. Reprinted from Canadian Historical Association *Report of the Annual Meeting, 1957.*

[1]G. Voigt, *Die Wiederbelebung des klassischen Altherthums oder das erste Jahrhundert des Humanismus* (Berlin, 1859).

[2]J. Burckhardt, *Die Cultur der Renaissance in Italien* (Basel, 1860).

[3]See W. K. Ferguson, *The Renaissance in Historical Thought: Five Centuries of Interpretation* (Boston, 1948).

mind, I shall limit my discussion to Italian humanism from about the middle of the fourteenth to the middle of the fifteenth century, the crucial period of the origins and early growth of the movement.

The first problem for the historian here, as always, is that of causation. What caused the literary world of Italy to turn with such enthusiasm to the study and imitation of the classical Latin and Greek authors? And why at this particular stage in the development of Italian culture? The contribution of Petrarch and the influence of his personality, which Voigt stresses so strongly and to which he devoted more than a fifth of his book, seems an inadequate explanation. True, it was Petrarch who first brought a new understanding and appreciation to the study of classical literature and by his indefatigable missionary zeal aroused the interest of Boccaccio and other contemporary scholars. It is true also that his personality did much to influence the direction in which humanism would develop. Yet, had empathetic love of the Latin authors been a mere personal idiosyncrasy, it would not have aroused a similar enthusiasm in so many of his countrymen.

A much more fundamental cause of the classical revival can, it seems to me, be found in the peculiar social development of Italy in the preceding period. The wealthy upper classes of the Italian cities had by the fourteenth century achieved sufficient cultural maturity and self-confidence to be ready to seek a culture suited to their peculiar needs. Lay education, fostered by large-scale business enterprise, was wide-spread among the middle and upper classes, while the concentrated wealth produced by capitalism furnished the means for patronage as well as the leisure to cultivate literature and the arts. But a society with new interests seldom creates a completely new culture. More commonly it will utilize its legacy from the past and adapt it to suit its own needs and tastes. Neither the chivalric nor the clerical literary traditions of the Middle Ages, however, could furnish an adequate foundation for a new urban culture. The upper class laymen of the Italian cities had lost contact with the feudal and chivalric *mores* that had produced the secular literature of medieval France, while at the same time they lacked the professional training and special interests of the clerical schoolmen. But if medieval traditions proved inadequate, the Italians had only to turn to a more distant past to find a more congenial inspiration in the culture of a society very much like their own. The literature of Roman and Greek antiquity was the product of a wealthy, aristocratic, secular, and predominantly urban society, a society in which the citizen's life was set in the framework of a non-feudal state; a society, in short, in which the upper classes of the Italian city-states could easily imagine themselves at home. They had only to approach it in a receptive spirit to find in it a storehouse of secular knowledge and human wisdom, the whole expressed in literary forms different from and, on the whole, more perfectly finished than those inherited from the Middle Ages.

So much has been written about the humanists' preoccupation with the form of classical literature[4] that it seems necessary to emphasize the fact that they were attracted to it by its intellectual content as well as by its aesthetic form. It was doubtless the beauty of Latin speech that first aroused the enthusiasm of Petrarch in his early youth and, poet that he was, he never ceased to revere the artistic mastery of the ancient writers. The influence of a classical sense of form was, indeed, apparent in his Italian poetry. But as he grew older he learned to value more and more what could be learned from the thought and the varied knowledge of the ancient authors. The exigencies of their craft forced his successors to become philologists, but only the pedants among them — and let that age which is without pedants cast the first stone — ever forgot that form and content were inseparable characteristics of the literature they so greatly admired. What the humanists sought in the classics was a foundation upon which to build a culture in the broadest sense. What they found in the ancient culture was a liberal education.

The term adopted by the Renaissance scholars to denote this form of culture and education based on classical studies was *humanitas* or *studia humanitatis*. It was a term much used by Cicero and was apparently introduced into Renaissance usage in the Ciceronian sense by Leonardo Bruni in a dialogue *De studiis et litteris* written in 1401. Somewhat later the term *humanista* or humanist was applied, on the analogy with the classification of law students as *jurista* or *canonista*, to students of the humanities. The modern derivative, humanism (*Humanismus*), is a product of nineteenth century German scholarship. Like many similar terms, it has been used in such varying senses that it seems worth while to define it carefully. Occasionally it has been used to denote mere philological classical scholarship. More frequently it has been applied to any philosophy which centers attention upon man. It has even been confused at times with an attitude that would more properly be called humanitarian. Even in antiquity some confusion as to its meaning apparently existed, since Aulus Gellius, writing in the second century A.D., felt it necessary to define the correct usage of *humanitas*.

> Those who have spoken Latin and have used the language correctly [he wrote]do not give the word *humanitas* the meaning which it is commonly thought to have, namely, what the Greeks called *philanthropia* signifying a kind of friendly spirit and good feeling toward all men without distinction; but they give to *humanitas* about the force of the Greek *paideia*, that is, what we call *eruditionem institutionemaque in bonas artes* or "education and training in the liberal arts." Those who earnestly desire and seek for these are most highly humanized, for the pursuit of that kind of knowledge, and the training given by it, have been granted to man alone among the animals, and for that reason it is termed *humanitas* or "humanity".[5]

---

[4]The charge that the humanists were interested in form only and cared little for the content of literature was a constant theme with nineteenth century historians and is still current. See, for example, Voigt, pp. 428 ff; F. de Sanctis, *Storia della letteratura italiana* (Naples, 1871; Eng. trans. New York, 1931), I. 373 *et passim;* P. Monnier, *Le Quattrocento* (1900; 2nd ed., Paris, 1924), I. 229 ff; R. Sabbadini, *Storia del Ciceronianismo* (Turin, 1885). For a vigorous rebuttal, see J. H. Whitfield, *Petrarch and the Renaissance* (Oxford, 1943).

[5]*The Attic Night of Aulus Gellius,* Eng. trans. by J. C. Rolfe (Loeb Classical Library, 1927), II, 457.

It was in this proud sense that the Renaissance scholars used the term, with
the additional limitation that for them "education and training in the liberal
arts" was inseparable from the study of classical literature. As a specific historical phenomenon, humanism or the *studia humanitatis* meant a fairly well
defined group of intellectual diciplines: grammar, rhetoric, history, poetry
and moral philosophy, all based upon the study of classical authors.[6]

It is this definition of humanism as the study of both the form and the
general content of the classical literature that differentiates Renaissance
humanism from the so-called clerical humanism of the twelfth century, and to
an even greater degree from the scholastic study of ancient Greek philosophy
and science. The clerical humanists of John of Salisbury's generation were
seduced by the beauty of classical Latin style and imitated it to the best of
their ability. But, as devout clerics, they were suspicious of the ideas expressed in pagan writings, or were simply indifferent to their secular content;
while, as products of a feudal age, they were incapable of understanding the
social milieu and the ways of thinking reflected in the classical authors. The
scholastic philosophers and theologians, on the other hand, who superseded the
clerical humanists in the thirteenth century were largely indifferent to classical style, but were deeply concerned with the content of certain aspects of
Greek thought, though only those which could serve the technical needs of
their specialized professional disciplines. Whether the scholastics were in
fact closer to the living tradition of antiquity than were the men of the Renaissance, as Etienne Gilson has contended, is a matter of opinion, but to call
them humanists is to rob the term of all specific meaning.[7]

Although they had their own group of disciplines, which they regarded
as within their province, the Italian humanists did not form an organized
academic profession. They had as yet no firmly established place in the universities, which in Italy were concerned chiefly with the professional courses
in law, medicine and natural philosophy. An occasional humanist might be
called to give a few lectures at a university, and several held fairly permanent
posts as professors of rhetoric, fulfilling the traditional function of the earlier
dictatores as teachers of formal composition for practical use. But, for the
most part, they functioned outside the universities, as independent men of
letters. As such, they have been regarded as forming a new class in society.[8]
Most of them were laymen, or if, like Petrarch they had taken minor orders as

---

[6]Cf. P. O. Kristeller, *The Classics and Renaissance Thought* (Cambridge, Mass.,
1955), p. 11.

[7]E. Gilson, "Le Moyen Age et le naturalisme antique," *Archives d'histoire doctrinale
et littéraire du Moyen Age,* VII (1932), 5-37; cf. J. Maritain, *True Humanism* (New
York, 1938) and critical review by G. G. Coulton in *Journal of the History of
Ideas,* V (1944), 415-33.

[8]P. O. Kristeller, *Studies in Renaissance Thought and Letters* (Rome, 1956, pp.
563ff rejects this interpretation and argues that the humanists were simply the
successors of the medieval rhetoricians; but see R. R. Bolgar, *The Classical Heritage
and its Beneficiaries,* (Cambridge, 1954) p. 329 for the uncertain and anomalous
position of the humanists in the universities.

a prerequisite to clerical patronage, their way of life was little affected thereby. After their work had made classical education fashionable in cultured society, some men with humanist training rose to high position in the Church, two or three even to the highest. But the majority of the humanists remained free-lance writers and teachers, seeking a living as secretaries in the papal *curia* or in the chancelleries of the Italian states, as state historians, as tutors to the children of princes and wealthy citizens, or simply by soliciting patronage from princes, prelates, businessmen and *condottieri* to whom they dedicated their written works. Under the circumstances it is not surprising that some of them were guilty of gross flattery of the rich and powerful, or that the highly competitive, uncertain and wandering life they led developed in them some unamiable qualities. Despite the high respect in which classical studies were held, the pay a humanist could claim was generally much less than that accorded to a jurist or a member of the other established professions. They felt, with some justice, that they were not appreciated at their true worth, and the feeling tended to make them arrogant and assertive. Competition for patronage, too, bred professional jealousies that sometimes found expression in literary feuds replete with obscene abuse. There seems no reason to believe that the humanists as a group were more immoral than any other social class, but their immoralities were better publicized. It is unfair, however, to judge the humanists, as Voigt and others have tended to do, by the most disreputable members of the class.[9] A more balanced view must also take into account such men of high character and sober purpose as Coluccio Salutati, the venerable chancellor of Florence, or the inspired teacher, Vittorino da Feltre.

It is unfair, too, to judge the humanists by the disparity between what they aspired to achieve and what they actually accomplished.[10] To reach a fair estimate of their achievement during this pioneering period, one must take into account the magnitude of their task. The restoration of all that survived of classical literature involved first of all a systematic search for manuscripts. The story of their search and its results is too well known to need repetition.[11] It was encouraged and financed by wealthy patrons who built up their libraries by buying rare manuscripts or having them copied. Nearly all the reigning princes, the Visconti, the Gonzaga, the Estensi, and such wealthy Florentine citizens as Niccolo Niccoli and Cosimo de' Medici collected libraries whch were made available to scholars. In mid-century Nicholas V founded the Vatican library, which soon became the largest public library in Europe. It is obvious, of course, that the classical authors discovered

---

[9]For a generally unfavorable picture of the character of the humanists, see Voigt, pp. 401 ff; Burckhardt (Eng. trans., London, 1921), pp. 273 ff; J. A. Symonds, *Renaissance in Italy,* II (London, 1897), 374 ff.

[10]Sabbadini, for example, called the learning of the humanists an immense illusion. See the Preface to his *Storia del Ciceronianismo,* cited above.

[11]The fullest account is in R. Sabbadini, *Le scoperti dei codici latini e greci nei secoli XIV e XV,* 2 vols. (Florence, 1905-14); see also J. E. Sandys, *A History of Classical Scholarship* (Cambridge, 1908), II, 24 ff.

by the humanists had not been literally unknown in the Middle Ages. Recent research, too, has shown that medieval scholars were fairly familiar with the main body of classical literature.[12] Still, a large number of minor works and some of major importance existed only in rare copies widely scattered and almost forgotten in decaying monastery libraries. What the humanists and their wealthy patrons did was to gather together and make available almost the whole surviving body of classical literature. When we remember that even Petrarch, who idolized Cicero, did not know the *Familiar Letters*, which Salutati discovered in 1392, we cannot doubt the importance of the collectors' work for the full understanding of antique civilization.

The collecting, copying and diffusion of manuscripts was, however, but a part, and not the most laborious part, of the task the humanists had set for themselves. Many of the manuscripts they found were defective, having been copied by monks whose knowledge of Latin was imperfect and who were frequently careless. Poggio complained that a codex of Cicero's *Philippics*, which he had found, was so full of errors that to emend it called for divination rather than conjecture. "There is no woman [he added] so stupid or ignorant that she could not have copied more correctly."[13] To secure a faithful text it was thus necessary to compare as many copies as possible, to emend faulty readings, to weed out interpolations and to reject forgeries. And this in turn required a minute study of the problems of paleography, orthography, grammar, syntax and usage, all without the aid of printed texts, manuals, dictionaries and all other aids regarded as indispensable to modern classical scholarship. In the process the humanists founded the science of critical philology. It was as yet a layman's science with little or no institutional organization, but their attitude toward it was not that of dilettanti. They brought to their task the patient and laborious devotion to *minutiae* which is the indispensable characteristic of the scientific scholar. When one considers the quantity of midnight oil sacrificed upon the altars of classical scholarship, the charge of frivolity so frequently brought against the humanists seems rather unfair.[14]

As philologists the humanists were forced to develop a discriminating critical sense. Apparent in nearly all of them, it reached its fullest development in this period in the work of Lorenzo Valla.[15] After having been brought up in Rome, Valla led a wandering life. He taught in various cities, spent some years under the protection of Alfonso of Naples and finally returned to Rome to spend his last years under the patronage of Pope Nicholas V. His widely ranging critical sense, reinforced by an irrepressibly combative

---

[12]Cf. M. Manitius, *Handschriften antiker Autoren in mittelalterlichen Bibliothekskatalogen* (Leipzig, 1935); J. W. Thompson, *The Medieval Library* (New ed., New York, 1957).

[13]Poggio Bracciolini, *Epistolae*, III, 17; quoted in Monnier, I, 264.

[14]See, for example, Voigt, p. 467.

[15]There is no good full length study of Valla. For a brief sketch see A. Renaudet, *La fin du Moyen Age* (Paris, 1931), pp. 517 ff.

spirit, brought him into conflict with jurists, philosophers, monks and theologians and even for a time with the papacy. In a treatise *On Pleasure* he examined in turn the ethical doctrines of Stoicism, Epicureanism and Christianity, and although he concluded that the last was superior to the other two systems, his sympathetic presentation of the Epicurean point of view shocked the serious-minded. He offended the theologians by exposing the writings of Dionysius the Areopagite as spurious and by questioning the tradition that the Apostles' Creed was actually composed by the Apostles. He also combined historical with philological criticism to demonstrate that the Donation of Constantine, the document on which papal claims to territorial sovereignty in Italy were founded, was an eighth century forgery. But, for all the diversity of his critical interests, Valla remained essentially a grammarian and philologist. His textual criticism of the New Testament, which later exerted a strong influence on Erasmus, was a work of pure scholarship without theological connotations. For the further development of humanism his most important work was the *Elegantiae linguae latinae,* a systematic survey of correct classical usage, based on an empirical study of the best classical authors. Its appearance marked a turning point in the development of humanist scholarship and literary taste. The early humanists had been eclectic in their choice of classical models, accepting as classical any pagan or Christian author, prior to the seventh century A.D. Valla, with his keen critical and historical sense, distinguished between the various periods in the development of Latin and gave his full approval only to the usage of the last century of the Roman Republic and the first century or so of the Empire. Although Valla would not have approved the exclusive Ciceronianism of some of the later humanists, his work marked a decisive step in the process which finally converted a living tongue into a dead language by electing one moment in its historical evolution as standard and by freezing it at that point.

The humanists of the first century of the movement, however, were still free from the cramping effects of a too exclusive classicism. But in their writing they did model their style on that of the ancient authors and thereby they laid themselves open to the often repeated charge that they were mere imitators, devoid of originality.[16] The fact is simply that they wanted to write well, and they could think of no better way of doing so than to write as much like the ancient masters as possible. The method they used to achieve that end, however, led to rather more literal imitation than was altogether beneficial.[17] It was their common practice to jot down in note books words, phrases, metaphors and turns of speech as well as all sorts of factual material and expressions of opinion culled from the classical authors. These they studied and committed to memory. In their own writing they drew upon this store-house, reassembling the fragments to suit their purpose. At the worst, this method led to writing that was little more than a mosaic of borrowed

---

[16]This charge was most common among nineteenth century Romantic critics who represented the classical revival as an interruption of the spontaneous development of the national literatures.

[17]For description of this method, see Bolgar, pp. 265 ff.

phrases, overloaded with an unnecessary burden of classical allusion. At the best this detailed analysis of classical style made the writing of the humanists more correct, more flexible, simpler and more artistically integrated. One has only to turn from the rambling incoherence of a medieval chronicle to Bruni's *History of Florence* or from the ponderous dullness of Gower's *Vox Clamantis* to Valla's dialogue *De libero arbitrio* to appreciate what the humanists had gained by their study of classical form, even though something of spontaneity might have been lost in the process. It was this minute study of classical authors, too, which enabled the humanists to recreate in their own minds so vivid an impression of the whole social and intellectual atmosphere of the ancient world. It must not be forgotten, either, that imitation of classical models reintroduced into literature a number of literary forms which had been neglected in the Middle Ages: the dialogue, the essay, the familiar epistle, comedy, tragedy, and the literary treatment of history, biography, moral philosophy and political theory.

Neverthelesss, the fact remains that little if anything of what the Italian humanists wrote during this period has remained a living part of the world's literature. And this fact has reinforced the charge that imitation of the classics robbed them of the originality they presumably might have had if they had used their native tongue. It may be true, indeed, that the task of restoring the ancient authors and of developing a classical style absorbed the energies of the humanists and directed them into scholarly rather than creative channels. The circumstances of their employment and patronage, too, forced them to write a great deal of occasional material that could have no interest for a later age. As masters of the classical style so highly prized by contemporary taste, they were called upon to compose endless orations, eulogies and manifestos for every public occasion. But perhaps the most important reason why these writers, who were so much esteemed in their own day, have been neglected by later generations is that what they found in the classics and strove to disseminate was then new but later became, thanks largely to their efforts, an integral part of European culture and as such seemed commonplace. It remains so even in our own generation when a classical tag no longer serves to point a moral or adorn a tale.

It seems to me that to have brought a fresh appreciation to classical poetry and prose, and fuller understanding of those aspects of antique thought that medieval scholars had neglected or had failed to comprehend, was surely in itself an original contribution. In the classical Latin literature, which had never been deeply influenced by the systematic Greek philosophy and science which attracted the scholastics, the humanists found a wealth of comment on moral philosophy, ethics, history, political theory and, in general, on the problems of men seeking a pattern for the good life as individuals or as citizens. For Petrarch and his successors Cicero was not only the supreme master of eloquence; he was also the *magister vitae,* the wise man who could teach men how to live. And it added to the charm of this ancient wisdom that it was presented in literary form, not in syllogisms or *summae* or the professional jargon of the schoolmen. It was a form which appealed strongly to laymen like the humanists and their patrons, most of whom were not trained in professional philosophy or theology.   Any educated man, living in a not too dissimilar society could read and appreciate Cicero's treatises *De amicitia, De senectute* or *De officiis;* and any humanist felt himself qualified, after intensive study of the ancient authors, to write similar treatises or to discuss the problems of the good life in elegant letters or dialogues.   Looking over lists of humanist writings one finds such titles as *De tyranno, De fato et fortuna, De avaritia, De re uxoria,* and many more of the same sort.   That the men who purveyed the ancient wisdom to their generation were not in all instances wise men is irrelevant.   Nor was it really important that most of them were not very original or systematic thinkers.   The turn of phrase was frequently an echo of a classical source and the ideas were selected in an eclectic and haphazard fashion from a variety of systems.   What is important is that they took from antiquity what suited the needs of their age as the scholastics had done before them.   In both cases there was imitation and excessive respect for antique authority, but in both cases also the creation of something new, without which the cultural evolution of Western Europe would have been different.

One of the services which the humanists performed in their capacity as moral guides to the urban society of Italy in this transitional age was to erect a secular ideal of virtue and the virtuous life alongside the Christian, a lay morality alongside the clerical and monastic, an ideal not so much in conflict with Christianity as independent of it.   The conceptions of the good life which they found in their classical models were based exclusively on experience in this world, the experience of thoughtful and responsible citizens. The ancient authors could speak directly to men who were trying, perhaps unconsciously, to reconcile their way of life with ideals inherited from the Middle Ages.   A strong strain of Franciscan idealization of poverty ran through the piety of fourteenth century Italy, and the medieval belief that monastic rejection of the world represented the highest form of religious life still haunted the minds of thoughtful men.   It certainly haunted the troubled soul of Petrarch, and in his dilemma he turned for guidance not only to St. Augustine but also to Cicero and Seneca.[18]   In the teaching of the Stoic sages that the wise man will be indifferent to poverty or wealth, to good or evil fortune, he found an ideal of virtue that accorded well enough with the Franciscan and monastic ideals, but which still left the door open for the acceptance of wealth and honour.   Among the vagrant humanists who followed him, the Stoicism they preached seems often no more than a pathetic justification of their actual poverty and the uncertainty of their lives.[19] Stoic indifference to honours and glorification of the contemplative life of the sage was frequently distorted into a justification for the neglect of all civic or family responsibilities. But, as the humanists, and particularly the Florentine group, learned to understand Cicero more fully, they found in that noblest Roman a positive

---

[18]See Petrarch, *Secretum,* Eng Trans. by W. H. Draper (London, 1911).

[19]Cf. C. E. Trinkaus, *Adversity's Noblemen: the Italian Humanists on Happiness* (New York, 1940), p. 56 f.

support for the active life of the citizen, and when, having recovered a knowledge of Greek, they went directly to the *Ethics* and the *Politics* of Aristotle, they found in his conception of moderate wealth as an aid to virtue an ideal more suited to the life of a mercantile society.[20]

The ancient Greek and Roman conceptions of citizenship found a particularly responsive echo in the Republic on the Arno around the turn of the century when Florence was fighting for her liberty against the expanding despotism of Giangaleazzo Visconti. In Florence more than anywhere else the humanists were closely associated with the upper class of citizens who dominated the government of the republic. A number of them — Salutati, Bruni, Marsuppini, Poggio—held office as chancellors of the republic. Others enjoyed the patronage of such wealthy families as the Strozzi, the Alberti, the Albizzi and the Medici and came to share their political and social attitudes. During the struggle against the Visconti despotism the Florentine humanists gained a new appreciation of the ideals of the ancient Roman Republic and applied them to the contemporary political scene with considerable propagandist effect. They also placed a new emphasis upon those aspects of antique thought which would give support to the bourgeois ideals of sober thrift and of responsible family and civic life and which would contribute to the education of good citizens. And these ideals of "civic humanism," as it has been called, were given a wider circulation by treatises in the vernacular such as Luigi Palmieri's *Della vita civile* and Leo Battista Alberti's *Trattato della cura della famiglia.*[21]

Aside from their eclectic borrowings from antique moral philosophy, the humanists absorbed many ideas and attitudes simply through breathing, although at second hand, the intellectual atmosphere of the ancient world. From their reverent communion with the great poets, moralists and historians they gained a heightened awareness of individual personality, an awareness particularly marked in Petrarch who was in this as in so many other respects the prototype of humanism.[22] With this went a desire for fame and for a secular form of personal immortality in the memory of posterity. The humanists not only yearned for immortal fame themselves; they believed it in their power to confer it upon others through their writings; and some, like Francesco Filelfo, were ready to sell their pens to the highest bidder. The humanists, it is true, were not responsible for the individualism which characterized Renaissance society — it was a natural outgrowth of the economic, social and political development of the age—but they did furnish it with models and with the authoritative sanction of antiquity. They also found in the fully

---

[20]Cf. H. Baron, "Franciscan Poverty and Civic Wealth as Factors in the Rise of Humanistic Thought," *Speculum*, XIII (1938), 1-37.

[21]The fullest discussion of Florentine civic humanism is in H. Baron, *The Crisis of the Early Italian Renaissance: Civic Humanism and Republican Liberty in an Age of Classicism and Tyranny*, 2 vols. (Princeton, 1955); see also E. Garin, *Der italienische Humanismus* (Bern, 1947).

[22]Voigt, pp. 80 ff., cf. H. Eppelsheimer, *Petrarca* (Bonn, 1926), pp. 157 ff.

developed and cultured personalities of the ancient world models for imitation more congenial to their age than the medieval ideals represented by the
feudal knight or the ascetic monk.   When the humanists argued, as Poggio
did in the dialogue *De nobilitate,* that nobility depends solely on personal
worth, they were merely applying concepts drawn from the pre-feudal society
of antiquity to the post-feudal society of the Italian cities.   Reverence for the
sages and the great men of antiquity, too, bred in the humanists a profound
sense of the dignity of man, which ran counter to the belief in man's innate
depravity that was one of the persistent strains in medieval thought.   It has
been argued recently that St. Thomas Aquinas presented a stronger philosophical defence of human dignity and individual worth than did the humanists, and in fact their ideas received philosophical formulation only in a later
generation in the *Oratio de hominis dignitate* (1486) of Pico della Mirandola.[23]   But it is significant that the early humanists founded their concept of
the dignity of man not upon man's place in a divinely ordained cosmic scheme
or great chain of being, but simply upon the potentialities of man as a human
being.   Finally, the humanists' acceptance of the classical pre-Christian
authors as moral guides led to an emphasis upon ethical and moral conduct as
ends in themselves, independent of their theological implications, which later
bore such diverse fruit as, on the one hand, Machiavelli's utterly secular conception of *virtù* and on the other, the lay piety of the Northern "Christian
humanists," with its Erasmian conception of religion as a matter of ethics
rather than dogma and of Christianity as the *Philosophia Christi.*

The reverence of the humanists for antiquity and their efforts to find in
it a pattern for life have led many historians to regard the classical revival as a
revival of paganism and to blame it for the irreverence and immorality, the
hedonism and worldliness they found in Renaissance society.[24]   After the
Romantic movement of the early nineteenth century there was long a tendency to picture the Renaissance as a peculiarly wicked age in contrast to the
Christian-ascetic Middle Ages.   There was certainly a good deal of conventional as well as original sin in Renaissance society, although whether there
was more than in the Middle Ages, or whether it was simply better publicized,
is open to question.   But there was no revolt against Christianity and very
little evidence of atheism or scepticism.   What there was would be found
among the Averroist schoolmen rather than among the humanists.   The paganism, in the strict sense of the word, to be found in humanist writings was
purely a matter of literary convention. The morality they drew from antiquity
was certainly not pagan in the nineteenth century sense of the word.   The
humanists were in fact, like other people, more or less religious according to

---

[23]Eng. trans. in E. Cassirer *et al.,* eds., *The Renaissance Philosophy of Man*
(Chicago, 1948), pp. 223 ff.

[24]The view expressed in Symonds, II, 12 f; 381, is typical of the nineteenth century.
L. von Pastor distinguished between the Christian and the pagan strains in humanism.
See the Preface to his *History of the Popes from the Close of the Middle Ages* (London,
1899).   For a sane reassessment of the problem, see Kristeller, *The Classics and
Renaissance Thought,* pp. 70 ff.

their individual temperaments. They were aware of no antagonism between Christian doctrine and the high-minded moral and ethical teaching they found in the ancient sages, so that they could devote themselves to their classical studies in the secure conviction that they could have all this and Heaven too. What they did introduce into the intellectual life of Renaissance Italy was not paganism but an enormously increased body of secular material and non-religious interests. Their influence greatly accelerated both the laicization and the secularization of culture, tendencies already apparent in the preceding generations and which would have developed in any case, although not so rapidly, as a result of the social changes which were transforming the medieval world. These secular interests competed with religion for the attention of lay society, but they were not in any positive way antagonistic to the Christian faith.

Recent research has established beyond doubt the fact that many of the humanists were deeply religious, and that characteristically medieval forms of religious thought may be found in Petrarch and many of his successors. And this discovery has led some historians to regard all signs of Christian piety among the humanists as evidence of the continuation of medieval traditions and as ground for annexing the Renaissance to the Middle Ages.[25] In this connection it is sometimes necessary to point out that Christianity was not a medieval invention and that the Middle Ages have not had a monopoly of Christian faith. It seems to me that the fact that many humanists were pious Christians is not sufficient reason in itself for regarding them as medieval. That some characteristically medieval traits persisted in humanist thought should not be surprising, since the transition from the Middle Ages to the Renaissance was neither sudden nor complete. But the preoccupation of the humanists with antique moral philosophy and classical scholarship could not leave their religious thought entirely untouched and it did in fact lead them with each generation further from the medieval norms. The results were not yet clearly apparent in the work of the Italian humanists of this first century of the movement, but their emphasis upon ethics rather than speculative theology and their philological interest in the works of the early Fathers, above all Valla's textual criticism of the New Testament, pointed the road along which Erasmus and the "Christian humanists" later travelled.

If the new learning, as the humanists liked to call their classical scholarship, was not antagonistic to Christianity as such, it was, however, positively antagonistic to medieval scholasticism. It was not the Christian content of scholastic thought that alienated the humanists. On the contrary it was the lack of concern with spiritual things in the so-called Averroists of the Italian universities that aroused the wrath of Petrarch and caused him to denounce them as materialists and little better than atheists. It must not be forgotten that theology never held the dominant place in the Italian universities that it did at Paris and the other northern schools.[26] The scholastic learning with

---

[25]For discussion of this tendency in recent scholarship, see Ferguson, pp. 344 ff.

[26]The best survey of the medieval universities is still H. Rashdall, *The Universities in the Middle Ages* (rev. ed., Oxford, 1942).

which the Italian humanists came in contact was largely concerned with law, medicine, and natural philosophy, subjects which made small appeal to the humanists who, as lay men of letters, were primarily concerned with the literary form and the ethical and moral content of classical literature. Petrarch spoke for the whole clan of the humanists when he called down a curse on all their houses: jurists, doctors of medicine, and philosophers alike. What could their knowledge contribute to the good life?[27] This was one of the crucial objections of the humanists to scholasticism as they knew it. Even the systematic theology of the schoolmen, so far as they were acquainted with it, seemed inadequately concerned with the immediate ethical and moral problems of human life. A second objection was to the form of scholastic learning, which was technical, syllogistic, and expressed in Latin that fell short of classical standards of elegance.

In rejecting scholasticism the humanists undoubtedly limited the scope of their intellectual interest. Recent historians of science have deplored their indifference to the natural sciences, the study of which was included under natural philosophy in the scholastic curriculum, and have tended to regard the whole period of humanist ascendance as a regrettable hiatus in the development of scientific thought.[28] The fact may be admitted and the explanation is simple. The humanists' interests lay elsewhere, within the circle of the *studia humanitatis*. It has also been charged that they contributed little, in this early period at least, to formal philosophy[29]. This, too, may be admitted. As philosophers they were amateurs[30]. Their philosophy was largely a matter of ethics and good sense, founded upon eclectic gleanings from the antique literary sources. Its aim was simply to aid men to live well.

The difference between humanist philosophy and that of the professional schools was reflected in the work of the humanists as educators.[31] Having rejected scholasticism and with it the educational methods and aims of the medieval universities, the humanists were forced to construct theories of education

---

[27]See Petrarch, *De suis ipsius et multorum aliorum ignorantia;* Eng. trans. in Cassirer *et al,* pp. 47 ff.

[28]See especially G. Sarton, "Science in the Renaissance," in J. W. Thompson, G. Rowley, F. Schevill and G. Sarton, *The Civilization of the Renaissance* (Chicago, 1929); and L. Thorndyke, *Science and Thought in the Fifteenth Century* (New York, 1929), pp. 1 ff.

[29]For a survey of literature on Renaissance philosophy, see P. O. Kristeller and J. H. Randall, Jr., "The Study of Philosophy of the Renaissance," in *Journal of the History of Ideas,* II (1941), 449-96. See also E. Garin, *La filosofia,* I (Milan, 1947); and G. Saitta, *Il pensiero italiano nell'umanesimo e nel rinascimento,* I (Bologna, 1949).

[30]Cf. Kristeller, *Studies in Renaissance Thought and Letters,* p. 561: "I should like to suggest that the Italian humanists were not good nor bad philosophers, but no philosophers at all."

[31]The best studies of humanist education are W. H. Woodward, *Vittorino da Feltre and other Humanist Educators* (Cambridge, 1921); and *Studies in Education during the Age of the Renaissance* (Cambridge, 1924).

and methods of instruction of their own. As was to be expected, they based their theories on classical models, drawing heavily upon Cicero's *De oratore* and Quintillian's *Institutio oratoris.* These works dealt primarily with the training of orators, that is, men equipped to take an active part in public affairs. Since the orator's function involved speaking well, training in literary composition was essential. But the ideal orator envisaged by Cicero and Quintillian was not merely a rhetorician, but a philosopher, a virtuous and broadly educated man. And the achievement of this ideal was the aim expressed in all the humanist treatises on education. In the civic humanist circle in Florence education was clearly designed to produce responsible and devoted citizens. Alberti in the *Trattato della cura della famiglia* insisted on the obligation of citizens to serve the state, and Palmieri in *Della vita civile* stressed the similar educational aim of fitting men for active life in society. In the courts of Ferrara and Mantua, where the two greatest schoolmasters of the Renaissance, Guarino of Verona and Vittorino da Feltre founded private schools for the education of the children of princes and courtiers, the aim of education was more specifically directed toward the formation of well rounded and harmonious personalities. Both gave due emphasis to bodily exercise as well as to intellectual discipline, to religion, morals and good manners as well as to book learning. Vittorino stressed above all the duty of the school master to consider the individual personality of his pupils and to develop their potentialities to the fullest extent. It was an educational program practical only in a small aristocratic school, and the finished product it aimed at was the perfect courtier as later described by Castiglione. Despite minor differences of aim and method, however, all the humanist educators were agreed that the essential basis of education was a thorough knowledge of the Latin and Greek classics, including the writings of the early Christian Fathers. From these could be derived everything that an educated man needed to know and all, too, that was needed for the formation of his character. Except for the emphasis on classical scholarship, it was in no way a technical or professional training, although it might serve admirably as a foundation to which professional training could later be added. The great humanist schoolmasters like Guarino, Vittorino and later Federigo of Urbino could obviously reach only a small number of students directly, but their educational ideals exercised a wide-spread and lasting influence. Neither their curriculum nor their educational aims would have seemed strange to a ninettenth-century head master of Eton or Harrow.

In this program of education for life and citizenship the study of history played an important part. The humanist educators urged the reading of the ancient historians as models of prose style, but also, as Bruni pointed out in his treatise *De studiis et litteris,* because history furnished an invaluable treasury of examples of ethical, moral and political behaviour from which citizens and statesmen could learn much to their advantage[32]. More important than this rather unoriginal recognition of the pragmatic value of history,

---

[32]L. Bruni, *De studiis et litteris ad illustrem Dominam Baptistam de Malatesta tractatulus,* ed. Israel (Zschopau, 1880), p. 10.

however, was the historical perspective the humanists gained from their classical studies. When the medieval world chroniclers turned to the distant past, writing the history of the world from the creation, they adopted the divine view of history—a view shared by too many of our students. A thousand years were as a day in their sight. Their conception of temporal distance was as uncertain as the notion of spatial distance indicated on a monastic *Mappa Mundi* or indeed, in any medieval painting.[33] Moreover, so long as they believed the Holy Roman Empire of their own day to be an unbroken continuation of the ancient Roman Empire, they were unable to envisage ancient civilization as a distinct historical phenomenon or as constituting a chronologically limited historical epoch. The Italian humanists, on the other hand, viewing the peaks of antique civilization across the gulf of medieval barbarism, were forced to form a new periodization of history based upon a clearer realization of chronological distance.[34] In their view, antiquity formed a distinct historical period, separated from them by a thousand years of darkness, during which all culture was dead or dormant, to be revived again only in their own day. Moreover, they had learned from their classical models to think of history, not as the divinely ordained history of mankind since the creation, but as the history of individual secular states. When they began to write history in the classical manner, they therefore wrote the history of their own Italian states, usually beginning with the decline of the Roman Empire. They thus took history out of the theologically oriented framework of the world chronicle in which Augustine had placed it and gave it a purely secular setting and content. In short, they replaced clerical history by lay history. The result was a revolution in historical thought, the beginning of modern historiography. Many critics have deplored the loss of local color which they felt resulted from the humanists' use of classical Latin in their histories,[35] but any loss in that direction was more than compensated by the coherence and historical insight they gained from their study of the ancient masters.

The first work to demonstrate the full effect of these various factors on historical writing was Leonardo Bruni's *History of the Florentine People*, written while he was chancellor of the republic between the years 1437 and 1444. Here Bruni set a standard of literary style, historical criticism, and coherent

---

[33]That there was a psychological relation between the lack of spatial and of chronological perspective in the Middle Ages has been suggested by E. Panofsky, *Studies in Iconology* (New York, 1939), p. 27 f: "Just as it was impossible for the Middle Ages to elaborate the modern system of perspective, which is based on realization of a fixed distance between the eye and the object, and thus enables the artist to build up comprehensive and consistent images of visible things; just as impossible was it for them to evolve the modern idea of history, which is based on the realization of intellectual distance between the present and the past, and thus enables the scholar to build up comprehensive and consistent concepts of bygone periods."

[34]For discussion of humanist historical writing and interpretation of history, with bibliography, see Ferguson, pp. 1 ff.

[35]See, for example, Burckhardt (Eng. trans.), p. 244 f.; Voigt, pp. 440 ff; V. Rossi, *Il Quattrocento* (Milan, 1933), pp. 169 ff; E. Fueter, *Geschichte der neueren Historiographie* (Munich, 1936), pp. 9 ff.

organization that differentiated his work clearly from even such late chronicles as that of Giovanni Villani, and made it the model followed by nearly all later humanist historians. Bruni's thought had been profoundly influenced by Aristotle's *Politics,* which he had translated, and by the political atmosphere of Florence in the period of its struggle against Visconti aggression. More than any other historian of his age he perceived the vitally important role of the free communes in the evolution of medieval Italy, and his conviction that political freedom was a necessary prerequisite to civic virtue and a vigorous culture led him to advance the novel theory that it was imperial despotism that was primarily responsible for the decline of Roman civilization. His rejection of the theory that the medieval empire was in fact a continuation of the Roman Empire, too, demonstrated the distance historical thought had travelled since Dante wrote the *De monarchia.*

The historical perspective which the humanists gained from literature and history was further reinforced by their eager study of the physical remains of the ancient civilization they so much admired and by their desire to envisage the life of ancient Roman society as concretely as possible. Niccolo Niccoli, the Florentine merchant turned humanist, collected antique sculpture, coins and medals as well as manuscripts, and made them available to students. Poggio was haunted by the spectacle of grandeur and decay presented by the ruins of the ancient Roman buildings and monuments and wrote a description of them in his treatise *De varietate fortunae.* The real founder of modern archaeology, however, was the indefatigable papal secretary, Flavio Biondo of Forli. With infinite labour and critical skill Biondo reconstructed the topography, monuments, manners and customs of ancient pagan and Christian Rome in two encyclopedic books: *Roma triumphans* and *Roma instaurata.* Then, enlarging the range of his research, he compiled a geographical and historical survey of Italy since ancent times under the title *Italia illustrata.* Finally, in his *History from the Decline of the Roman Empire* he furnished a factual account of Italian history from the sack of Rome by the Visigoths to his own time. This was a scholarly work, founded upon critical examination of the sources, but it lacked the literary style, the coherent organization and the historical insight of Bruni's work. Later humanists scorned its pedestrian style but borrowed from it freely, usually without acknowledgement.

The foregoing discussion has dealt primarily with the humanist interest in classical Latin literature and ancient Roman civilization, for that was as yet the most important part of their recovery of the antique heritage. The first half of the fifteenth century, however, also witnessed the first decisive steps in the rediscovery of ancient Greek literature. This was in a much more literal sense a recovery of something that had been lost than was true of the revival of classical Latin. For centuries knowledge of Greek had almost disappeared in Western Europe[36] Despite their dependence on Aristotle and other Greek authorities, which they read in translations of uneven value, few of the medieval schoolmen could read Greek, and of Greek literature as

---

[36]L. R. Loomis, *Medieval Hellenism* (Lancaster, Pa., 1906).

such they knew little. Nor would they have been greatly interested had it been available. The humanists, on the other hand, were eager to recover just those parts of Greek literature that the schoolmen had ignored; not logic, metaphysics and science, but history, biography, poetry, drama, and works of moral philosophy. These were the aspects of Greek culture that had exerted a powerful influence on the Latin writers of the classical age, and no ardent admirer of Cicero could avoid having his curiosity aroused about the literature which that master of eloquence had regarded as the most perfect expression of *humanitas*.

There were, however, serious obstacles in the way of the Italian students who first desired to master Greek. They were starting from scratch. Greek manuscripts were rare in Italy and such aids as manuals, grammars and dictionaries were practically non-existent. That Petrarch, with all his linguistic talent and enthusiasm for antiquity, never learned Greek is a measure of the difficulty involved. He treasured a manuscript of Homer, which he had acquired, but to the end it remained Greek to him. What the Italian scholars needed was a competent teacher to give them a start, and the real introduction of Greek studies into Italy can be dated from the appointment of a distinguished Byzantine scholar, Manuel Chrysoloras, to a chair in the Florentine university in 1397. At the news of his arrival scholars came from all over Italy to sit at his feet. Pier Paolo Vergerio resigned his post as professor of logic at Padua and Leonardo Bruni abandoned his legal studies to come to Florence to seize the unprecedented opportunity.

Chrysoloras lectured for only three years in Florence and for three more in Milan and Pavia, but before he returned to Constantinople in 1403 he had sown the seed which others could now cultivate. Once started, the Greek revival progressed steadily. Guarino and Filelfo followed him to Constantinople to complete their training, and returned to teach. Bruni mastered Greek sufficiently to translate a number of Greek works. Both Guarino and Vittorino gave the study of Greek an important place in the curriculum of their schools. The hunt for ancient manuscripts now included the Greek, and a number were imported from Constantinople. Thus, when an ecumenical council of the Greek and Roman churches met in Ferrara and Florence in 1438 and 1439 in a vain attempt to heal the schism, Italian scholars were already prepared to make the most of the opportunity to fraternize with the learned Byzantine delegates, some of whom also remained to teach after the council had ended. The fall of Constantinople to the Turks in 1453 came too late to be of decisive importance for Greek studies in Italy, but it did help to accelerate the movement. The refugees brought many more Greek manuscripts, and they swelled the number of Greek teachers, editors and translators, but that is all.

Although Greek studies were well founded before 1453, the influence of Greek culture on humanist thought was still relatively slight.[37] The number of Italian scholars who could read Greek well enough to be influenced by Greek style was still fairly small, and the work of translating, which spread

---

[37]Cf. Bolgar, pp. 276 ff.

the influence of Greek thought to a larger audience, did not get well under way until the second half of the century. On the whole, it seems to have been the Greek prose writers — the historians and philosophers — who were most widely read in this period. Since Petrarch, the humanists had nourished a prejudice against the philosophical and scientific works of Aristole, which they identified with scholasticism, but they seized upon the *Ethics* and *Politics* and the Pseudo-Aristotelian *Economics* and incorporated them into their eclectic system of moral philosophy. Many of the humanists, it is true, professed a preference for Plato over Aristotle. They were charmed by his literary style and found the dialogue form of his works more to their taste than Aristotle's textbookish treatment, but the systematic study of Platonic and Neoplatonic philosophy did not begin till after the middle of the century.

In conclusion, then, how should we assess the achievements of the first century of humanism? It must be admitted that the humanists of this period added little to systematic philosophy, science, or religious thought, and that they wrote little that proved of lasting literary value. But they did achieve what, above all, they set out to achieve, and no one questioned the magnitude of that achievement until with the Romantic movement a generation arose to call them damned. They assembled, edited, and made permanently available almost the whole body of classical Latin literature and they reintroduced the study of Greek in Western Europe. They established the study of both the form and the content of the classics as the indispensible basis of a liberal education, and they found in the sane and broadly human *Weltanschauung* of the ancient world a lay morality and a model and a justification for the secular life. Their exclusive preoccupation with the classics cut across the literary traditions of the Middle Ages. They broke the scholastic monopoly of learning, and they also put a period to the chivalric cult of courtly love and the literary tradition of the *Roman de la rose* with all its machinery of dream sequence and allegory. Romantic critics have blamed the classical revival for interrupting and distorting the natural evolution of the national literatures; but what emerged when the humanist movement had run its course was a vernacular literature, both in Italy and the North, which was greatly enriched in content and in aesthetic discipline, a literature which no longer expressed the exclusive attitudes of a single social class, as did the feudal and clerical literatures of the Middle Ages, but could appeal to all educated men. Finally, as a result of their classical studies, the humanists developed a new critical sense and historical perspective and founded the modern disciplines of philology, historiography and archaeology. Taken all together, what the humanists accomplished was surely an original achievement; and I would like to quote in conclusion the pertinent comment of a distinguished historian of humanism:

> The effect of the classics on Renaissance thought and literature may show us that it is possible to learn from the past and be original at the same time. Originality is greatly to be admired, but it is a gift of nature or providence; it cannot be taught, and I doubt if it is harmed by knowledge or increased by ignorance.[38]

[38]Kristeller, *The Classics and Renaissance Thought,* p. 89.

THE INTERPRETATION OF
ITALIAN HUMANISM:
THE CONTRIBUTION OF HANS BARON*

The interpretation of humanism has from the beginning occupied a central position in the historiography of the Renaissance. Time was, indeed, when the two terms were practically synonymous, when the Renaissance was regarded simply as *la renaissance des lettres,* plus the simultaneous revival of art under the influence of classical antiquity. For the past hundred years or so, however, since the publication of Burckhardt's epoch-making essay and Georg Voigt's scarcely less influential book, *Die Wiederbelebung des classischen Alterthums, oder das erste Jahrhundert des Humanismus,* historians have generally treated the humanist movement as a distinct phenomenon, a part only, although a very important part, of the broader cultural complex of the Renaissance. Nevertheless, as the most articulate representatives of their age, the humanists have continued to serve as the principal touchstones by which scholars have assessed the intellectual atmosphere of the Renaissance and have attempted to measure the extent and direction of its departure from the norms of medieval civilization. Historians' views of humanism have therefore veered with all the varied winds that have driven the concept of the Renaissance upon its erratic course. On one point, however, there has been general agreement, unless with Jacques Maritain[1] one identifies true humanism with scholasticism. Whether they liked it or not, historians have agreed that Renaissance humanism was in its origins an Italian movement, and that when it spread northward it assumed forms which differentiated it in fundamental ways from the Italian prototype. The characterization of humanism as an historical movement must therefore begin with Italy, and our discussion here will be limited to consideration of humanism as an Italian phenomenon.

So long as humanism was treated simply as the literary and scholarly

---

*Read before the American Historical Association, December 1956. Reprinted from *Journal of the History of Ideas,* XIX, 1958.

[1] J. Maritain, *True Humanism* (New York, 1938). But see the criticism of Maritain's position by G. G. Coulton, "The Historical Background of Maritain's Humanism," *Journal of the History of Ideas,* V (1944), 415-33.

aspect of the revival of antiquity, the humanists held a secure place in the history of culture as the agents whose devoted labours restored and perserved the classical heritage for the modern world. Not much else was required of them. Scholars who had been influenced by Romanticism, it is true, frequently deplored the interruption of the native tradition of literature in the *volgare* which resulted from exclusive preoccupation with classical forms. But even the Romantics regarded the restoration and preservation of the classical heritage as, in itself, an achievement of great value. There could, indeed, be no serious depreciation of the humanists' achievement so long as the classics remained the basis of all liberal education. It is only in our own time that a generation has arisen that knows not Cicero.

With the crystallization of the periodic concept of the Renaissance, however, it became necessary to fit humanism into the broader context of *Kulturgeschichte*. The first step in this process was to relate the humanists to the secular, individualistic spirit of the Renaissance as Burckhardt had conceived it. There followed from this a shift in emphasis from the philological achievements of the humanists to their personalities as individuals, with some rather paradoxical results. Most of the historians in the half century after 1860, while still admiring the humanists for their restoration of classical culture, and their development of a critical spirit in philological scholarship, characterized them as for the most part irresponsible individualists, profligate, conceited, scurrilous, and indifferent to religion, if not positively pagan. Burckhardt himself painted the humanists in a generally unfavorable light, despite his intense admiration for what they accomplished as philologists. While admitting that there were exceptions, he felt that "many, and among them the loudest speakers, were guilty" of the charges brought against them. "Three facts," he concluded, "explain and perhaps diminish their guilt: the overflowing excess of favour and fortune, when luck was on their side; the uncertainty of the future, in which luxury or misery depended on the caprice or malice of an enemy; and, finally, the misleading influence of antiquity. This undermined their morality, without giving them its own instead."[2]

The unflattering portrayal of the humanists as people, however, together with the emphasis on their personalities as significant factors in the culture of the Renaissance, probably owed more to Voigt than to Burckhardt. In Voigt's history of the first century of humanism, Petrarch's successors are completely overshadowed by their great prototype. And it was Petrarch's self-conscious personality that most attracted Voigt's admiration. This, he concluded, was Petrarch's most significant achievement. It was what made him "the prophet of a new age, the ancestor of the modern world."[3] For, it was Petrarch's egocentric individualism that first broke the bonds of

---

[2] J. Burckhardt, *The Civilization of the Renaissance in Italy,* trans. by S. G. C. Middlemore (London, 1921), 273f.

[3] G. Voigt, *Die Wiederbelebung des classischen Alterthums oder das erste Jahrhundert des Humanismus* (Berlin, 1859), 81.

medieval corporate consciousness. After him, the later humanists could do no more than tread in his footsteps, imitating his less admirable personality traits without his genius, and also without the soul struggle which had ennobled his obsessive preoccupation with his own complicated state of mind. Voigt's humanists were mostly frivolous *dilettanti* without originality or integrity, devoted to literary form to the exclusion of serious concern for content. Neither here nor in the literary histories which followed during the next half century was much attention given to the ideas of the humanists, nor to what they wrote except as critical philologists. At the turn of the century, Philippe Monnier could dismiss them with the damning phrase: "Having nothing to say, they said it interminably."[4]

Since the beginning of the present century, this conception of the character of the humanists and their contribution to the Renaissance has been gradually supplanted, not by one, but by a number of different interpretations. The new developments, interacting upon one another, arose from a number of factors: greatly intensified research into the sources of both medieval and Renaissance culture; the opening up of new fields of economic, social, and intellectual history, and, above all, from the tendency, stemming in large measure from Dilthey's school of the *Geisteswissenschaften,* to seek the key to an understanding of a given civilization in the types of *Weltanschauung* which characterized it. With this tendency went a conviction that there is a relation between all aspects of the life of the spirit and between the higher forms of culture and the social and political milieu in which their roots are nourished. The result was a series of new interpretations of humanism, as well as of art, philosophy and other forms of culture, new because set in frames of reference that were unfamiliar to the historians of the nineteenth century and which they had neither the data nor the methodological concepts to construct.

One of the first results of the shift in emphasis from the personality of the humanists to their thought, or more precisely to that combination of consciously held ideas with unconscious preconceptions which *in toto* constitutes *Weltanschauung,* was a reversal of the time-honored conception of the humanists as irreligious, semi-pagan, or at best but indifferent orthodox sons of the church. This revision of the traditional interpretation coincided with and supported the contemporaneous tendency to annex the Renaissance to the Middle Ages as a kind of anti-climactic epilogue, a tendency fostered by the recent scholarly enthusiasm for the Middle Ages, by the conviction of the evolutionary rather than revolutionary nature of historical development which was inherent in late nineteenth-century historicism, and, perhaps, also by a waning appreciation of the significance of the recovery of classical culture. Thus Alfred von Martin found in Salutati "a classical example of medieval *Weltanschauung,* that is, of conscious medieval Catholicism."[5] And Ernst

---

[4]P. Monnier, *Le Quattrocento, Essai sur l'histoire littéraire du XVe siècle italien* (Paris, 1910, new ed. 1924), I, 228.

[5]A. von Martin, *Mittelalterliche Welt- und Lebensanschauung im Spiegel der Schriften Coluccio Salutatis* (Munich, 1913), viii.

Walser demonstrated by a detailed study of humanist literature that the paganism of the Renaissance *literati* was merely a superficial literary fashion and that the content of humanism was largely medieval, having nothing that was not common to medieval learning except a new artistic appreciation of the formal beauty of antique letters and art.[6] This interpretation, while rehabilitating the religious character of the humanists, robbed them of what originality Voigt had left them. They were now depicted as unoriginal, not merely because they imitated the classics, but because they continued to think as their medieval predecessors had thought. In much the same way, the historians of science, seeking in the writings of the humanists for evidence of an interest in the natural sciences, and seeking in vain, came to the conclusion that the whole humanist movement was a frivolous aberration of the human spirit which had little to contribute to the scientifically oriented modern world.

Not all the attempts to place humanism in new frames of reference had, however, this rather depreciatory effect upon the evaluation of the humanist movement as a whole. For, one result of the new interest in the ideas of the humanists, which opened the way to fruitful re-examination of their rôle, was the belated recognition of diversity in a movement which had commonly been treated as a unified entity. Once historians began to examine closely what individual humanists actually wrote, they found that they could not dismiss them as merely less gifted Petrarchs, but that they would have to be considered as individuals or at least classified in groups at different chronological stages in the development of humanism. Walter Goetz, Ernst Cassirer, Giovanni Gentile, Guiseppe Saitta, de Ruggiero, and, more recently, Paul O. Kristeller and Eugenio Garin, among others, have found in the humanists more or less original and positive ideas in regard to religion, philosophy, education, the place of man in society, and the dignity of human life in this mortal world. From all this there has resulted a certain rehabilitation of humanism and a tendency to see in it something more than critical philology and unbounded admiration for antiquity coupled with unquestioning acceptance of medieval religious attitudes—something more, in short, than a medieval *Weltanschauung* masquerading in an ill-fitting toga.

It is in this context of new frames of reference, of close examination of the texts and recognition of different lines and stages of development, that I want to discuss briefly the contribution of Hans Baron to the interpretation of Italian humanism.

Although Baron would no longer wish to be classified as an adherent of the Burckhardtian tradition, unless the only alternative were to be ranged among those who denied any validity to Burckhardt's conception, he has never wavered from the conviction that something happened during the Renaissance which justifies the characterization of the Italians as, in Burckhardt's

---

[6]See especially E. Walser, *Poggius Florentinus, Leben und Werke* (Leipzig, 1914); and *Lebens- und Glaubensprobleme aus dem Zeitalter der Renaissance* (Marburg, 1926); *Studien zur Weltanschauung der Renaissance* (Basel, 1920).

phrase, "the first born among the sons of modern Europe." Writing nearly thirty years ago, he stated the position which may be taken as the point of departure from which his later historical thought evolved:

> The picture of the Renaissance and Humanism that Jacob Burckhardt and Georg Voigt painted more than sixty years ago still serves today as the great, safe road for our research, aside from which one may indeed take interesting expeditions into unknown lands, yet without any of these having as yet opened up an alternative road to a general view of the spiritual world of the Italian Trecento, Quattrocento and Cinquecento.[7]

Since then the direction of his research has been motivated apparently less by a conscious effort to revise or modify the interpretation of the Renaissance and humanism which dominated the late nineteenth century than by the necessity he felt of adjusting his ideas progressively to the evidence of the sources, to contemporary trends in research and interpretation, and to concepts which had played little part in the Burckhardtian tradition. In 1950 he could sum up the experience of his generation as follows:

> Some of us may not have wondered until after many years of study how far we had travelled from Burckhardt's position. We had not set out, I think, to supply any elements missing from Burckhardt's synthesis; our problems sprang from the conditions of twentieth-century scholarship.[8]

The gradual evolution and progressive crystallization of Baron's conception of the character of Italian humanism and of its relation to the social developments and political events of the Quattrocento can be traced through a long series of publications, beginning with the introduction to his edition of Leonardo Bruni's *Humanistisch-Philosophische Schriften* in 1928 and culminating in his two recent books: *The Crisis of the Early Renaissance: Civic Humanism and Republican Liberty in an Age of Classicism and Tyranny* and *Humanistic and Political Literature in Florence and Venice at the Beginning of the Quattrocento,* both published in 1955.

Two of Baron's basic conceptions for the characterization of Quattrocento humanism as an original and creative force appeared quite early in works written while he was still in Germany. The first of these was his conviction of the unique character of Florentine "civic humanism" (Bürgerhumanismus) from Salutati and Bruni to Ficino. In the republic on the Arno, he argued, the humanist circle was closely associated with the ruling class of wealthy citizens, shared their ethical and political interests, and hence developed a positive evaluation of social and political activity, which was possible only in a free republic and which differentiated them from the rootless *literati* who found an uncertain patronage in the courts of the Italian despots. Even the Medicean domination did not completely destroy the old republic or change the ideals shared by citizens and humanists. As a result of this close association with civic life in a republic, the Florentine humanists

---

[7]H. Baron, "Renaissance in Italien. Literaturbericht," *Archiv fur Kulturgeschichte,* XVII (1927), 226.

[8]H. Baron, "The First History of the Historical Concept of the Renaissance," *Journal of the History of Ideas,* XI (1950), 500.

developed a new and essentially modern historical outlook. This idea, suggested in the introduction to his edition of Bruni's works,[9] Baron developed further in 1932 in an article entitled "Das Erwachen des historischen Denkens im Humanismus des Quattrocento," in the *Historische Zeitschrift*.[10] Petrarch had made the first break with medieval historical tradition by abandoning the theologically oriented belief in the continuity of the Roman Empire down to his own time; but the decisive break came in the early fifteenth century when Bruni and other Florentine humanists placed the decline of Roman culture and the subsequent revival of literature and art in historical perspective and related them to natural social and political causes. As citizens of an independent republic, they ascribed the decline of ancient civilization to the psychological effects of the loss of freedom under the Empire, and the revival of cultural life in Italy to the rise of the free communes.

A few years later, Baron developed further his conception of the peculiarly civic nature of early fifteenth-century Florentine humanism, illustrating by specific examples the effect upon humanist thought of the attitudes toward political and social life which the humanists had absorbed from their republican bourgeois environment. In an article on "Cicero and the Roman Civic Spirit in the Middle Ages and the Early Renaissance," published in 1938,[11] he traced the radical change in the humanists' conception of Cicero's character which took place at the beginning of the Quattrocento. Where the Middle Ages had seen in Cicero only the aloof Stoic sage, and Petrarch, who had gained the first real understanding of him through his letters to Atticus, was shocked and repelled by Cicero's passionate interest in politics, the Florentine humanists of Bruni's generation found in Cicero's combination of political with literary activity the perfect expression of their own ideal. Then, turning from the political to the economic interest of burgher humanism, in an article published in *Speculum* in the same year,[12] Baron analysed the changing attitudes toward the possession of wealth to be found in humanist literature during the fourteenth and fifteenth centuries. Here he argued that the Franciscan doctrine of poverty united with the Stoic contempt for riches and worldly status to justify in the minds of the vagrant humanists of the fourteenth century their own uncertain social position and their rejection of the active life and of all family, social or political responsibility. Here again Baron found the decisive break with tradition in the early years of the fifteenth century. It was stimulated by Bruni's discovery of the civic virtues of the antique *polis* in Aristotle's *Ethics* and *Politics;* but Baron felt

---

[9]H. Baron, ed., *Leonardo Bruni Aretino, Humanistisch-Philosophische Schriften* (Leipzig, 1928), xiff.

[10]H. Baron, "Das Erwachen des historischen Denkens im Humanismus des Quattrocento," *Historische Zeitschrift*, CXLVII (1932), 1-13.

[11]H. Baron. "Cicero and the Roman Civic Spirit in the Middle Ages and the Early Renaissance." *Bulletin of the John Rylands Library*, XXII (Manchester, 1938), 72-97.

[12]H. Baron, "Franciscan Poverty and Civic Wealth as Factors in the Rise of Humanistic Thought," *Speculum*, XIII (1938), 1-37.

that the principal reason for the new attitude toward material possessions was "the participation of citizens in intellectual life" which "explains the suddenness and the depth of the change which took place in the character of humanism in the fifteenth century."[13]

In both of these articles Baron not only emphasized the fundamental nature of the changes he observed in humanist thought, but also reasserted, though with altered chronological limits, the Burckhardtian conception of the Renaissance as a period distinct from the Middle Ages. In the article in *Speculum* cited above he noted the fact that discoveries of the survival of a medieval *Weltanschauung* in early humanism had led many scholars to reject Burckhardt's conception of the Renaissance "on the ground that it makes the transformation of intellectual life from the Middle Ages to the Renaissance appear too much as a sudden revolution. May it not, they say, be accepted today that the humanistic world slowly developed from that of the Middle Ages? Is it not an error to regard the Renaissance as a fundamental break with medieval tradition, a new edifice on changed foundations?" To the view thus stated he replied: "There is one obstacle in the way of these conclusions. The great transformation from medievalism to the Renaissance actually took place in two different stages. . . . Only the second of these stages changed the whole trend of cultural life in Italy by leading back to the pure traditions of antiquity and forward to a new and realistic observation of man and the world: and this second stage did not begin till about 1400."[14] Again, in the article on "Cicero and the Roman Civic Spirit", he reiterated his conviction that "The old conception of the Renaissance as a fundamental break with medieval traditions, as a new edifice on changed foundations, was not entirely wrong. It was only erroneous in so far as that break was placed at too early a date. A complete revolution in intellectual life did indeed take place, but not until the end of the fourteenth century, not until the very moment when Petrarch's humanism was transplanted into civic surroundings— first and foremost into the civic world of Florence."[15]

At the time when these articles in English were being published, Baron was evidently working away from the tendency, inherent in much of German *Geistesgeschichte,* to treat intellectual developments in a social and political vacuum. From this point on, he laid increasing emphasis on the relation between the revolution he observed in humanist thought and specific political and social events. In an article on "The Historical Background of the Florentine Renaissance," also published in 1938, he introduced the idea, which was to dominate much of his later interpretation, that it was the crisis provoked by the threat of Visconti aggression which brought Florentine humanists and citizens together in a common defence of civil liberty against tyranny.

---

[13]Ibid., 18.

[14]*Ibid.,* 1f.

[15]*Bulletin of the John Rylands Library.* XXII, 88.

In the stormy years when Florence was defending her heritage of liberty
[he wrote] her intellectual life took a new direction. The conception of an
education arose, whose object was not only to train learned men but to
produce good citizens; an education which inspired men to take part in the
activities of daily life, and in the public affairs of the community. At this
point the citizens' ideas merged into the humanist mode of thought. In the
works of Aristotle and Cicero could be found the classical conviction that
the personality of the individual only grows to maturity—both intellectually
and morally—through participation in the life of his "polis" and "Respublica." The humanism of the fourteenth century, which had retained
the characteristics of medieval aloofness from the world, was now transformed into a civic humanism.[16]

A year later, approaching the problem for the first and almost the last
time from a sociological point of view, Baron sought to find in the economic
and social history of Florence an explanation for the changes in the tone of
humanism around the beginning of the fifteenth century. Here he argued
that the great merchant bankers of the Calimala, who had dominated Florence
in the generation of Dante, were in fact "typical products of the feudal age."[17]
Their fortunes originated in trade, but their immense wealth was largely the
product of usurious money-lending to kings, princes, nobles, and prelates.
They were, in short, feudal financiers and they adapted themselves to the
manners and customs of the nobility. "Forming, as they did, a foreign body
in the noble feudal world and yet living at its expense, they were not the
potential bearers of a new outlook on economic life."[18] It was only after the
bankruptcy of the great Florentine banking houses in the 1340's that leadership in Florence passed to the new class of merchant industrialists in the *Arte
della lana,* and "it was this growth of industrial interests in the state which
primarily determined the economic ideas of the Florentine Renaissance."[19]
The bourgeois ethic of civic humanism, then, was the product of an interaction between the humanist discovery of the Roman civic virtues and the
high value placed upon thrift and labour by an industrial society. The influence of Max Weber is clear here and possibly also that of Alfred von Martin's
Soziologie der Renaissance.

In later articles Baron returned to what had apparently become his major
interest: the relation between humanist thought and the political evolution of
fifteenth-century Italy, with the addition of a growing conviction that the survival of republican and monarchical states side by side in a balance of power
was a fundamental prerequisite of Renaissance culture, and the factor that in
the truest sense made Italy the prototype of the modern world. In an article
entitled "Toward a More Positive Evaluation of the Fifteenth-Century Renaissance," published in 1943, he developed the idea that "it is because of this

---

[16]H. Baron, "The Historical Background of the Florentine Renaissance," *History,*
N. Ser. XXII (1938), 320.

[17]H. Baron, "A Sociological Interpretation of the Early Renaissance in Florence,"
South Atlantic Quarterly, XXXVIII (1939), 428.

[18]*Ibid.,* 431.

[19]*Ibid.,* 433.

survival of civic initiative in geographical proximity to bureaucratic-unifying absolutism that the whole range of modern political experience was traversed in the fifteenth century."[20] And again, "it is not only in diplomatic technique ... but in the inherent dynamics of international relations that Renaissance Italy foreshadowed the character of the family of Western nations."[21] As the second World War progressed, and Hitler spread his New Order across Europe, the conviction that there was a parallel in fifteenth-century Italy to the state system of modern Europe grew stronger, and in an article published in 1944 Baron announced the thesis that the failure of Italy to achieve national unity through Visconti aggression was not a catastrophe, as Italian historians had thought since the Risorgimento. On the contrary, he asserted, "without Florence's survival in the decisive hour, there would not have been in the Quattrocento anything like the outburst of cultural energies that we call the Renaissance."[22] Finally, in a long article in the *American Historical Review* in 1953, Baron filled in the historical background of the period in which the two great commercial republics, Florence and Venice, stood together as defenders of the *Libertas Italiae* against the Milanese aggressor.

I have traced the evolution of Baron's ideas in chronological order, because it seems to me that thus we can see most clearly the way in which his attempt to interpret Quattrocento humanism in a frame of reference of civic and political life led step by step to an essentially novel conception of the interaction upon one another of humanist thought and political events, and hence to a reinterpretation of the intellectual and political history of Italy in the fifteenth century. Such a treatment was also necessary to indicate the priority of his interpretation in relation to the somewhat similar views expressed by Eugenio Garin, Rudolf Stadelmann, and Nino Valeri in books published since the war.[23]

In Baron's major work on the early Italian Renaissance, the interpretations outlined in the preceding articles were brought together in a synthesis, amplified in detail and supported by a formidable mass of documentation. Here the cumulative effect of their reiterated juxtaposition added immeasurably to their persuasive force. In particular, the author's belief that the struggle of the Florentine Republic against Giangaleazzo was essentially an ideological conflict, at least in the minds of the literary protagonists, emerges more clearly and convincingly. So, too, does his conviction of the crucial im-

---

[20]H. Baron, "Toward a More Positive Evaluation of the Fifteenth-Century Renaissance," *Journal of the History of Ideas,* IV (1943), 26.

[21]*Ibid.,* 27.

[22]H. Baron, "Articulation and Unity in the Italian Renaissance and in the Modern West," *Annual Report of the American Historical Association,* III (1942), 135.

[23]See, for example, E. Garin, *Der italienische Humanisms* (Bern, 1947), and *La Filosofia,* I, *Dal Medio Evo all'Umanesimo* (Milan, 1947); R. Stadelmann, *"Persönlichkeit und Staat in der Renaissance," Die Welt als Geschichte,* V (1949), 137-155; N. Valeri, *L'Italia nell'età dei principati dal 1343 al 1516* (Milan, 1950).

portance of the struggle. It is difficult to deny that "the growth of the Renaissance would have been nipped in the bud if Florence had become a provincial town within an Italian kingdom under despotic Viscontian rule,"[24] although one may ask whether it was Florentine civic humanism and the sentiment for republican liberty that was the essential prerequisite to the flowering of the Renaissance or simply the survival of Florence as an independent state, albeit under Medicean dictatorship.

In assessing Baron's contribution to the interpretation of Italian humanism and its place in Italian history, I shall be forced to take more or less for granted the mass of detailed information, based on original research and a profound knowledge of the sources, which comprises most of the *Crisis of the Early Italian Renaissance* and, to an even greater degree, of the companion volume, *Humanistic and Political Literature in Florence and Venice at the Beginning of the Quattrocento.* Baron's construction of a solidly based chronology for the humanistic literature of the early fifteenth century is in itself a contribution to our knowledge of the field which no scholar can afford to ignore. Here, however, I can consider only the main lines of his interpretation, attempt to place it in the perspective of recent Renaissance scholarship, and raise some questions concerning its validity.

In the first place, Baron's interpretation of humanist thought and *Weltanschauung,* in the frame of reference of political events and the citizens' participation in the active life of the state, undoubtedly adds a facet to the rounded picture of the Renaissance, and one which had hitherto been ignored or inadequately treated. The fuller understanding of both humanism and the Renaissance achieved by twentieth-century scholarship has been largely the product of such additions to the total picture as the result of seeing it from a new point of view. Such, for example, was Henry Thode's perception of the influence of the Franciscan spirit on Renaissance art, or Walser's discovery of medieval traits in the humanist *Weltanschauung.* But, while such reinterpretations have not only added to our knowledge, but have also corrected many previous misconceptions, they have proved inadequate to serve as the basis for a complete reinterpretation of the age or even of the humanist movement as a whole.

It is perhaps too early to pass final judgement on the significance of Baron's contribution, even if I were equipped to do so, for much work along the lines he has opened up still remains to be done, as, I am sure, no one is more keenly aware than Baron himself. It may be that his most important contribution will prove to be the stimulus his ideas will give to future research, and perhaps as much in the field of political history as in that of humanism. As his work stands at present, however, it raises certain questions in my mind regarding his interpretation of Italian humanism and its relation to the Renaissance. Granted the validity of his conception of civic humanism for Bruni and the Florentine circle in the first half of the fifteenth century, does it help to clarify our view of humanism elsewhere, or even at a later date

[24]H. Baron, *The Crisis of the Early Italian Renaissance* (Princeton, 1955), 384.

in Florence itself? Or could the application of a similar politically oriented frame of reference serve to cast new light on the humanism of the princely courts or of the Platonic Academy? Perhaps so. Nevertheless, Baron's contention that the most important factor in shaping the type of classicism which dominated the literature and art of the Quattrocento and distinguished it from the preceding century was "a new position assumed by the Florentine city-state Republic" seems to me as yet inadequately demonstrated, as does also his assertion that "the most significant effect for the future was that from Florence ideas and interests spread through all Italy such as could develop only in the society of a free city," and that "this influence changed most of the ideas held by the humanists of the Trecento."[25] Again, granted that the attitude toward the active life of the citizen underwent a revolutionary change among the Florentine humanists in Bruni's generation, and possibly also among others in Venice and elsewhere who followed their leadership, is this sufficient to warrant a conception of the Renaissance as a period divided from the Middle Ages by a sharp break at the beginning of the fifteenth century, even if one correlates the new civic humanism with contemporaneous developments in art, as Baron does in passing? I am myself loath to yield Petrarch to the medieval *Anschluss,* and I would prefer to regard Dante rather than Petrarch or Salutati as the transitional figure. Baron is on safer ground, I think, when he argues that the revolution in historical thought and the historical perspective achieved by Bruni and his successors represented a new and essentially modern view of the world, which had a wide-spread and lasting influence.

The questions I have raised should not be taken as minimizing the debt Renaissance scholarship owes to Baron for new insights, for new points of view, as well as for much hitherto unknown factual material. His work constitutes an invaluable chapter in the intellectual history of Florence and in the political history of Italy in the fifteenth century. It seems to me, however, that the synthesis that will place the whole movement of Italian humanism in relation to the economic, social, political, and cultural evolution of the Renaissance must be based upon a broader frame of reference, although such a synthesis will necessarily include that aspect which Baron has perceived and demonstrated with irrefutable proofs.

---

[25]*Ibid.,* 4ff.

Essays in Interpretation and Synthesis

THE INTERPRETATION OF THE RENAISSANCE: SUGGESTIONS FOR A SYNTHESIS*

The attempt to find an historical interpretation of the Renaissance, or of any other age, is predicated upon the acceptance of certain methodological assumptions. We must assume first the value of periodization and of synthesis, and the possibility of achieving both in a significant way. Few historians would now deny the value of periodization, though there are some who would still argue that the historian's task consists simply in recounting events as they occurred. But, in fact, periodization is an intellectual tool, essential to the historian's trade. Its use, to quote Collingwood's dictum, "is a mark of advanced and mature historical thought, not afraid to interpret facts instead of merely ascertaining them."[1] Whether his periods be decades, centuries, or larger chronological areas such as the Middle Ages or the Renaissance, the historian cannot think about history without them, much less interpret it for others. There is perhaps less agreement concerning the need for synthesis, particularly among scholars who are concerned primarily with one discipline or one aspect of history. Yet even for specialists, some general notion of the character of the age they deal with, and of the relation of their own field of interest to the total complex of civilization, seems to me essential. Without some such general conception, the specialist may well find himself operating in an historical vacuum, in which the gravity of all objects seems equal.

A synthetic interpretation, which includes all aspects of a given civilization, is especially important for its bearing upon the problem of causation, even in the most restricted fields of enquiry. Painting, sculpture, music, poetry, science, philosophy, or theology may each develop to a certain extent along lines dictated by the discipline itself, either by a kind of inner logic, or as the result of the contribution of individual men of genius. Yet the general direction taken by any one of these can never, I believe, be fully understood or explained without consideration of other contemporaneous or antecedent changes in economic activity, political institutions, social configurations, and

---

*Paper read at Modern Language Association, annual meeting, Dec. 28, 1950. Reprinted from *Journal of the History of Ideas,* XII, 1951.

[1] R. G. Collingwood, *The Idea of History* (Oxford, 1946), 53.

religious beliefs, or in those more imponderable shifts in ways of thinking which we classify under the heading of climates of opinion, or which we designate, such being the poverty of the English language, as the *Zeitgeist*, or the *Weltanschauung* of the age. The interrelation of these various forms of historical activity may be difficult to establish with certainty; but the scholar who ignores the possibility of causal relation between them and the subject of his own special interest, or who is content to recount *what* occurred without venturing to suggest *why* it may have occurred, is, I think, using the concept of scientific objectivity as a pretext for avoiding the necessity of thought.

But, if we admit the value of periodization and the desirability of synthesis, can these be applied satisfactorily to the concept of the Renaissance? In many disciplines, especially the history of art and music, the term Renaissance has been commonly used as a style concept, as distinguished, for example, from Late Gothic or Baroque. In other fields, notably the history of literature and the history of ideas, it has been used to designate a movement of thought, something which may influence, coincide with, or run counter to, such contemporaneous movements as the Reformation. Such uses of the term, if consciously defined, are justified within the framework of the particular discipline, and in both instances there is an implicit periodization, since certain chronological limits are assumed. For purposes of synthesis, however, the term Renaissance should, I think, be given a broader and more specifically periodic connotation, and be applied to the entire civilization of the age. It is as a period in the history of Western civilization, then, that I shall discuss it. Nor shall I pause here to justify the use of the term in this connotation, unfortunate though it be in many respects. I suspect it is here to stay. There is, in any case, little to be gained by re-enacting the miracle of the confusion of terms. The real problem is not what the age should be called, but what were its most characteristic traits and its chronological boundaries. How, in short, can we establish a periodic concept of the Renaissance that will prove a useful tool for the historian, and have practical value for the interpretation of history?

It would seem at first glance, that the primary problem in periodization is to establish the chronological limits of the period in question. But that cannot be done without first forming some idea of what are the characteristics that distinguish it from the preceding and following ages. To serve the purpose of historical thought, a period must possess for the historian some conceptual content. It must correspond to a significant stage in the development of a civilization or a part thereof. Otherwise it is merely an arbitrarily selected and meaningless section of time. But significant periods do not emerge of themselves out of the unbroken flow of historical activity as it occurred from day to day and from year to year. It is the task of the thoughtful historian to discern, by close study of the facts, noteworthy changes in the course of history; and this he cannot do without at the same time forming a concept of the nature of these changes. Having determined to his own satisfaction what are the fundamental characteristics of a particular stage in historical development, he may then determine more exactly the chronological limits of the period to which these characteristics apply. This process should not be regarded as the imposition upon historical reality of an arbitrary scheme, founded upon *a priori* reasoning. All that is meant is that in the interpretation of history, as in the study of the natural sciences, an hypothesis must arise out of observation, if the infinitude of isolated facts is to be arranged in some coherent pattern and so be made accessible to thought.

To return to the problem of the Renaissance, the first step in establishing a period that will have practical value for the historian must be to form, from the infinite variety of available fact, an hypothesis concerning its essential character. Divergence of opinion in this respect is, indeed, the principal cause of the bewildering diversity of opinion regarding the chronological scope of the Renaissance. When the Italian Renaissance first emerged, like Pallas Athene, full-grown from the head of Jacob Burckhardt, it possessed certain traits that were regarded as characteristic of Italian culture during the whole period from Dante to the Counter-Reformation. Of these traits, individualism was, in Burckhardt's synthesis, the determining factor. He regarded this as primarily the product of the unique social and political organization which had shaped the genius of the Italian people, but he also attributed it in secondary degree to the revival of the classics. The influence of the latter, he thought, was predominant in the most characteristic forms of Renaissance literature and art, and also gave rise to the pagan spirit that was commonly regarded as an essential element of Renaissance culture. The periodic concept of the Renaissance thus continued to be attached, more or less, as was the older and narrower conception of the *renaissance des lettres,* to the revival of antiquity. When northern scholars strove to establish a Renaissance period for their own countries, they found that equivalent phenomena occurred much later than in Italy, and largely as importations. They thought of the Renaissance as having crossed the Alps at some time around the middle or end of the fifteenth century. The chronological beginnings of the Renaissance thus varied from country to country by a century or more. Still other scholars, reacting against the significance traditionally assigned to the revival of antiquity, thrust the beginnings of the Renaissance back to St. Francis, or continued the Middle Ages through to the Elizabethans. And some, particularly the historians of the natural sciences, regarding humanist culture with a bilious eye, looked before and after and pined for what was not, with the result that for them the Renaissance disappeared entirely, or became at best a kind of middle age, a regrettable lapse of time between two great periods of scientific thought.

Much of this chronological confusion arose, it seems to me, from constructing the concept of the Renaissance upon too narrow a foundation. If we take into consideration the total complex of European civilization, it will become evident, I think, that all the countries of Western Europe entered upon a decisive change about the beginning of the fourteenth century. The character as well as the rate of change varied from country to country, and from one type of culture, or institution, or form of activity, to another. But wherever we look, the typically medieval forms begin to disintegrate, while new and recognizably modern forms appear, if only in embryo. At the same time the centre of gravity shifts noticeably from the social and cultural factors that had been dominant in the Middle Ages to those minority phenomena that were to assume a leading role in the modern period. To define the Renaissance in a sentence seems rather like rushing in where not only angels but even fools would fear to tread. To avoid doing so at this point, however, would savour of moral cowardice. Viewing the Renaissance as an age in the history of Western Europe, then, I would define it as the age of transition from medieval to modern civilization, a period characterized primarily by the gradual shift from one fairly well co-ordinated and clearly defined type of civilization to another, yet, at the same time, possessing in its own right certain distinctive traits and a high degree of cultural vitality. And on the basis of this concept or hypothesis, I would set the arbitrary dates—1300 to 1600—as its chronological boundaries. To invest this definition with any significant content, however, and to pin down the weasel words, it is necessary, first of all, to indicate what may be considered the prevailing elements of both medieval and modern civilization, and then to trace the main lines of development within the transitional period.

In the broadest terms, then: the two dominant institutions of the Middle Ages were the feudal system and the universal Church. Between them, they determined both the social structure and the ideological content of medieval civilization. And both, in their institutional aspects, were founded upon an agrarian, landholding economy. Feudalism, indeed, took shape in the early Middle Ages very largely because it was the only possible means of maintaining social and political organization in a moneyless economy — an economy in which the land and its produce were almost the sole form of wealth—commerce, industry and normal city life having virtually disappeared. Lacking financial resources in fluid form, central government was unable to maintain effective political or judicial authority, and was forced to relinquish these into the hands of the great land-holders. Lay society was divided into two hereditary classes of widely divergent status: the land-holding nobility, whose duty it was to fight and govern; and the peasants, more or less servile, whose duty it was to work the land. Only one other class had a useful service to perform: the clergy, whose duty it was to pray and to care for the souls of men. Having no other means of support, the clergy necessarily became a landholding class, and, as land-holders, the officers of the Church became feudal lords. On the material side, then, the Church was deeply involved in the feudal system. At the same time, the Church had inherited from its origins in the Roman Empire a principle of universality and a centralized, hierarchical government, which it never lost. But this universal authority was of too large a sort to come into direct conflict with the highly localized government of the feudal nobles. Feudalism and the universal Church, indeed, could live more or less harmoniously together as *concordantia oppositorum*.

Into this agrarian, feudal society the commercial revival of the eleventh and twelfth centuries introduced the new and alien elements of commerce and skilled industry, with the resulting growth of cities and the expansion of money economy. This was followed by a notable increase in the prosperity and fluid wealth of the landholding classes. It was also accompanied by a great quickening of cultural activity, by that full development of clerical and feudal culture that made the twelfth and thirteenth centuries the classic period of medieval civilization. The economic stimulus which spread from the growing cities, together with the heightened tempo of intercommunication along the lines of trade, was, I think, the material factor that made possible the immense cultural vitality of these two centuries. But the content and spirit of that culture did not emanate from the urban classes. Learning remained the exclusive monopoly of the clergy. Art and music served the Church. And vernacular literature expressed the ideals of feudalism and chivalry. Exceptions to these broad statements will, of course, leap to mind immediately. It is my contention, merely, that the elements of medieval civilization which I have mentioned were the most general and the most characteristic.

When we turn to the modern age, say by the beginning of the seventeenth century, the general complex of European civilization has changed so radically that it amounts to a change in kind rather than in degree. The economic balance has shifted from agriculture to commerce and industry. Money economy has become almost universal, and capitalism has replaced all but the vestigial remnants of medieval economic organization. On the political side, the national states with centralized government have taken the place of feudal particularism, while at the same time the unity of Christendom has been decisively broken. Beside the Catholic Church stand the Protestant churches and sects, in their infinite variety. The social balance has shifted, so that the urban classes are no longer a minor element in society, but are prepared to assume political and cultural leadership. The clerical monopoly of learning has been broken, and laymen have replaced the clergy as the most numerous and influential group, both as patrons and creators of the higher forms of culture. The secular elements in literature, learning, and general *Weltanschauung* now decisively outweigh the transcendental; and the natural sciences have replaced theology as the dominant form of knowledge.

Compared with the revolutionary changes in the character of Western European civilization between the years 1300 and 1600, the changes in the following three centuries are changes in degree rather than in kind. Despite the increasingly rapid tempo of development, the evolution of modern civilization has followed, or did follow at least until our generation, lines already clearly established by the beginning of the seventeenth century. It is my contention, then, that medieval and modern civilization, despite the common elements that have remained constant in the Western world for the past two thousand years or more, are, in effect, two different types of civilization, and that the change from the one to the other occurred during the three centuries of the Renaissance.

But, in thus asserting the transitional character of the Renaissance, I have done no more than lay the ground work for an interpretation of the age itself. The mere characterization of the types of civilization that preceded and followed it suggests the lines of change within the transitional age, but does nothing to indicate how or why the changes took place. Here we must face the fundamental problem of causation. What were the dynamic forces that disintegrated the medieval social structure, and as a result altered medieval ways of thinking, gradually at first, but in the long run so profoundly as to create a new type of culture? In thus framing the question, I am, of course, implying a partial answer to the problem of causation, for there is implied in the question the assumption that the fundamental causes of change in the forms of culture are to be found in antecedent changes in economic and political institutions and in the whole structure of society. This is an assumption that many scholars, notably those imbued with the traditions of Hegelian or Thomist idealism, would be loath to accept. Yet it seems to me that, if we regard the whole complex of European civilization in this period, social change everywhere precedes cultural change, and that what is new in Renaissance culture, including novel adaptations of inherited traditions, can most readily be explained as the product of a changed social milieu.

Let me repeat my earlier generalization—that medieval culture was predominantly feudal and ecclesiastical, the product of a society founded upon an agrarian, landholding economy. By the beginning of the fourteenth century that society had already been replaced in Italy by an urban society, constructed upon an economic foundation of large-scale commerce and industry, and with rapidly developing capitalist institutions. In the northern countries the expansion of money economy worked more slowly, but by 1300 it was already disintegrating the landholding basis of feudal society, and had at the same time made possible the effective exercise of central government in the great national or territorial states. Both politically and economically, the feudal nobles were losing ground to the rising forces of monarchy and the bourgeoisie. Meanwhile the Church was also entering upon a period of profound crisis when, with its moral prestige sapped by a monetary fiscal policy, it was forced into a losing battle with the newly arisen political power of the national states. Though it survived as a universal Church for about a century after the Council of Constance, it never recovered the prestige and authority lost during the period of the Babylonian Captivity and the Great Schism.

The changes in the social structure and in the balance of the social classes, which resulted from these economic and political developments, were not reflected immediately or in equal degree everywhere by changes in the forms of higher culture. But, with due allowance for a normal cultural lag, it seems to me that as the economic, political, and social balance shifted, the leadership in all forms of intellectual and aesthetic activity also shifted in the same directions: from the clergy to the laity, from the feudal classes to the urban, and from the isolation of monastic foundations and baronial castles to the concentrated society of cities and of royal or princely courts.

One of the ways in which the influence of economic and political change worked most directly upon Renaissance culture was through the spread of lay education and lay patronage of art, learning, and letters. And this, I think, was clearly the result of the massing of population in cities, of the growth of large private fortunes, and of the concentration of both fluid wealth and political power in the hands of kings and princes. Under the conditions of feudal life, the noble classes made no pretence to intellectual eminence or scholarship sublime, and as Professor Pollard once remarked, even today a little thinking goes a long way in rural England. Not only did ideas circulate more rapidly in an urban atmosphere, but capitalist enterprise necessitated a general literacy among the middle and upper classes of the cities, while at the same time it furnished the most prosperous of the urban patriciate with the means for liberal patronage. In similar fashion, the growth of centralized state governments, supported by taxation, opened up careers to laymen trained in law and administration, and also created new centres of lay patronage. The princely courts of Italy all became active centres of lay culture, and had also, incidentally, broken completely with the feudal traditions that had inspired the greater part of lay culture in the Middle Ages. The royal courts of the North, and semi-royal courts like that of the Dukes of Burgundy, retained the forms of a feudal and chivalrous society, but the literary reflections of these forms had by the fifteenth century lost the vitality that had inspired the feudal literature of the twelfth and thirteenth centuries. The forms of feudalism and chivalry no longer bore a close relation to social reality. Economic and political pressure combined to transform the semi-independent baron of the Middle Ages into the Renaissance courtier. The ranks of the nobility were being infiltrated by the *nouveau riche,* and beside the remnants of the old *noblesse d'épée* now stood the wealthy and highly cultured members of the *noblesse de la robe.* To maintain their position at court, scions of the old nobility were being forced to don a veneer of education and cultured taste, and to extend their intellectual interests beyond the spheres of courtly love and refined homicide which had been the principal themes of medieval feudal literature. The spread of lay education among the upper ranks of both the bourgeoisie and the nobility thus served not only to break the ecclesiastical monopoly of learning and the patronage of art, but also to modify radically the feudal and chivalrous spirit of vernacular literature. As higher education was adapted increasingly to the needs of a lay society, even the clergy were exposed more than ever before to secular learning, so that their contribution to Renaissance culture was in many instances indistinguishable from that of the educated layman.

The increasing laicization of education and of learning, literature, art and music was accompanied, almost inevitably, by an expansion of their secular content, and frequently by the introduction of a more secular tone. By this I do not mean to imply that the men of the Renaissance were, in general, less religious than those of the Middle Ages. There has been enough nonsense written about the pagan spirit of the Renaissance without my adding to it. On the other hand, it seems to me equally nonsensical to seize upon every evidence of religious feeling or belief in the Renaissance as proof that its culture was still basically medieval. Christianity was not a medieval invention. The Christian tradition certainly continued from the Middle Ages through the Renaissance—and beyond—but it did not continue unaltered, nor did it in the same degree dominate the culture of the age. In the first place, the greatly increased participation of laymen introduced into learning, literature and art whole areas of secular knowledge and subjects of general human interest which, if not wholly lacking in the Middle Ages, were yet inadequately represented. In the second place, the writer or artist, who worked for a predominantly lay audience or for lay patrons, had to meet the demands and satisfy the taste of men not trained in theology nor bound by clerical traditions. Even the religious art of the Renaissance gives frequent evidence of consideration for the taste of lay patrons. Finally, religion itself was in some degree laicized. This is evident, in the fourteenth and fifteenth centuries, in the growth of anti-clerical sentiment, and in revolts against the hierarchical authority of the Church and the sacramental-sacerdotal aspects of medieval religion. The Wycliffite and Hussite heresies are extreme cases. But even within the bounds of orthodoxy, such movements of popular mysticism as the *Devotio Moderna* in the Netherlands show a tendency toward the development of a peculiarly lay piety. The religious writing of the Christian humanists offers further examples of an increasingly independent participation of laymen in the shaping of religious thought. These men were deeply pious, but they had little in common with Thomas Aquinas or Innocent III. The Protestant Reformation itself was in part a revolt against the sacerdotal domination of religion. In proclaiming the priesthood of all believers, Luther placed the believing laymen on an even footing with the cleric. The whole problem of the relation of the Reformation to both medieval and Renaissance culture is, however, too complex to be discussed here. For the present, I can do no more than assert the opinion that it can be fully understood only if it is considered in relation to the changes that had altered the whole structure of European society and the character of European culture since the beginning of the fourteenth century. In short, I think that the Reformation must be interpreted as one aspect of Renaissance civilization, rather than as something running counter to it.

The emphasis I have placed upon social and cultural change, upon the decline of medieval and the rise of modern elements, is in accordance with my conception of the Renaissance as a transitional age. But, as I defined it, the Renaissance was also an age which possessed, aside from the uneasy co-existence within it of medieval and modern characteristics, certain distinctive traits and a high degree of cultural vitality. Here I can do no more than suggest answers to a few of the innumerable questions posed by this latter aspect of the problem. In the first place, whence came the cultural vitality of the Renaissance? Having no time for any but the briefest and most dogmatic of statements, I would say that it was made possible by unprecedented wealth and by the participation of an unprecedented variety of social types. I would say, further, that it drew its positive inspiration from the intellectual excitement caused by the challenge of new conditions of life, of new potentialities in every field of culture, and, in general, of a sense of breaking new ground and of scanning ever-widening horizons. Within the civilization of the Renaissance there were, of course, innumerable cross-currents, inconsistencies, and apparent reactions. These, I think, were the natural results of the conflict, more intense in this age than in any other

since the dawn of Christianity, between inherited traditions and a changing
society. The Renaissance was an age of moral, religious, intellectual and
aesthetic crisis. This has been recognized often enough. What has not
always been so clearly recognized in this connection is that it was also an age
of acute crisis in economic, political and social life.

In the second place, was the Renaissance an age marked to a peculiar
degree by the spirit of individualism? This is a difficult question to answer,
for individualism is a perilously protean concept. It is also more than a
little shop-worn, and it bears the marks of much careless handling. In any
case, I find it difficult to think in terms of *the spirit* of the Renaissance, just
as I find it impossible to envisage *the Renaissance man.* Such a complex and
vital age must have had many spirits, good and bad, though probably few
indifferent. Nevertheless, it does seem to me that there was in this transitional age a growing awareness of personality and a keener sense of individual autonomy than had been possible in the social and cultural conditions
of the Middle Ages; and it may be that this trait was more strongly marked,
more aggressive, in the Renaissance than in later ages, when the individual's
right to self-determination was more easily taken for granted. To individualism, thus defined, many factors contributed, in addition to those mentioned
by Burckhardt; for there were more changes in the heaven and earth of
Renaissance men than were dreamed of in Burckhardt's philosophy—for
example, the growth of a lay piety that stressed the individual man's direct
communion with God, and, at the other end of the moral spectrum, the
development of a capitalist spirit that stressed the individual man's direct
communion with Mammon. With the dislocation of European society that
accompanied the breaking up of medieval institutions, men were left more
dependent than before upon their own personal qualities, while the increasing
complexity of social organization opened up a wider choice of careers, and
more varied opportunities for the development of personal tastes and interests.

Finally, what is the rôle in the Renaissance of the revival of antiquity?
That I have left discussion of the classical revival to the last does not mean
that I regard it as unimportant. Rather the reverse. But I do think that its
causative force, great though it was, was of a secondary character; that, indeed,
the enthusiasm with which classical literature and learning were seized upon
was itself caused by antecedent changes in the social structure, which became
effective first in Italy, and later in the North. That men should love the
classics, once exposed to them, has always seemed to classicists an obvious
fact needing no explanation. Yet I think that the intense, almost excessive
enthusiasm for classical culture, which was peculiar to the Renaissance, can
be explained only by the fact that it was perfectly designed to meet the
needs of educated, urban laymen, of a society that had ceased to be predominantly either feudal or ecclesiastical, yet had in its own immediate past
nothing to draw upon for inspiration but the feudal and ecclesiastical traditions of the Middle Ages. I am not forgetting that the twelfth century also
had its clerical humanists, notably John of Salisbury, but their humanism was
of a different sort, and between them and Petrarch fell the shadow of schol-

asticism. The humanism of the Renaissance was not a clerical humanism, though there were clerical humanists—and it was certainly not feudal. It cut across the most characteristic of medieval traditions. When the mania for antiquity had passed its peak, and the writers of the sixteenth century were laying the foundations for the modern national literatures, they wrote not for one class only but for all cultured people.

Without minimizing the importance of the revival of antiquity, it is also worth noting that, even where the classics exerted no direct influence, as in music, the Renaissance broke new ground, and exhibited enormous vitality. This was the age that witnessed the greatest strides in the development of polyphony and the work of a long line of brillant composers, from Machaut to Palestrina. Here, as in so many other aspects of Renaissance culture, the increasing participation of laymen, and the growth of lay patronage, was accompanied by the development of new forms and by the introduction of a larger proportion of secular content and tone. Music in the Renaissance was a social art, and a fair mastery of its techniques was an essential qualification for the successful courtier or indeed for any cultured person. Any account of sixteenth century social life leaves the impression that wherever two or three were gathered together they sang four or five part polyphony. I make no apology for thus ending my discussion of the Renaissance on a musical note. That any synthesis should leave an adequate place for music is, indeed, a point that I wish to emphasize; for it is one of the peculiarities of the traditional schools of *Kulturgeschichte* that, while giving full consideration to all the pictorial arts, they have scarcely afforded a passing word for music, the most closely related of all the arts to the life of the people.

In conclusion, may I disclaim any pretension to having solved all the problems of the Renaissance. The interpretation I have suggested is no more than a frame-work, within which there is room for much variation in treating the individual aspects of Renaissance civilization. Yet I feel that to approach the problems presented by the history of intellectual and aesthetic disciplines, of morality and religion, as well as of economic, political and social institutions from the point of view I have suggested will lead to a clearer understanding of the relation of each of these to the others and to the main currents of historical development. There is implied in this point of view a theory of historical interpretation, but not historical determinism. I would maintain, for example, that the growth of a wealthy urban society might well be regarded as a necessary conditioning factor in the development of Quattrocento art, whereas I find it difficult to see how the development of the art of the Quattrocentro could have been a necessary conditioning factor in the growth of a wealthy urban society. Yet, I also see no reason to believe that such a society must necessarily have produced Donatello or Ghirlandajo. To say that things happened thus does not imply that they could not have happened otherwise. In seeking to discover the causes of cultural phenomena, the historian must often be content with permissive or partially effective causes. He may be able to assert with some confidence what made a specific development possible, or even what determined its general direction, and what were the boundaries beyond which it could not go.   But within that framework, he must always leave room for the unpredictable activity of the human spirit.   He may be able to explain why the achievements of Michelangelo or Machiavelli, of Josquin des Prez or Erasmus were possible and why they would have been impossible a hundred years earlier or later, but what in these men was peculiar and personal eludes him.   Realization of the fact that he cannot hope to explain everything fully, that history is not an exact science, should not, however, cause the historian to lose confidence in his craft or cease his endeavor to understand what can be understood.   The historian's reach must exceed his grasp, or what's the study of history for?

TOWARD THE MODERN STATE*

In this second symposium, as in the first, we are gathered together to discuss a crucial period in the history of western civilization. Broadly interpreted, the Age of Diocletian marked a decisive stage in the transition from the classical, the Greco-Roman, civilization of the ancient Roman Empire to the Christian-Germanic civilization of the early Middle Ages. Similarly interpreted, the age of the Renaissance marked the transition from the fully developed civilization of the Middle Ages to the modern world. In planning these symposia, the directors of the Metropolitan Museum have followed, whether consciously or not, a notable precedent. Nearly a hundred years ago, that great pioneer in the field of cultural history, Jacob Burckhardt, chose these two periods for his most significant historical works. In the first of these, *The Age of Constantine the Great,* published in 1852, his aim, as expressed in the preface, was "to portray the half century from the rise of Diocletian to the death of Constantine in its peculiar character as an age of transition." In the second, *The Civilization of the Renaissance in Italy,* published in 1860, he strove to analyze the spirit of Italian culture in the age which he considered to be the birth hour of the modern world. And in both works Burckhardt undertook, as we shall undertake in these discussions, a topical treatment of the various aspects of the civilization in question, beginning with the political background.

The introduction of Burckhardt's name at this point is not entirely irrelevant, nor is it inspired solely by the piety that would have us praise famous men and our fathers that begat us. It is, in fact, difficult to discuss the interpretation of the Renaissance without mentioning Burckhardt. Wherever two or three Renaissance scholars are gathered together his name keeps cropping up in the conversation—like King Charles's head. For Burckhardt was not only a great Renaissance historian; he was also, in a sense, the creator of the Renaissance considered as a period in the history of European civilization. And almost all the historians of the Renaissance since his time have taken his work as a starting point and have labored to amplify, modify, or reject his interpretation of the age. Thanks to the impression made by his great

*Reprinted from *The Renaissance: A Symposium,* the Metropolitan Museum of Art, New York, 1953.

essay, historians remained for a long time in a happy state of agreement concerning the general character, cultural content, and chronological scope of the Renaissance. When they talked about the Renaissance, however much they might disagree in matters of detail, they were at least talking about the same phenomenon. Their Renaissance was Burckhardt's, even when it was carried across the Alps and naturalized somewhat uneasily in the northern countries. But that idyllic condition no longer exists. In recent years the traditional conception of the Renaissance which Burckhardt crystallized has been modified so drastically and in so many different ways that it has become all things to all men. Some scholars would even deny that it ever existed. That such variety of interpretation was inevitable, and possibly even desirable, Burckhardt himself recognized. In the introduction to *The Civilization of the Renaissance in Italy,* he wrote:

> The intellectual outlines of any cultural period will probably present a different picture to the eye of each beholder; and, moreover, when we are dealing with a civilization which, as the mother of our own, continues to exert its influence upon us, subjective judgments and feelings must constantly intrude themselves upon writer and reader alike. Many are the paths and various their directions, which thread the wide sea on which we venture forth, and it is possible that the same materials which served in the preparation of this work might in other hands not only be subjected to an entirely different treatment and turned to a different purpose, but might also lead to essentially different conclusions.[1]

I may add that this prophetic intuition has been amply borne out by experience. I need not, however, labor further the point that historians have not always interpreted the Renaissance in the same way. It will probably become obvious enough as our symposium proceeds. Nor shall I attempt to outline for you all the conflicting tendencies of interpretation that have characterized Renaissance scholarship during the past half-century.[2] As a German friend once said to me in reply to an innocent question concerning the nature of existentialist philosophy, "That is something you are as well without knowing anything about off." I mention the subject only because, as the introductory speaker in this symposium, I feel that I should warn you not to be surprised if my learned colleagues should prove not to be in entire agreement concerning the character or even the chronological scope of the Renaissance. My own problem, if not altogether simple, is at least relatively uncontroversial. I have been asked to present some aspects of the political background of the Renaissance, and most historians would agree that in this field the development of greatest significance during the period was the emergence of states of a modern type, though not all would agree with the dates I assign to that development, nor with my conception of its causes.

The Renaissance, it seems to me, was, in a peculiar way, an age of transition. Every age is, of course, more or less transitional, since it is the nature of history to be constantly changing. The fleeting present is ever the transi-

---

[1] J. Burckhardt, *Die Cultur der Renaissance in Italien* (Basel, 1860), p. 1.

[2] For review of these see W. K. Ferguson, *The Renaissance in Historical Thought* (Boston, 1948).

tional link through which all our yesterdays flow uninterruptedly into the infinite succession of tomorrow and tomorrow and tomorrow. But there are few periods in the history of western civilization—I would venture to say not more than two, unless our own age should prove to be a third—in which the transition from the preceding to the following age makes so complete a transformation that it may be regarded as a change in kind rather than in degree. Such a change was involved in the transition from medieval to modern civilization. And the Renaissance owes much of its peculiar character, I think, to the uneasy coexistence within it of medieval and modern elements, of decaying or obsolescent institutions and ways of thinking, together with new institutions and ideas still imperfectly formed. For the history of political institutions, the first decisive stage in the transition may be dated from about the beginning of the fourteenth century. The process was virtually complete by the end of the sixteenth century. We have then a period of roughly three hundred years to consider.

Unfortunately, we cannot limit our discussion to those three hundred years, long though that period is and short the time at our disposal. The causes and the character of the changes that took place in the transitional period cannot be made clear without some description of the political institutions of the Middle Ages. Briefly stated, the predominant factor in medieval political life was that muddled complex of personal relations, private jurisdictions, and local particularism known to us as the feudal system. This was a method of organizing government, evolved out of that necessity which is the mother of invention, during the early Middle Ages, at a time when there was little regular commerce, when normal city life had almost disappeared, and when all classes depended for their living largely on the cultivation of the soil, either directly as workers or indirectly as landholders. From this economic situation two facts emerge which have a direct bearing on the formation of feudal government: first, the fact that land represented the only considerable form of wealth and, second, the fact that, since each rural community was to a large extent self-sufficient, there was little need for money as a medium of exchange and hence very little money in circulation. Services of any kind could therefore be paid for, as a rule, only by grants of land; and conversely, rent for the use of land could be paid only by services, whether manual, religious, or military. Allowing for the inconvenient exceptions that partially vitiate any generalization about medieval society, the exchange of land for services obtained from top to bottom of the feudal system, including the manorial organization which was its economic base. And this exchange involved a personal relation between the grantor of the land and the tenant, which on both sides tended to become hereditary. The king was thus forced to grant land in fief to great lords in payment for military service and for the administration of justice and the maintenance of law and order. Lacking the monetary revenue to maintain these essential functions of government, the king could scarcely do otherwise. The lords who thus became his vassals-in-chief in their turn granted parts of their land to vassals of their own on similar terms, and for similar reasons. That, at least, is the feudal theory. In actual practice what probably happened was that landholders of all grades usurped the functions and exercised the authority of government on their own lands because they alone were in a position to do so. And if they held their land in tenure rather than free ownership and did military service for it, they did so because they needed protection, because they felt a vague need for a legal theory to bolster their *de facto* power, and because society could not have been held together in any other way. The result of the process, at any rate, was the decentralization of government and the dismemberment of the state into a host of private jurisdictions. As stated by feudal lawyers, the basic principle of government was that every baron is sovereign in his own barony.

Needless to say, this system implied a severe curtailment of the king's authority and at times, as in tenth and eleventh century France, it came close to destroying his authority entirely. The king was the ultimate feudal lord, the apex of the feudal pyramid, but in practice he could exercise direct authority only over those lords who held their land directly from him. A chain of command ran downward from the king to the smallest *seigneurie,* but the chain was no stronger than its weakest link, and few would bear any great strain. Nevertheless, even in the most chaotic period of feudalism, the king was still the king, that is, he was something more than a suzerain to whom vassals as powerful as himself owed a vague obedience. Some imponderable element of prestige clung to the royal title. There was a kind of divinity that did hedge even a feudal king. He was the Lord's anointed, consecrated at his coronation as was Saul by the prophet Samuel. The monarchy thus survived until a change in the economic situation made possible the re-establishment of effective central government.

Signs of the economic change that would eventually produce that result began to appear in the eleventh century, or as Mr. Lopez would argue,[3] as early as the tenth century. Commerce began to revive in Western Europe and introduced a new era of expanding prosperity. Throughout the twelfth and thirteenth centuries inter-regional trade grew steadily in volume; old cities came back to life and new cities were founded; a growing urban population of merchants and skilled craftsmen exchanged goods with the surrounding countryside; and money began to circulate more and more freely as buying and selling gradually replaced barter, and rents and wages began to take the place of tenures and labour services. Kings began to enjoy larger revenues and used the power of money to expand the scope of their government. But the feudal system did not wither away in proportion as the conditions which had made it necessary disappeared. The independence and the private jurisdictions which the landholding class had acquired during the early feudal period were now sanctioned by generations of custom and precedent. They were sanctioned still further by the universal prevalence of feudal ways of thinking from which even kings were not immune. Medieval men thought of government in terms of feudal relations as naturally as we think of it in terms of democracy and citizenship. Moreover, the king's ability to increase his revenue was strictly limited by the nature of the feudal

---

[3]R. Lopez, "Still another Renaissance," *American Historical Review* LVII (1951), 1-21.

contract between himself and his vassals, the form of which had been fixed at a time when money was unavailable. The king's vassals owed him military service and certain occasional aids, but no regular taxes; and the king could not go over their heads to tax their dependents without infringing upon their sovereign rights in their own fiefs.

There was a limit, then, to the extent to which the central government of the state could augment either its revenue or its effective authority within the framework of the feudal system. And by the end of the thirteenth century that limit had been reached in both France and England and to a lesser extent in the other kingdoms and principalities of Western Europe. Any further development of royal power would necessitate a breach with the fundamental concepts of feudal government, and further development was inevitable. The change to a money economy from an economy founded on land and services strengthened the monarchy while it weakened the nobility, and that change was destined to continue with increasing rapidity. Loosely organized though it seemed to be, the feudal system possessed a certain tough vitality that enabled it to absorb the alien economic force of money for more than two centuries without apparently fatal results, but by the end of the thirteenth century it had reached the saturation point. From that time on, the economic foundations on which feudalism rested were in the last stages of distintegration and the structure reared upon them could not long endure.

The general tendencies which were common to all Western European countries were, of course, modified and conditioned by the particular political circumstances prevailing in each state. Only in France and England did the feudal state evolve directly into national monarchy. In Germany the imperial government had been permanently wrecked in the thirteenth century as a result of the emperor's commitments in Italy and the long struggle with the papacy. The tendency toward the centralization of government operated there only within the smaller area of the territorial states which had been the great feudal fiefs of the medieval Empire. In the Low Countries a group of counties and duchies, fiefs either of France or the Empire, were in the fourteenth and fifteenth centuries welded together to form a rich and strongly governed state under the Dukes of Burgundy. Spain did not exist as a national state until near the end of the fifteenth century, when Ferdinand of Aragon and Isabella of Castile united their states by marriage and expanded them by the conquest of Navarre and Granada. In central and northern Italy a unique situation had led to the decline of feudalism at an unusually early date. It had been replaced, however, not by strong central government but by a host of independent urban communes, turbulent little city-states, the wealthiest of which expanded by conquest to form territorial states of a quite unmedieval sort. In the time at our disposal we cannot hope to trace the evolution of all the European states. I propose, then, with your permission, to concentrate attention on the two most distinct types: first, France and England, the feudal kingdoms which evolved into national monarchies, and, second, Milan, Venice, and Florence, the medieval communes which evolved into territorial states.

The process by which the kings of France and England recovered the governmental functions that had been parcelled out among the landholding lords and the self-governing commmunes operated especially in the four more or less distinct spheres of the administration of justice, military organization, economic regulation, and the collection of taxes. Of these the last was of the most all-pervasive importance. Without some revenue the kings of the twelfth and thirteenth centuries could not have begun the task of expanding the scope of royal justice and of organizing an army on a national scale; but, having begun, they needed more and more revenue to meet the rising costs of government. In short, the more responsibilities the national governments assumed, the more revenue they had to have, and there seems to be a kind of iron law of fiscality according to which the financial needs of government always grow a step or two in advance of income. It is a problem not unfamiliar in our own age. The financial problems of the fourteenth and fifteenth century governments were also made even more acute than they otherwise might have been by the fact that the technique of warfare was changing in ways that made it increasingly expensive, a situation with which we are also not unfamiliar.

It was in the administration of justice that the kings first succeeded in making serious inroads upon the jurisdiction of the feudal lords. As the supreme feudal lord, the king could claim the right to hear appeals from the courts of his vassals and sub-vassals, and as the consecrated king he had not only the right but the duty to see that justice was done to all within his kingdom. The practical problem was to build up a royal government strong enough to enforce these claims, and this was a very gradual process, involving among other things the acquisition of increasing revenues. But the actual administration of justice placed no particular financial strain on the government, since the courts paid their way by levying fines and fees. In England, where the Norman conquest had introduced a more centralized form of feudalism than that prevailing on the continent, royal justice spread rapidly in the twelfth century. Under Henry II the system of sending out travelling justices from the king's court spread a uniform royal law, the common law of the land. At the end of the thirteenth century Edward I, the English Justinian, codified the common law in the form of statutes, and virtually completed the absorption into the royal courts of all important criminal and civil cases. What remained of feudal jurisdiction was taken over in the following centuries by the justices of the peace, local gentry appointed by the crown, who served without pay but on the whole with admirable loyalty to the state.

In France, where feudalism was much more fully developed—that is, more decentralized—the triumph of royal justice was later and less complete. The French kings of the twelfth century had little jurisdiction beyond their own domain lands, a small area around Paris. During the following centuries, however, they expanded the domain to include one great fief after another and thus expanded the scope of their jurisdiction until it included the whole of the kingdom. But, even within the domain, feudal and seigneurial courts still existed and were never completely destroyed until the French Revolution. Nevertheless the king's justice spread steadily through his assertion of his right to hear appeals from the courts of his vassals and sub-vassals. In practice this process was carried out chiefly by a host of administrative officials, who were paid by receiving a portion of the fees and fines levied in the royal courts and so were eager to enlarge the business of these courts by extending royal jurisdiction as far as possible. These were the termites who nibbled away the foundations of feudal jurisdiction and carried on a ceaseless war of attrition against both seigneurial and communal courts. By the sixteenth century, in France as well as in England, one of the most essential functions of government had been recovered by the national state from the landholding lords who had usurped it in the early Middle Ages.

Along with the administration of justice and the maintenance of law and order, an equally important function of government is the defense of the state against the attacks of enemies from without or rebellion from within; and we can scarcely conceive of a state in which the central government does not assume full responsibility for the organization, equipment, and pay of the country's armed forces. Nor can we easily envisage a state in which all able-bodied citizens are not liable for military service. Yet in the early feudal state the king neither paid nor equipped an army, and he could do little to shape or control its organization. All he could do was call upon his vassals-in-chief to do the military service they owed—forty days, or so, a year—accompanied by such of their vassals as they could force to abandon their private feuds for a few weeks to serve the state. For all practical purposes, only the nobles were liable for military service, and they made up the only effective branch of the army, the heavy cavalry composed of armored knights. Most of the people in the early feudal period were serfs and hence not expected to fight. In a national emergency the king could call upon burghers and other freemen to serve as infantry, but these militia forces were poorly armed and poorly trained. Altogether, feudal armies were generally small, unreliable, undisciplined, and unmanageable on the field of battle. They were fit only for the local warfare that was the normal state of feudal society. For war on a national scale they were totally inadequate.

With increasing revenue, the kings of the twelfth and thirteenth centuries made some improvement in this situation by hiring foreign mercenaries and by paying a small permanent force, as well as by offering partial pay to vassals or commons who served beyond the customary time. The first decisive step toward the formation of a really national army did not, however, come until the last years of the thirteenth century, and then only in England. It was Edward I who reorganized the English army for his long campaigns in Wales and Scotland, and it was with this new type of royal army that his grandson, Edward III, later invaded France, where it demonstrated its decisive superiority over French armies that were still largely feudal in form and imbued with the undisciplined spirit of feudal chivalry.

Regular payment of wages on a graduated scale was an essential part of the new military organization. This made it possible to hold the army together for long campaigns. It also made possible the organization of the army into companies under royal officers who could impose discipline. Without pay, too, it would have been difficult if not impossible for many knights to bear the rapidly rising cost of armour, in this period when heavy plate was beginning to replace the simpler chain mail of the crusading era. Fully equipped knights were, of course, expensive, and the king of a relatively poor country like England could not afford many of them. Edward I probably had no more than 500 to 1000 knights for any of his campaigns, and his grandson's cavalry force at Crécy probably consisted of no more than 1200 knights and perhaps twice as many mounted sergeants. What made the English armies of this period so formidable was the fact that the small but well equipped and trained cavalry force was supported by a much larger force of equally well trained and disciplined infantry, who were armed, moreover, with the first really effective missile weapon known to the Middle Ages, the deadly longbow. This weapon, the use of which the English had learned the hard way from their troublesome Welsh neighbours, was greatly superior to the ancient short bow, which was all that Locksley's grandsire could possibly have drawn at Hastings. It was also far superior in both range and rapidity of fire to the crossbow commonly used by continental archers. It had a range of something up to 300 yards, and a skilled archer could loose ten or twelve shafts a minute. It was, however, a weapon that could be used effectively only after years of practice. It would not have spread terror through France for more than a hundred years had not the English archers been picked men, carefully selected by royal officers from the growing class of free yeomen farmers, who had made archery their national sport and who, since the days of Edward I, had formed a permanent militia reserve on which the king could draw at will.

With all due respect to the longbow and the skill of the English yeomen, however, there was a more fundamental reason for the consistent victories of the English army over much larger French forces during the greatest part of the Hundred Years' War. It was the balanced combination of cavalry and infantry tactics that destroyed the chivalry of France on the fields of Crécy and Poitiers. And tactics of any kind were possible only in a permanently organized and disciplined army. The Englishmen who fought from Crécy to Agincourt were professional soldiers who had taken the king's shilling and learned to obey commands. The French army, it is true, was also paid by the king and commanded by royal officers. The growing cost of armour, together with the general impoverishment of the nobility from economic and social causes too complex to discuss here, had made it necessary to pay even the king's noble vassals. The cost of warfare was, indeed, placing a crushing burden on the financial resources of the French government. But neither the French nobles nor the king could escape from the prejudices and traditional *mores* of feudalism sufficiently to adjust themselves to the new type of warfare. In the early days of the war the French army was not organized in uniform companies on a permanent basis. It was simply a paid feudal array, and the heavy cavalry was still regarded as the only important arm. At Crécy no use was made of the infantry, except for a few hundred mercenary Genoese crossbowmen, whom the French knights rode down when they got in the way. With no thought of tactics, and at Crécy against the express orders of the king, the French knights charged in massed formation again and again, only to be cut down in thousands by the hail of cloth-yard arrows from the English bowmen. In the years following Poitiers, Charles V abandoned the feudal levy and put the French army on something like a professional basis. He enrolled companies of native men-at-arms, as well as foreign mercenaries, and placed them under the command of Bertrand du Guesclin, a hardened old campaigner of relatively humble birth. It was not a very satisfactory system, for the mercenary companies were almost as destructive to French life and property as were the English enemy, but it was successful. While avoiding pitched battles, du Guesclin wore the invaders down by constant pressure, and when Charles V died in 1380, the English had lost everything they had gained in the early years of victory. In the long period of truce with England and civil war at home, which lasted through most of the reign of the mad king Charles VI, no further advance was made in the development of a national army. On the contrary, there was a kind of feudal revival, and when Henry V invaded France in 1415 the French commanders seemed to have forgotten the lessons of the previous century. Agincourt was a repetition of Crécy and Poitiers. The tide was finally turned against the English and the war brought to an end only after national sentiment had been rallied by the inspired patriotism of Joan of Arc, and Charles VII had organized a national army on a permanent basis, adequately paid and maintained by the state.

I have dealt at some length with the changes in military technique and organization because of the decisive part they played in shifting the balance of power within the state from the feudal nobility to the national monarchy. Let me underline some of the implications of this and add a point or two. Obviously, the substitution of a royal army for the more or less voluntary service of noble vassals was a triumph for the monarchy and a blow to both the prestige and the real power of the feudal lords. Obviously, too, the emergence of the infantry as an effective branch of the army was a blow to the nobles' monopoly of military force, on which their political power and independence had long rested securely. But there was more than this involved in the change. Infantry were effective only if well trained and well equipped and when used in fairly large bodies. That meant a permanent, paid force, which only a government supported by state taxation could afford. The introduction of firearms during the fifteenth century added further to the cost of maintaining infantry, and, incidentally, forced the knights to adopt heavier and heavier armour until it became a crushing burden in both the physical and financial sense. Finally, the development of artillery, chiefly as siege weapons, gave to state governments, which alone could afford such expensive pieces, the means by which to batter down the castles of rebellious nobles. Warfare, in short, was becoming a big business, too expensive to be indulged in as a private sport, as it had been in the feudal age. The wars of the sixteenth century were mostly international wars, fought by state governments, even when the motives might be religious or dynastic rather than national.

I need not, I think, labour further the point that as the central governments assumed more and more responsibilities they also required greatly increased revenues. The royal governments of this transitional period existed in a state of perpetual financial crisis. I cannot attempt to describe the various forms of taxation introduced in this period of fiscal experimentation by royal ministers who were prepared in their desperate need to try almost anything at least once. I would like, however, to point out briefly some of the ways in which the imposition of non-feudal taxes affected the evolution of national government.

In the first place, the central government could tax the great majority of the population only by going over the heads of the king's vassals to collect taxes directly from their dependents. This meant a vital infringement upon the private jurisdictions of the feudal lords, especially in France, where the royal government had less direct authority than in Norman England. It introduced the king's agents into every fief and *seigneurie*. And it established the direct contact between the king and the great mass of his subjects that was essential to the growth of a strong centralized state. So alien was state taxation to the ways of thinking of feudal society, however, that it could be introduced only as an extraordinary measure to meet some special emergency; and long after such emergencies had become normal annual occurrences, the subsidies the king demanded were still represented as extraordinary aids to the crown for the defense of the realm. For the same reasons, the kings in this transitional period found it advisable to negotiate with their subjects and to present their demands for taxes under the polite fiction that they were requests to which they asked the consent of clergy, nobles, and commons.

A second result of the king's growing need for taxes, then, was the development of representative institutions on a national scale: the English Parliament and the French Estates General. These institutions were an expansion of the king's feudal council by the addition of elected representatives of the non-noble bourgeoisie and, in England, of the landholding gentry also, who were empowered to give consent that would be binding upon the classes they represented. This, it is true, was not the only reason why kings of the fourteenth century chose to summon representatives of the non-noble property-owning classes to their council. It was an important step in the process of establishing direct contact between the royal government and the people, or such of them at least as were economically, and therefore politically, important. But the problem of consent to taxation was always a primary consideration.

In France a fatal division of interest between the first two estates, the clergy and the nobles, both of which were composed largely of noble landowners, and the third estate, which represented the commercial bourgeoisie, prevented the Estates General from maintaining the advantage they had won in the fourteenth century. By the fifteenth century the French kings found it possible to levy direct taxes without consulting the Estates, and thereafter ceased to summon them with any regularity. The Estates, then, had simply enabled the monarchy to bridge the gulf between feudalism and absolutism.

Having served the king's purpose, they ceased to exist. In England, on the other hand, where landholding gentlemen who shared the economic and social interests of the lords sat with representatives of the bourgeoisie in the House of Commons, Parliament was a more united and more genuinely representative body than the French Estates, and the kings were never able to ignore it with impunity. It would be sheer anachronism to think of Parliament in the first three centuries of its existence as a democratic body directing the affairs of the state. The most significant development of these centuries was the growth of the monarchy as an effective central government, which culminated in the semi-absolutism of the Tudors. Nevertheless, in the crowded chapter house at Westminster, seeds of representative government were planted that would eventually bear fruit throughout the English-speaking world.

One final by-product of the perpetual concern of royal government with the problem of revenue deserves mention, for it had an importance out of all proportion to the fiscal needs that inspired it. It was in these centuries that the central government gradually concentrated in its own hands the regulation of commerce and industry and shaped the national economic policy generally known as mercantilism. This development, too, had other causes than the king's need for taxes. It was, indeed, almost inevitable that as royal government grew stronger it would encroach upon the autonomy of the towns and cities which, in the feudal age, had been left almost entirely free to regulate their own economic life. Mercantilism was in many ways no more than the transference of the strict regulation of trade and the exclusive protectionism practised by the medieval cities to the larger area of the state. Still, it was the fact that commerce and industry produced wealth in readily taxable form that first attracted the solicitous attention of money-hungry monarchs. Even when tariffs and other regulations were ostensibly designed to promote the general prosperity of the commonwealth, the royal government was primarily interested in the resulting revenue. Edward I and his successors would have been less interested in regulating and promoting the wool trade if the export tax on wool had not formed so large a part of the royal income.

With the assumption of economic control by the central government, the triumph of the state over the local authorities that had dominated life in the Middle Ages was virtually complete. Thereafter the form of government might change, either by gradual evolution, as in England, or by revolution, as in most other European countries, but the state would remain the essential unit for the organization of modern society.

When we turn from the national states of the North to Italy, we find a very different situation; yet there, too, the Renaissance witnessed the development of a system of territorial states, though these were less than national in scope and they grew, not by the centralization of feudalism, but rather by the transformation and expansion of urban communes. The states of Renaissance Italy were necessarily different from those of the North, because the past history of Italy was so different, and that difference was partly the result of two purely political facts: first, the fact that from the tenth to the thirteenth century Italy was annexed to the German Holy Roman Empire, and, second, the fact that the popes ruled a territorial state stretching right across the center of the peninsula. Both emperor and pope claimed universal authority, and the inevitable conflict between them furnished the central theme of medieval Italian history, filling the land with sound and fury, but in the end signifying very little. The combined effect of the imperial *Anchluss* and the temporal sovereignty of the popes was to make the evolution of a national state in Italy impossible. That, however, is only half the story and perhaps not the most important half. It was a purely economic fact—the extraordinarily early and vigorous development of Italian commerce, a commerce built on the exchange of goods between the eastern Mediterranean and the lands of Western Europe—that was responsible for the growth of rich and populous cities in the tenth and eleventh centuries. And it was the cities which, in the last analysis, were the decisive factor in the political life of central and northern Italy. They were the primary cause for the early decline of Italian feudalism, for as the cities grew in wealth and power the nobles were drawn into them as though by a golden magnet. And they were the real victors in the struggle between the Empire and the Papacy, for by playing off one against the other and exploiting the weakness of both, the cities were able to win for themselves a practically complete autonomy. When imperial power in Italy was permanently broken in the second half of the thirteenth century, and when the papacy was transferred to Avignon at the beginning of the fourteenth century, the political void was filled by dozens of quarrel· some little city-states, each ruling the land around it and each pressing against its neighbours for more land to feed its people or for the control of essential trade routes.

Originally, these little city-states were self-governing communes with a republican form of government. This was a common medieval phenomenon. Except for the degree of their independence and the fact that they ruled the land around them, they were not very different in actual form of government from communes elsewhere in Europe. But just at the beginning of the Renaissance a vitally significant transformation was taking place in the majority of the communes, as republican government collapsed and was replaced by the rule of despots, or, to use the less prejudiced Italian term, of *signori*. This change, which marks the first clear break between the medieval commune and the Renaissance state, is the outstanding fact in the political history of Italy in the fourteenth century, as many historians have recognized by calling this period the Age of the Despots. As we shall see presently, the foundation of the despots' power was not quite as illegitimate as Burckhardt and Symonds make it appear. Yet it is true that they ruled largely because they were able to do so, which argues a certain force of character and a considerable endowment of cunning, if not a high order of intelligence. On the whole, the despots were colorful characters, patrons of art and letters and much given to original sins, and they furnished inspiring material for those Romantic historians who like to think of the Renaissance as a wicked age, in which art and vice attained an equal degree of aesthetic refinement.

Once despotic government was established in a city, a new despot might take over by inheritance, conspiracy, conquest, or simply by purchasing it from the current incumbent. The questions of prime interest to the historians, however, are why did republican government fail, and how were the despots able, in the first place, to acquire dictatorial power? It is a question certainly not without interest in the twentieth century. A number of factors enter into this extremely complicated problem. The bitter animosity of the Guelf and Ghibelline parties inherited from the days when pope and emperor had partisans in every city, family feuds that grew into factional struggles, the danger of conquest by neighboring states, the action of strong personalities, all these contributed to the disintegration of the republics. But it seems to me that the fundamental factor was the division of the city population into distinct economic and social classes with divergent interests, which they were unwilling to sacrifice for the common good. As a rule, the *signori* first gained power in those cities in which the various classes were most evenly balanced, so that it proved impossible to maintain stable government, and the citizens, having lost faith in republican government and having grown weary of perpetual civil strife, permitted some strong man to assume control of the state.

This situation seems to have been particularly prevalent in the inland communes of Lombardy, of which Milan is the most famous example. Here a wealthy upper class had gained control of the city government in the period when the communes were struggling for independence. They had earned their right to power by bearing a large part of the cost of war and by serving as cavalry in the communal militia. This class was composed partly of old merchant families and partly of nobles who had moved into the city. By the thirteenth century they had mingled to form a purely urban aristocracy, which monopolized the government offices and dictated the city's policies. Meanwhile, as a result of the expansion of commerce and the growth of capitalist forms of business enterprise, new families were rising to wealth. There were thus two wealthy classes: the old and the new rich, the former clinging to political power and living more and more on inherited wealth and investments in land, the latter aggressively active in commerce and equally aggressive in demanding the share in political power to which their wealth entitled them. United, these two classes might have dominated the government securely. Divided, they opened the road to popular revolution, as the growing class of small shopkeepers and skilled artisans organized to fight for the political power that would enable them to protect their interests against the rich.

From this insoluble conflict of classes, complicated always by party and factional strife, the rule of one man emerged at first as a temporary measure. In one city after another the upper classes agreed to invite some distinguished foreigner to come in as a *podestà,* to take over the government for a one-year term and to impose peace on the troubled city. In many places, too, a popular revolution gave a similar temporary dictatorship to the leader of the popular party, the *capitano del popolo,* to whom the victorious *popolani* gave unlimited power so that he might wreak vengeance on their enemies. These offices were never intended to be held permanently, but once the citizens had surrendered the government to one man, it was difficult to recover it. The capacity for self-government tends to atrophy unless constantly exercised. Sooner or later, the offices of *podestà* or *capitano del popolo* would become hereditary. At some point in this process the original title of office would be allowed to lapse and the dictator would be proclaimed *signore,* that is, lord of the city, and he would be invested with full and unlimited powers of government by the formal vote of the Great Council or some other body representing the citizens. How free such popular actions may have been we need scarcely question, nor does there seem much point in wondering what would have happened to any hardy citizen who voted against the *signore.* But the fact remains that he ruled by the consent, even if it was only the passive consent, of the people. Once established, the *signori,* scorning the base ascents by which they climbed, proceeded to obliterate as rapidly as possible all traces of the popular origin of their office. They secured a new legal sanction by purchasing the title of vicar from the emperor or the pope. Then, as the richer and more enterprising of them conquered other cities and built up a territorial state, they purchased the more resounding titles of marquis or duke from their territorial overlords. They were now princes, with all the semblance of legitimate sovereignty and the undisputed authority of absolute monarchs. Such were the Visconti and Sforza Dukes of Milan, the Estensi Dukes of Ferrara, and the Gonzaga Marquises of Mantua, and a score of petty princelings in the papal states.

So much for the question of why republican government failed in so many Italian communes. Despotism was the logical successor to a democracy that was not democratic and to a republic that had committed suicide. But the republics did not all collapse, nor did all Italians put their trust in princes. Our picture of the Italian states would be incomplete without some account of those republics that survived, especially Venice and Florence, the republics that grew into large territorial states.

Of all the Italian republics, Venice was the most stable, the most strongly organized, but also the least democratic. Venice was a commercial city in a sense that was scarcely true anywhere else. Having no land, it lived by commerce, and from the beginning its commerce was monopolized by a group of merchant families who formed the city's aristocracy. To protect their commercial monopoly, these patrician families established a water-tight monopoly of political power and opposed a united front against all demands by the mass of the populace for a voice in the government. In 1297, the Great Council was closed to all but the descendants of the families then in power. And, since the Venetian fleets were owned and controlled by the state, only members of the governing families were able to trade, so that no new families arose to threaten their power. Venice remained a republic, but a republic ruled by an oligarchy as arbitrary as any single despot.

The political history of Florence is much more complicated, partly because her economy was more complex and still in process of evolution in the thirteenth and fourteenth centuries, but partly also because the Florentine citizens seems to have combined with their unusual intellectual and aesthetic interests a passion for politics. At times, indeed, they demonstrated an ingenuity in the construction of involved political institutions that fell just short of lunacy.

Florence was a commercial city, but it was not a seaport, and its great economic expansion in the late thirteenth and early fourteenth centuries resulted from a combination of commerce with banking and large export industries, of which the woolen cloth industry was by far the most important and employed about a third of the city's ninety thousand population. This adventurous and many-sided capitalist economy afforded unusual opportunities for the creation of new fortunes, and as a result the composition of the class of wealthy merchant bankers and industrialists who generally succeeded in dominating the city's politics was constantly changing. New families rose to wealth, while old families went bankrupt or invested their inherited wealth in land and rents, or simply frittered it away. In the last years of the thirteenth century the new rich combined with the middle class of guildsmen to disenfranchise the old aristocracy and set up a government controlled by the merchant guilds, with a minor share allotted to the lesser guilds of shopkeepers and artisans. The great mass of proletarian workers in the woolen industry, who were not permitted to organize in guilds, were excluded entirely from active citizenship. One of the chief reasons why the merchant employers in the great wool guilds felt it necessary to control the government was to keep these restless workers in subjection. The middle class of small guildsmen also feared the violence of the woolworkers who crowded the slums of the city, and so they generally followed the lead of the merchant industrialists. For a time in the middle of the fourteenth century, when the merchant class was weakened by depression and a series of bank failures, the lesser guilds gained a larger share in the government, but even then its policy was generally dictated by the merchant oligarchy.

The fact that executive power in the republican government was vested in a committee of priors, elected afresh every two months, made it almost inevitable that some extra-constitutional group should direct policy and give it some continuity. As a result, the vicissitudes of Florentine politics were caused more by changes in the composition of the ruling clique than in the republican constitution itself. When in 1434 a group of new families headed by the banker Cosimo de Medici, took control from a clique of older families led by the Albizzi, there was no revolutionary change in the constitution. To quote Schevill, "the new government was the old government operated by a different set of beneficiaries."[4] Under four generations of Medici leadership the republic still maintained the semblance of democracy, though the sham became increasingly apparent, while the Medici directed affairs without holding actual public office, much after the manner of a modern municipal boss. It was in foreign policy especially, where continuity was absolutely essential, that the Medici made themselves indispensable. They were not *signori* in the ordinary sense of the word, but they took their place as equals among the princes of Italy.

---

[4]F. Schevill, *History of Florence* (New York, 1936), 355.

Foreign policy was becoming a matter of increasing importance to every Italian state in the fifteenth century, for by the beginning of that century the whole political structure of Italy had changed radically and was still changing. During the fourteenth century most of the petty despotisms of northern Italy had disappeared, swallowed up by the more powerful lordships of Padua, Verona or Milan. At the end of the century nearly all of Lombardy, as well as a large part of Tuscany, had been drawn into the expanding state of Giangaleazzo Visconti, Duke of Milan. When he died in 1402 his personally acquired state broke up, but it had lasted long enough to alarm Venice by the fear that a large state in Lombardy might cut off her food supply and her trade routes to the Alpine passes. The merchant republic therefore embarked on a policy of landward expansion and proceeded to seize a large part of eastern Lombardy. Florence, too, took advantage of the temporary collapse of Visconti power to conquer all of Tuscany except Siena and Lucca. Nearly half a century of warfare finally ended with the Peace of Lodi in 1454, by which time all of Italy north of the papal states was divided between Venice, Milan, and Florence, with three or four small states maintaining a precarious existence between them. For the next forty years, until the arrival of the French invaders under Charles VIII, these states, together with the Papal States and the Kingdom of Naples, kept a fair degree of peace by carefully maintaining the balance of power. It is, I think, the first example of consciously calculated balance-of-power politics in the history of modern Europe.

My time is nearly up, but I should like to say something about the interrelated problems of military force and revenue in the Italian states, as I did in relation to France and England, for it is the secret of much of their strength and their weakness. The Italian states of the Renaissance had no such difficulty with the introduction of a system of regular taxation as did the feudal kingdoms. The medieval communes had grown up with a money economy, and the citizens were accustomed to taxation as a normal instrument of political life. The oligarchical republics like Venice and Florence had only to rationalize and refine older customs. As for the despots, they took over going concerns and had only to use reasonable discretion to operate them at a profit. The successful despot was necessarily a good businessman, with a sharp eye on income, for in the Renaissance states money was the indispensable source of power. The citizens still paid taxes, but they no longer served in the armed forces of the state, as they had done in the heroic age of the communes. Instead, the states of the fourteenth and fifteenth centuries depended for military force entirely on hired mercenaries, homeless soldiers of fortune from every country in Western Europe. The *condottieri*, who commanded these mercenaries and sold their services to the highest bidder, were essentially capitalist entrepreneurs. They conducted war as a business, for a profit. They fought only for pay, and the pay was high. From this situation two things followed: first, that whoever controlled the treasury of the state, whether despot or oligarchy, also controlled the state's only armed force, before which the citizens were helpless; and, second, that small and poor states could not compete with larger and richer states which could hire more soldiers. The conquest of the poorer states by the richer was an inevitable result, as was demonstrated by the expansion of Venice, Milan, and Florence. At the same time, any mercenary army these states could afford was inadequate protection against the national armies of France and Spain. The invasion and subjection of Italy in the sixteenth century resulted not only from the inability of the Italians to unite against the foreigner, but also in large part from the fact that the Italian people had long since left the business of warfare to mercenaries and had lost the art of self-defence.

There are a good many more things I should like to say about the transition from the medieval to the modern state, if time permitted. I have said little or nothing about the sixteenth century; but that, I feel, is justified by the relatively greater genetic importance of the earlier and more formative period. The most essential steps in the transition took place during the fourteenth and fifteenth centuries. The sixteenth century simply completed the process, consolidated the authority already won by the central governments, established a state system in Western Europe based on the balance of power, and raised to a more conscious level the national sentiment bred in the conflicts of the preceding centuries. The feudal concept of the state as a complex of personal relations finally gave away in the North, as it had already done in Italy, to the concept of the state as a single political entity. In the sixteenth century, when every prince read Machiavelli or acted as though he had done so, when international wars and diplomacy held the center of the European stage, and when all men looked more and more to the government of the state for the regulation of their economic and social life, in that century the modern state came of age. This was the century in which national literatures finally triumphed over the Latin culture common to all Christendom. Even religion assumed a national character and fell to a certain extent under the control of the state. The Protestant Reformation destroyed the unity of the Christian faith and replaced it with national churches organized under the authority of the state. Where the old church survived it was forced to compromise and to share its authority with the state. In the sixteenth century feudal particularism and the universal Christian commonwealth both disappeared, leaving in their place the national state to form the matrix in which modern civilization would be cast.

THE CHURCH IN A CHANGING WORLD: A CONTRIBUTION TO THE INTERPRETATION OF THE RENAISSANCE*

The historical interpretation of that phase in the development of European civilization represented by the fourteenth, fifteenth, and sixteenth centuries poses a problem that has aroused much interest and no little controversy among scholars in the ninety-odd years since Burckhardt first treated these centuries as a period in the history of Italian civilization and labeled it the Renaissance. Since then, scholars who did not share Burckhardt's preconceptions, or who were interested primarily in other countries or in some particular aspect of culture, have presented widely divergent views of the spirit, content, and chronological limits of the Renaissance,[1] with the result that the value of the concept for purposes of periodization has been greatly vitiated. Much of the confusion concerning the Renaissance arises, I think, from the fact that it has been used indiscriminately as a style concept or to denote an intellectual movement, and that, when considered as a historical period, it has commonly been regarded from the point of view of one country or one particular cultural or religious interest, so that its interpretation has been constructed upon too narrow a foundation. It seems to me that, if we consider the economic, social, and political, as well as the intellectual, aesthetic, and religious life of the centuries from 1300 to 1600, we shall find a certain unity of development in all the countries of Western Europe. It seems to me, too, that, if the various aspects of their civilization are related to one another in a reasonably well co-ordinated synthesis, these three centuries may be treated as a period in the history of Western European civilization as a whole, and that such a periodic concept may have sufficient validity to serve as a useful, if not indispensable, instrument of historical thought. For this period the term Renaissance may not be well chosen, but it is still the only commonly accepted term we have for a crucially important historical period, and one

---

*Read at the Renaissance Conference of the Middle Eastern States held at the University of Pennsylvania, April 21, 1951. Reprinted from *The American Historical Review*, Vol. LIX, No. 1, October, 1953.

[1]For review of the major trends in the interpretation of the Renaissance, see W. K. Ferguson, *The Renaissance in Historical Thought* (Boston, 1948).

that cannot be treated satisfactorily by the simple device of attaching it to
either the medieval or the modern age, or by dividing it between them.

It is, indeed, the distinguishing characteristic of these centuries that they
are neither medieval nor modern, but represent a transitional stage which
has a character of its own. In a paper read at the meeting of the Modern Language Association in December, 1950,[2] I defined the Renaissance as a period
characterized by the gradual shift from one fairly well co-ordinated and
clearly defined type of civilization to another, yet at the same time possessing
in its own right certain distinctive traits and a high degree of cultural vitality.
As a more precise hypothesis I suggested that it was a transition from a
civilization that was predominantly feudal and ecclesiastical in its social,
political, and cultural manifestations and agrarian in its economic foundations, to one that was predominantly national, urban, secular and laic, in
which the economic centre of gravity had shifted from agriculture to commerce and industry and in which a simple money economy had evolved into
capitalism. What I want to consider here is the problem of the Church and
the papacy in this synthesis. To what extent do they fit? And to what extent does this approach to the interpretation of the Renaissance serve to illuminate a crucial segment in the history of the Church?

The conception of this period as peculiarly an age of transition makes it
necessary to establish first of all a fairly definite idea of the nature of the
civilizations that preceded and followed it. But, since historical thought
tends naturally toward a genetic treatment and, indeed, cannot avoid the
problem of causation, the interpretation of a transitional age is necessarily
bound up more closely with the age out of which it grew than with that into
which it later developed. By far the greater part of the controversy over
the character of the Renaissance has concentrated attention upon its relation
to the Middle Ages. This is the essential problem of the Renaissance scholar.
The question of the relation of the Renaissance to the following period be-
longs rather to scholars whose field of interest is the early modern period.
That is their genetic headache; let us leave it to them. This may seem an
irresponsible attitude, and I may be following too closely the example of that
little bird, the prototype of all historians, who always liked to fly backwards,
because he didn't care where he was going but liked to see where he had
been. I think, however, that in so far as our interest is concentrated upon
the transitional age itself, we must consider of first importance the question
of what were the causes, nature, and extent of change. And that leads us
back inevitably to the Middle Ages. As Carl Becker once remarked, a historian can describe anything only by first describing what it successively was
before it became that which it will presently cease to be.

The origins of the Church, of course, carry us back to a period before
the Middle Ages. From that early period it inherited not only its basic doctrine but also the concept of universality and the hierarchical organization

[2]W. K. Ferguson, "The Interpretation of the Renaissance: Suggestions for a
Synthesis," *Journal of the History of Ideas*, XII (1951), 483-95. See above, pp. 125 ff.

that have remained constant throughout its history. In considering what was peculiarly medieval in the Church, however, and therefore likely to change with the passing of medieval civilization, we need go no further back than the centuries in which feudalism was taking shape, that is, roughly the eighth, ninth, and tenth centuries. In these centuries, if we accept Pirenne's thesis, Western Europe had been reduced to an almost purely agricultural economy. And I think we might describe feudalism as fundamentally the adaptation of social and political organization to an economy in which land was almost the only form of wealth. Under these circumstances, central governments lacked the financial resources to govern effectively, so that legal jurisdiction and governmental authority were parceled out among the great landholders. Under these circumstances, too, the clergy, as one of the two classes that did not work the land yet had a very important function to perform, became a landholding class. Even earlier, in the Merovingian period, bishops had become administrative officers with secular rule over their cities. Now, as feudal lords, the bishops and abbots became the rulers of fiefs, barons ecclesiastical with sovereign rights in their baronies. From this period on, the Church was committed to the exercise of temporal authority and to great possessions. But, by the nature of feudal tenure, a lord was also a vassal. And the barons ecclesiastical were at the same time vassals of secular lords: kings or emperors. From this arose much interference by laymen in the election of church officals, and the ill-omened figure of Simon Magus cast its shadow across the Church. This was the period in which the Church was most completely feudalized. In their dual capacity as feudal vassals and church officers, prelates were forced to divide their services, often somewhat unequally, between God and Mammon, but they also exercised a great deal of independent authority. The utter inadequacy of fiscal income made effective central government almost impossible for either the papacy or the monarchies, so that the conflict of secular and spiritual interests operated on the level of diocese and fief rather than of Church and state in the broader sense.

The eleventh century marked the beginning of a tremendous revival in every branch of medieval civilization. Regular commercial relations were reestablished between Italy and the Levant. From the seacoasts trade spread inland until the whole of Western Europe was covered with a network of trade routes along which traveled not only merchants but also pilgrims, crusaders, students, and churchmen on official business. At intervals along these trade routes old cities revived or new ones sprang up. They became centers of local trade and skilled industry and, at the same time, furnished a market for surplus agricultural products. The twelfth and thirteenth centuries were characterized by a steadily growing prosperity in both country and city. The population of Western Europe probably doubled during this period. Money economy, reintroduced through commerce and industry in the cities, spread to the countryside and made possible the partial conversion of landed wealth into fluid wealth that could be mobilized and concentrated. But, though this economic revival received its initial impetus from trade and depended for its continuing growth on the growth of cities, European society still retained in main outlines the structure which had been given it by the feudal system and the Church. The vigorous culture which made the twelfth and thirteenth centuries the classic period of medieval civilization was pre-eminently the culture of the feudal nobility and the clergy.

Feudalism, indeed, lasted long after the passing of that condition of almost exclusive agricultural economy in which it had been formed and which had justified its existence. The rights and privileges of the dominant feudal classes were protected by their monopoly of military force, by long-established jurisdictional authority, and by custom so ingrained that no other form of social and political organization could be imagined. As Joseph Calmette has observed, feudalism had become a kind of Kantian category, in terms of which the medieval mind perceived the social world.[3] Nevertheless, the growth of a money economy made possible, even in this period, the gradual recovery by central governments of some of the powers that had been lost in practice, if not in theory, during the early feudal era. In the early stages of this development, however, the government of the Church was in a position to take advantage of the new situation to better effect than were the feudal monarchies. Though partially feudalized in practice, the Church had never been as feudalized in theory as were the secular states. Its hierarchical principle was deeply rooted in both tradition and dogma. The feudal system, it is true, was also in theory hierarchical; but the feudal hierarchy consisted of a fortuitous network of personal relations which changed its form with each generation and which the accidents of marriage and inheritance rendered increasingly chaotic. The hierarchy of the Church, on the other hand, was a rationally organized administrative system, modeled upon that of the Roman Empire. Whereas the secular monarchies could establish effective state government only by destroying the feudal hierarchy as a political reality, the ecclesiastical monarchy had only to tighten its control of the hierarchy to make it an effective instrument of central government.

Even so, this was no easy task, for the officers of the Church were also vassals of emperors or kings. Bishops resisted the extension of papal authority not only because it infringed upon their independent diocesan jurisdiction but also because, in many cases, they felt a prior loyalty to the king or emperor who had nominated and enfeoffed them. This was the most serious obstacle to the growth of a strong centralized government in the Church. The vigorous assertion of the papal monarchy by Gregory VII led inevitably to the Investiture Controversy with the emperors and to less overt conflicts with other kings and princes. It also led to an unprecedented expansion of the claims of papal supremacy from the ecclesiastical into the temporal sphere. For, so long as the officers of the Church were also temporal lords, whose support was essential to secular rulers, the government of the Church could not be disassociated from that of the state. An effective papal monarchy within the Church could, therefore, be achieved only by establishing papal supremacy over the secular states. In this the popes were never

---

[3]Joseph Calmette, *Le Monde féodal* (Paris, 1946), p. 169.

entirely successful, but in the age of Innocent III they came very close to the fulfillment of their ambition. In their contest with the powers of this world the popes could count on the immense spiritual authority conferred upon them by unchallenged faith in the saving power of the Church. Their spiritual weapons were not yet blunted by overuse. They enjoyed the prestige of leading the military might of Christendom against the infidel; and they were actively supported by all the reforming elements in the monastic orders, by the doctors of the new scholastic learning, and by the development of canon law in the new universities. It must not be forgotten that the assertion of papal supremacy began as a reform movement at a time when reform of the Church was sadly needed. There is something, too, in Heinrich von Eicken's theory that the supremacy of the Church over temporal governments was the logical extension into practice of the ascetic conviction of the worthlessness of all things worldly.[4] At any rate, the concern with temporal affairs, which threatened eventually to secularize the Church, had in the twelfth century the full support of St. Bernard and all the most ascetic elements in both the secular and regular clergy.

Despite all these advantages, it is doubtful whether the papacy or the Church as an institution could have achieved the dominant position they held in the age of Innocent III if political and social life had not still been cast in the feudal mold—and that not only because secular governments were still too much weakened by feudal particularism to resist the encroachments of the spiritual authority upon the temporal sphere. The privileged legal status of the clergy fitted naturally into a society in which all legal status depended upon social status. The immunity of the clergy from secular jurisdiction was only one of many immunities, akin to that of the burghers or any other corporate body. The ecclesiastical courts and canon law competed not with state courts and state law but with a bewildering variety of feudal and urban courts and laws. Everywhere the Church had the advantage that its institutions were universal, while those of the secular world were local and particular. The universality of the Church, indeed, found its perfect complement in the particularism and localism of feudal society. There could be little real conflict between a knight's loyalty to his immediate lord and the Christian's loyalty to the head of the *Respublica Christiana*. Seldom did these centuries witness any type of warfare between the extremes of the localized feudal brawl and the crusade against the infidel. Finally, it was largely due to the conditions of life in a feudal society that the clergy were able to maintain a practical monopoly of education. As the only class in society which had a felt need for these things, the clergy became the principal protagonists of learning, music, and art. They were thus able to give them a direction consonant with their own interests, and to place upon them the stamp of a universal uniformity that did much to impede the growth of national sentiment or national cultures. The feudal nobility had their vernacular literatures—troubadour lyric, chanson, romance, or Minnesang—but serious

---

[4]Heinrich von Eicken, *Geschichte und System der mittelalterlichen Weltanschauung* (Stuttgart, 1923), pp. 325 ff.

thought served the Church. The best brains of Europe functioned below a tonsure. And what medieval men had of visual beauty or the concourse of sweet sounds they owed to the universal Church.

The conditions so uniquely favorable to papal supremacy and to the dominant position of the Church in European society lasted until about the end of the thirteenth century. Even before that time, however, there were signs, though the cloud was no larger than a man's hand, that the halcyon days were passing. The conflict between the thirteenth-century popes and the viper brood of the Hohenstaufen ended in the practical destruction of the Empire. But, in the process, the papacy lost something of the moral prestige that had been its greatest asset in the days of the Investiture Controversy. A moral conflict had degenerated into a squabble over territorial sovereignty in Italy. The spiritual weapons of the Apostlic See had been used too freely in defense of the material patrimony of St. Peter, and popes had too often cried crusade when there was no crusade. So far as any contemporary could observe, however, the papacy was stronger than ever. The Empire was shattered, and, during the greater part of the thirteenth century, France was ruled by a saint and England by a pious fool, neither of whom would offer effective resistance to the spiritual ruler of Christendom. When in 1300 Boniface VIII proclaimed the first Jubilee Year, it seemed as though all Europe had come to Rome to pour its coinage into the papal coffers. Two years later, in the bull *Unam Sanctam,* Boniface proclaimed in uncompromising terms the subjection of the temporal to the spiritual authority and, concluded by declaring that, for all human creatures, obedience to the Roman pontiff is altogether necessary to salvation. The storm that broke immediately thereafter indicated the extent to which conditions had changed. Philip the Fair was no saint, and Edward I no pious fool. Nor were these sovereigns content to act as mere feudal suzerains within their kingdoms. The reigns of these two kings mark the first decisive stage in the transition from feudal to national monarchy, and a national monarch, determined to be master in his own state, could scarcely tolerate either the papal claims to supremacy or the immunity of the clergy from royal jurisdiction and royal taxation. In the rising national monarchies the papacy met for the first time a secular power too strong for it. The arrest of the aged pope at Anagni marked the end of a period which had opened with an emperor standing barefoot in the snow before the gates of Canossa.

The crisis precipitated by the conflict between Boniface VIII and Philip the Fair led to a series of events which seriously undermined the authority and prestige of the papacy: the long exile at Avignon under the shadow of the French monarchy, the scandal of the Great Schism, the conciliar movement, and the anarchy in the Papal States. All of these events aggravated the difficulties inherent in the position of the Church in a changing world. Yet their significance may easily be exaggerated. The anarchy in the Papal States which made Rome unsafe was not new. There had been schisms before the Great Schism, and antipopes before Clement VII. As Guillaume Mollat has recently pointed out, the absence of the popes from Rome was not unprecedented nor necessarily disastrous.[5] It has been calculated, indeed, that "between the years 1100 and 1304, that is, two hundred and four years, the popes lived one hundred and twenty-two outside Rome and eighty-two in Rome: a difference of forty years in favor of absence."[6]

What seems to me more significant than these external events in the history of the papacy is the profound though gradual change which took place in the whole civilization of Western Europe in the three centuries following 1300. It was a change caused by the interaction of political and social factors, complicated by shifts in the social balance and by the imponderable element of a changing *Weltanschauung*. But one factor at least was, I think, of basic importance: the expansion within feudal society of a money economy during the preceding two or three hundred years. By the end of the thirteenth century it had begun to distintegrate a system never intended for it. Even before that time, the manorial system, with its exchange of labor and produce for the use of land and its closely integrated relation of landholders to dependent workers, had begun to be replaced by a system of cash payments—of rents, leases, and wages. The result was a fundamental change in the economic and social foundations of feudalism. The disrupting effect of this change was aggravated by widespread famines in the early years of the fourteenth century, by the depopluation of Europe resulting from the Black Death and the succession of only relatively less fatal epidemics that followed, by the devastation of France during the Hundred Years' War, by the cessation of colonization and of the assarting of waste land, in short by a series of economic crises and depressions which bred intense social unrest and seriously undermined the economic stability of the feudal classes, including the land-holding clergy, and loosened their hold upon the land and its people.

At the same time that the economic and social foundations of feudalism were crumbling, the political and jurisdictional powers of the feudal nobles were being absorbed by the central governments in the great national states and in the smaller principalities of Germany and the Netherlands, as they had been already in the city-states of Italy. The money economy which undermined the independence of the feudal classes served to increase the powers of central government. Money furnished the sinews of administration as of war, and though the total wealth of the European states may not have increased materially during the period of economic crisis from 1300 to about 1450, governments everywhere were learning to utilize the available wealth to better effect by levying new taxes, by imposing import, export, and excise duties, by borrowing from the great Italian banking houses, and, in general, by evolving a more efficient fiscal system. The change in military technique from the feudal array to the royal armies and mercenary companies of the Hundred Years' War is but one symptom of a process which, by the end of the fifteenth century, had subordinated feudal particularism to royal absolut-

---

[5]Guillaume Mollat, *Les Papes d'Avignon* (Paris, 1949), pp. 9 ff.

[6]Louis Gayet, *Le Grand Schisme d'Occident* (Florence, 1889), p. 3.

ism and had transformed the feudal vassal of the Middle Ages into the courtier of the early modern period.

Meanwhile, in the urban centers of commerce and industry an equally fundamental change was taking place. Even before 1300, in Italy and the Netherlands, a simple money economy had begun to develop into an embryonic capitalist system. That development continued steadily during the following centuries and spread to all parts of Western Europe. The first hundred and fifty years or so of this period, it is true, lacked the steadily expanding prosperity of the preceding centuries. There were periods of acute depression and social unrest in all the great commercial and industrial cities during the fourteenth century. Some cities declined, while others grew. It is difficult to estimate how much the wealth of the cities actually increased during this period. There is, however, ample evidence of an increasing concentration of wealth and of a revolutionary development in the techniques of capitalist business enterprise. One result, the cultural and religious implications of which I shall return to later, was the spread of lay education in the cities; another, the growth of an urban patriciate composed of laymen who had the wealth, leisure, and cultivated taste to fit them for active participation in any form of intellectual or aesthetic culture. Still another result, the implications of which are more germane to my present argument, was the evolution by merchants, bankers, and financiers of new and more efficient methods of bookkeeping and accounting, as well as of more efficient techniques for the mobilization and transportation of money in large quantities. The development of state fiscal systems, the more rational accounting introduced into state chanceries, the hard-headed calculation behind the pious façade of royal policies, even the national bankruptcies that mark this period, are all evidence of the application to public finance of techniques and attitudes first worked out in the domain of private capitalist enterprise.

All of these changes operated, directly or indirectly, to alter the character of medieval society; and, inasmuch as the Church had adapted itself with remarkable success to medieval conditions, any change was almost certain to be prejudicial to it. And, in fact, it did become increasingly difficult for the Church to maintain its dominant position in society and for the papacy to maintain the temporal supremacy it had won in the feudal era. At the same time, the papacy could not conceivably abandon without a struggle powers and privileges which the Church had possessed for centuries and had exercised for the good of the Christian community and for the salvation of souls. Not only would the abandonment of its traditional policy have involved encroachment upon too many vested interests; it would also have involved a grave dereliction of duty, the abdication of a responsibility for the moral government of Christendom that had been asserted by saints and popes and rationalized by centuries of canon law and scholastic argument. But to maintain its position under the new conditions, the government of the Church would have to fight with new weapons. It would have to meet the growing centralization of state administration with an increased centralization in the administration of the Church; and, as money became more and more the essential source of power, it would have to rival the fiscal system of state governments by establishing a more efficient fiscal system of its own. Or so it must have seemed to anyone likely to achieve high office in the Church. There were mystics, like the spiritual Franciscans, who felt differently, and reformers, like John Wycliffe, whose conviction that wealth and power were a hindrance rather than a help to the Church drove them into heresy. But mystics are seldom successful politicians, even ecclesiastical politicians, and spiritually-minded reformers who advocated a return to apostolic poverty or the abandonment to Caesar of the things that were Caesar's were not likely to rise to positions of great authority in an institution committed to great possessions and to the exercise of temporal power. Yet the fiscal system and the concentration of administrative authority in the papal curia, both of which were developed with such skill by the fourteenth and fifteenth century popes, should not be considered simply the result of official will to power or avarice in high places. To the hierarchical mind there must have seemed no alternative. The changing policy of the Church as it strove to meet changing conditions must have seemed merely the continuation through new methods of the traditional policy of the preceding centuries. No Biblical injunction warned of the danger of putting old wine into new bottles.

Nevertheless, the development within the Church of a highly organized and centralized fiscal system implied more than the mere adaptation to old ends of a new means. Hitherto, the papal supremacy had been founded largely upon moral authority. The wealth of the Church had remained, even after the reintroduction of money economy, to a great extent decentralized. It was wealth drawn largely from land and held by the officers of the local church organizations. By the end of the thirteenth century, however, the increased circulation of money, together with the growth of new techniques of bookkeeping, banking, and exchange, had made possible an effective system of taxation in both Church and state. Thereafter, the centralization of governmental authority and the elaboration of a fiscal system went hand in hand. In this the papacy was simply keeping pace with the secular governments. But the results were different, for the Church was not a secular institution devoted solely to secular ends, though its officers may occasionally have lost sight of this fact in their preoccupation with *Realpolitik*. The possession of wealth had always carried with it the threat of a materialism that might sap the spiritual vigour of the Church. Since the days of Peter Damiani preachers had complained that men were inspired to seek office in the Church by avarice and ambition. So long as the wealth of the Church remained decentralized, however, its central government had remained relatively uncontaminated. Under the new conditions not only the wealth but the materialism that went with it seemed to be concentrated in an unprecedented degree in the papal curia. Contemporary wits noticed that the word Roma furnished an acrostic base for the apothegm *radix omnium malorum avaritia.*

Nor did the danger end there, for the blight of fiscality spread throughout the Church. The increasing demands of the papal curia forced preoccupation with finance upon all the officers of the Church down to the parish level. And the effort of the papal chancery to introduce a fiscal system into an institution that had never been designed for it led inevitably to the systematization of simony and to traffic in spiritual goods. The fourteenth century popes, it is true, were very largely successful in gaining that control of the nomination of prelates for which the medieval popes had labored in vain. But, as Dean Inge once remarked, in matters of religion nothing fails like success. The reservation to the papal curia of the right of nomination to vacant benefices throughout Christendom did not achieve a reform of the Church. On the contrary, fiscal pressures, diplomatic negotiations with secular princes, and nepotism in the curia made papal provisions the source of new abuses: absenteeism, duplication of offices, traffic in expectancies, the outright sale of benefices, and close calculation of the financial value of every office. Through the imposition of annates and *servitia* the system also imposed a crushing tax upon benefices, so that many of the charitable and other services expected of the local clergy were left undone. I need not describe here the fiscal expedients to which that financial genius, John XXII, and the other popes of this period resorted. Nor need I emphasize their deleterious effects upon clerical morality. These things are well enough known. Conditions were doubtless never as bad as the reforming preachers would have us believe. One cannot, however, entirely ignore the evidence of a cloud of witnesses to the effect that secular and material interests had done much to corrupt the spiritual character of the clergy, high and low. The pamphlet literature of the conciliar movement furnishes ample evidence of a widespread demand for reform of the Church in head and members, and of a growing conviction that reform could be achieved only by depriving the papal monarchy of some of its sovereign powers.

The conciliar movement, however, was by its very nature doomed to failure. Its constitutional theory ran counter to the trend of growing absolutism in the state as well as in the Church. The position of the bishops had been weakened by many of the same political and economic factors as had undermined the independence of the feudal nobles. The principle of free canonical election, for which the councils strove, had for centuries been no more than partially realized, and it was now a lost cause. It served the interest of the kings no more than of the popes. Finally, the whole conception of the ecumenical council as an international body governing a universal Church had become partially anachronistic. In practice, at any rate, it was vitiated by the intrusion of national governments, national interests, and national sentiments, which divided the councils and frustrated the attempt to impose a permanent control upon the papal executive.

The popes were thus able to weather the storm of the conciliar movement, and they emerged with their theoretical sovereignty intact and with a stronger hold than ever upon the administration of the Church. If so much was won, however, much also was lost. During the crisis years of the Captivity and the Schism the popes had gradually abandoned in practice their claims to supremacy over secular rulers. The fifteenth-century popes made their peace with kings and princes through a series of tacit agreements or formal concordats, by which they shared the nomination of church officers and the taxation of the clergy with the secular rulers. In England, the Statute of Provisors, which the fourteenth-century parliaments had used as an instrument to check papal provisions to English benefices, was allowed to become a dead letter. The English kings were content to leave to the popes the right of provision, and incidentally the annates or *servitia* paid by those who received their benefices by papal collation, on the tacit understanding that a certain number of royal ministers or favorites would be nominated. A similar tacit agreement to share some of the fruits of the papal right of provision in Germany with the emperor and the electors underlay the formal Concordat of Vienna of 1448, by means of which Nicholas V won the emperor Frederick III away from the Council of Basel. The French monarchy, long accustomed to special consideration by the Avignonese popes, proved more difficult to deal with. The Pragmatic Sanction of Bourges in 1438 was a unilateral assertion of the liberties of the Gallican Church, and for more than half a century it remained a threat to the principle of papal sovereignty. The theory of papal authority was finally saved by the Concordat of Bologna in 1516, but only at the cost of surrendering to Francis I the most profitable fruits of control of the national church.

In the system of concordats the papacy made its first adjustment to a world of strong secular states. The popes made such practical concessions as were necessary, without apparent impairment of their own *plenitudo potestatis*. For an estimate of the results we can scarcely do better than quote Professor McIlwain's masterly summary:

> They were concessions only. But they were concessions guaranteed by a bilateral document in the nature of a treaty, which implies two treaty-making powers. The concordats were in fact the price the Papacy paid for its victory over the councils and it was a price heavier than appeared at the time. They were a tacit acknowledgement of the sovereignty of national states and they mark the virtual end of the medieval theory that Christendom in its secular aspect is one great state as in its spiritual it is a single Church. From such an admission the logical inference must come sooner or later that the Church is *in* every nation instead of embracing all nations, and this can ultimately mean only that its functions are primarily spiritual and that its participation in secular matters is never justifiable except for a spiritual end—*ad finem spiritualem.*[7]

That was undoubtedly the ultimate result; but it was not the moral immediately drawn from the situation by the popes in the century between the Council of Basel and the Council of Trent. Having failed to maintain the universal sovereignty that had been possible in the feudal age, they concentrated their attention upon restoring their temporal sovereignty in their own states. In this transitional stage, the popes became Italian princes. They suppressed the independent despotisms in the Papal States by force; they employed armies of mercenaries, waged wars, made and broke alliances,

---

[7]C. H. McIlwain, *The Growth of Political Thought in the West* (New York, 1932), p. 352.

and in general took their place as one of the powers in the state system of Europe. In this period political expediency dominated papal policy, though fiscal considerations were not neglected. The College of Cardinals now included members of the ruling families of Italy and the chief ministers of the great European states. Never before had the papacy seemed so securely established as a temporal power, but never before had its power seemed so purely temporal as it did in the age of Alexander VI and Julius II. This was its period of greatest peril. On the one hand, the pope, as temporal ruler of the States of the Church, was no more than a third-rate power, on the level more or less of Milan or Florence. In the game of power politics he was no match for France or Spain. In 1527 the papacy that had chosen to live by the sword came very close to perishing by the sword, and thereafter the popes, as temporal rulers, were drawn into the Spanish sphere of influence, becoming satellites whose foreign policy was dominated by Spanish kings. On the other hand, the preoccupation of the papal curia with temporal politics during these crisis years made it peculiarly unfitted to combat the spiritual revolution that broke out in Germany and that, within two generations, separated half of northern Europe permanently from the Church of Rome. The papacy survived this crisis too, with its sovereignty over what remained of the Church strengthened rather than weakened; but it did so only by ceasing to compete with secular states upon their own terms, by withdrawing into the spiritual sphere in which its authority was unchallenged, by restating the doctrines of the Church in the spirit of the great scholastic age, by employing the militia of the Society of Jesus rather than hired mercenaries, and by leaving coercive jurisdiction to the secular arm of state governments. Not that the temporal power of the papacy, the privileged status of the clergy, and the great possessions of the Church were completely abandoned in the Counter-Reformation. Much remained that would be whittled away only very gradually in the following centuries. But, by the end of the sixteenth century, the main lines which were to be followed in the Church's adjustment to the modern world were already clearly indicated. The transition from medieval to modern forms was nearly complete.

So far I have concentrated attention primarily upon the papacy and the Church in their relation to the secular states. That, however, is only a part of the problem of assessing the position of the Church in the changing civilization of the Renaissance. The relation of the Church to contemporary changes in culture, religious sentiment, and general *Weltanschauung* is of equal if not greater importance, but it is less easy to summarize in a brief paper. Here I can do no more than make a few general observations.

One factor of primary importance for the whole cultural evolution of the Renaissance period, it seems to me, was the growth of lay education. This was not an entirely unknown phenomenon in the Middle Ages. As James Westfall Thompson and others have demonstrated, there was more literacy, at least, among medieval laymen than historians used to suppose, though

that is not saying very much.[8] Nevertheless, the magnificent intellectual and
aesthetic achievements of the twelfth and thirteenth centuries, if we exclude
the vernacular literature of chivalry, was almost entirely the work of clerics
and was patronized, organized, and directed by the Church *ad majorem Dei
gloriam*. Under feudal conditions the nobles had little use for learning and
less for art, while the burghers had not yet acquired the wealth, social security,
or independent cultural tradition that would enable them to compete with
the clergy in this sphere. In Italy, however, before the end of the thirteenth
century, and in other countries of Western Europe somewhat later, the social
and economic development of the cities had reached a point where literacy
was a necessity, and higher education a possibility, for the middle and upper
classes of the urban population. To this end the growth of communal
governments staffed by lay administrators, increasing prosperity, and the
gradual evolution of a more self-confident burgher tradition all contributed.
But on a purely material level the major factor, I think, was the expansion of
business enterprise which accompanied the transition from itinerant to sedentary commerce, and the growth of capitalist forms of business organization. This involved, on the one hand, bookkeeping, written instruments of
credit and exchange, accurate calculation of profit and loss, complicated
negotiations with distant agents or partners, and a much more precise definition of civil law, all of which made literacy indispensable for everyone
connected with business in any managerial capacity and also called into
being a numerous learned class of lay lawyers, scribes, and notaries. On the
other hand, it resulted in the concentration of wealth and the accumulation
of surplus capital which furnished the means for lay patronage of literature,
learning, and the arts. It also created a new class of leisured *rentiers*, who
lived on inherited wealth and were free to devote themselves to intellectual
or aesthetic interests. The concentration of both wealth and political power
in royal or princely courts served the same purpose in slightly different
ways. Such courts became centres for the patronage and dissemina-
tion of lay culture, and so exposed the courtly nobility to a wider range of
cultural interest than had been available in the isolated baronial castles of
the feudal era. After 1450 the invention of printing vastly increased the lay
reading public and tipped the scale decisively in favor of lay participation
in all forms of literary culture; but that epoch-making invention was itself
the answer to a demand already large enough to ensure its being a profitable
venture.

The spread of lay education and lay patronage and the growth of a distinct class of lay men of letters greatly expanded the secular content of
Renaissance culture. This does not imply any necessary decline in religious
sentiment. On the contrary, it was accompanied in many places by a pro-
nounced growth in lay piety. Nevertheless, it was detrimental in many ways
to the dominant position which the Church had acquired in medieval society.
It deprived the Church of its exclusive control of higher education and the
clergy of their monopoly of learning and serious thought. And it created a

---

[8] J. W. Thompson, *The Literacy of the Laity in the Middle Ages* (Berkeley, 1939).

rival, if not an antagonist, to the ecclesiastical culture of the preceding centuries. Evidence of this may be found everywhere in Renaissance music and art, as well as in literature and learning. The revival of antiquity is but one aspect, if the most prominent, of this general trend. Humanism grew up largely as a lay interest, the offspring of lay education, though many humanists were technically clerics. It was, at any rate, not controlled and directed by the Church as scholasticism had been, and it may even be said to have imposed itself upon the Church in the person of such popes as Nicholas V and Pius II and the scores of humanists highly placed in the ecclesiastical hierarchy. In the long run, humanism of the Erasmian variety inspired the most telling attacks upon the temporal power, wealth, and materialism of the Church in the period just preceding the Protestant Reformation.

The reforming Christian humanism of the Erasmian circle represents another aspect of the danger to the medieval Church inherent in the spread of lay education. As I noted in passing, this was accompanied in many places by a distinct revival of lay piety. But the lay piety inspired by mystical preachers like Eckhart and Tauler, and represented by such movements as that of the Friends of God in the Rhineland or the *Devotio Moderna* in the Netherlands, was in large part a reaction against the sacerdotalism of the Church, its mechanization of the means of salvation and the materialism of the contemporary clergy. It is clear that in these years of crisis the Church was not satisfying the spiritual needs of many thoughtful and pious laymen. Left to find their own way toward a sense of personal communion with Christ, they read the New Testament and devotional works which, while entirely orthodox, still had the effect of shifting the emphasis in religious thought from the services of the Church to the inner life of faith and a loving devotion to the person of Christ. It was this peculiarly lay piety that Erasmus, who had been taught in his early years by the Brethren of the Common Life, introduced to a wide circle of educated readers in the *Enchiridion Militis Christiani* and a score of other works less ostensibly devotional.

It may be, too, that the growing bourgeois ethic, if I know what I mean, was in these centuries drifting away from the moral teaching and ascetic ideals of the medieval Church. The pious burgher, sober and hard-working, may well have resented the attitude of the doctors of the Church who barely tolerated commercial activity; and he may also have been tempted to regard the monks, especially such monks as he saw about him, as men who had not so much fled the pleasures and temptations of the world as escaped from its responsibilities. Finally, the intellectual independence which education gave to laymen, together with the individualism fostered by a complex and changing society, might well have made men less ready to accept without question the absolute authority of the Church in matters of doctrine or the claim of the clergy to be the indispensable purveyors of the means of salvation. There has, I think, been a good deal of confused thinking concerning the relationship of capitalism to Protestantism. Nevertheless, I think there can be little doubt that the economic and social conditions which made possible a widespread lay literacy and stimulated a growing sense of self-confident individualism did, at the same time, create an intellectual and moral atmosphere favorable to the reception of Luther's doctrine of the freedom of a Christian man and the priesthood of all believers.

Consideration of the Protestant Reformation, however, except as it affected the Catholic Church, lies beyond the scope of the present discussion. The Church survived this crisis also, with its membership sadly diminished but with its divinely inspired authority strongly reaffirmed. Though papal infallibility was not yet a dogma, the popes after Trent enjoyed an absolute authority in matters of faith and morals greater than that of even their most authoritative medieval predecessors. In the cultural and religious, as well as in the political and administrative fields, the Counter-Reformation completed the Church's adjustment to the modern world. Since then it has changed but relatively little. Yet, if I have assessed aright the predominant characteristics of modern civilization, it was no more than a partial adjustment, and was in some respects a reaction. It was certainly no surrender to the new elements that had grown up within Western civilization since the High Middle Ages. It was rather an orderly retreat to a previously prepared position. The withdrawal of the Church into the spiritual sphere in which its authority could still be exercised in absolute fashion involved not only the abdication of temporal supremacy but also the partial rejection of the secular philosophies, the natural sciences, and large areas of the autonomous lay culture that grew out of the Renaissance. While making concessions where concessions were unavoidable, and abandoning such claims to authority in secular matters as changing conditions had made untenable, the Church returned after the Counter-Reformation, though in a more purely spiritual sense, to the conception of its nature and function that had been formulated in the twelfth and thirteenth centuries. What it could not dominate it rejected, and so maintained, in an ever-shrinking sphere, the authoritative direction of human activity that, in the Middle Ages, had approached a universal domination of the temporal as well as the spiritual life of the Christian community.

But if the Church thus finally succeeded in adapting the medieval ideal to the realities of the modern world, it did so only after a series of well-nigh disastrous crises, which lend to its history during the transitional period a special character. If we consider the events and the changes in ecclesiastical polity that fill the years between the death of Boniface VIII and the period of reconstruction after the Council of Trent, and if we take as the common factor in all of them the efforts, often misguided or self-defeating, of the Church and the papacy to maintain the position they had achieved during the Middle Ages in the midst of a social complex that was being radically altered by new economic, political, and cultural forces, we may, I think, safely conclude that the three centuries of the Renaissance constitute a distinct period in Church history, and that to treat them as such will serve to clarify much that might otherwise remain obscure. The Renaissance Church and the

Renaissance papacy were neither medieval nor modern; rather they were caught in a state of uneasy maladjustment between two worlds. It is the distinguishing mark of a genuinely transitional period that the unresolved conflict between traditional institutions and ways of thinking on the one hand, and, on the other, changing economic, political and social conditions creates a state of acute crisis. The Renaissance was such a period, and the effects of the conflict, as well as the fundamental causes, are, I believe, no-where more clearly evident than in the history of the Church.

70 71 72 73   12 11 10 9 8 7 6 5 4 3 2 1